How Children Learn

Series in Critical Narrative
Donaldo Macedo, Series Editor
University of Massachusetts Boston

Now in Print
The Hegemony of English
　　　by Donaldo Macedo, Bessie Dendrinos, and
　　　Panayota Gounari (2003)
Letters from Lexington: Reflections on Propaganda
　　　New Updated Edition
　　　by Noam Chomsky (2004)
Pedagogy of Indignation
　　　by Paulo Freire (2004)
Howard Zinn on Democratic Education
　　　by Howard Zinn, with Donaldo Macedo (2005)
How Children Learn: Getting Beyond the Deficit Myth
　　　by Terese Fayden (2005)
The Globalization of Racism
　　　edited by Donaldo Macedo and
　　　Panayota Gounari (2005)
Critical Literacy: What Every American Ought to Know
　　　　Eugene F. Provenzo Jr. (2005)
Humanizing Pedagogy Through HIV/AIDS Prevention:
Transforming Teacher Knowledge
　　　coordinated by the American Association of Colleges
　　　for Teacher Education with Carl A. Grant and
　　　Liane M. Summerfield (2006)

Forthcoming in the series
Science, Truth, and Ideology
　　　by Stanley Aronowitz (2006)
Pedagogy of Dreaming
　　　by Paulo Freire (2006)
Dear Paulo: Letters from Teachers
　　　by Sonia Nieto (2006)

How Children Learn

Getting Beyond the Deficit Myth

Terese Fayden

Paradigm Publishers
Boulder • London

Copyright © 2005 Paradigm Publishers

Published in the United States by Paradigm Publishers, 3360 Mitchell Lane, Suite E, Boulder, CO 80305 USA.

Paradigm Publishers is the trade name of Birkenkamp & Company, LLC
Dean Birkenkamp, President and Publisher.

Library of Congress Cataloging-in-Publication Data

Fayden, Terese.
  How children learn : getting beyond the deficit myth / by Terese Fayden.
    p. cm. — (Series in critical narratives)
  Includes bibliographical references and index.
  ISBN 1-59451-104-7 (cloth) 1-59451-105-5 (pbk)
    1. Multicultural education—United States—Case studies.   2. Minorities—
Education (Elementary)—United States—Case studies.   3. Learning,
Psychology of.   4. Literacy.   5. Pueblo children—Education—Case studies.   I.
Title. II. Series.
  LC1099.3.F39 2005
  372.1829—dc22

                                                                    2005003198

Printed and bound in the United States of America on acid-free paper that meets the standards of the American National Standard for Permanence of Paper for Printed Library Materials.

Designed and Typeset by Kärstin Painter.

09 08 07 06   2 3 4 5

For my mother

"If the Great Spirit had desired me to be a white man he would have made me so in the first place. He put in your heart certain wishes and plans, and in my heart he put other different desires. Each man is good in his sight. It is not necessary for eagles to be crows."

—Sitting Bull, 1876

Contents

Lilia O. Bartolome

Foreword

*E*ducators and the general public typically do not understand that the solutions to many of the educational challenges facing Native American and other subordinated students are not purely technical or methodological ones but are, instead, rooted in discriminatory ideologies and practices. In her book, *How Children Learn: Getting Beyond the Deficit Myth*, Terese Fayden courageously challenges the reader to acknowledge the continuing existence (and vigorous resurgence) of cultural and linguistic deficit views of Native Americans as well as its myriad manifestations in schools. However, Fayden does not stop at merely naming and critiquing these deficit views at a theoretical level; she also presents empirical counterevidence in the form of a descriptive research study in which she demonstrates that Native American kindergarten students are intelligent, articulate, and strategic language users and thinkers. Furthermore, Fayden links her research findings to an extensive body of literature on Native Americans and offers numerous suggestions for improving the education of Native Americans and other linguistic and cultural minority students. In particular, Fayden identifies key social constructivist teaching and learning principles and explains their potential for informing successful educational programs, specific educational curricula, and pedagogical approaches. Thus, Fayden operates on numerous levels ranging from the theoretical to the practical in this highly informative and insightful book

I applaud Fayden's courage and willingness to resist constructing solutions to academic challenges in purely technical and methodological terms that are dislodged from the sociocultural reality that shape them. In fact, in my work I also maintain that teaching methods, in and of themselves, may not be the most significant factors in improving minority students' academic performance. The actual strengths of the methods depend, first and foremost, on the degree to which they reject a deficit orientation and reflect a humanizing pedagogy that builds and extends upon the students' background knowledge, culture, and life experiences. It is erroneous to assume that blind replication of instructional methods—and there are numerous potentially promising approaches as cited in this book—that will, if linked with other sociocultural factors, guarantee successful student learning, especially when we are discussing cultural groups that historically have been mistreated and miseducated by the schools. One starting point for demystifying what I term the "methods fetish," as Fayden models, is to name and interrogate the typically negated but ever present deficit views of Native American and other minority students.

The deficit model has the longest history of any model discussed in the education literature and the fact remains that these negative views of difference are deeply imprinted in our individual and collective psyches. As Fayden eloquently explains, the deficit model explains the academic problems among students from low status groups as largely due to "pathologies" or deficits in their sociocultural background (e.g., cognitive and linguistic deficiencies, low self-esteem, and poor motivation). Different yet equally offensive deficit-based descriptors have been used to describe Native American and other low-SES nonwhite students and range from "mentally retarded," "linguistically handicapped," "culturally and linguistically deprived," and "semilingual" to the current deficit euphemism, the "at-risk" student (Flores 1982).

Fayden questions how deficit views may or may not be affecting our work with minority students and focuses specifically on linguistic deficit explanations of Native American educational failure. In her discussion of cultural differences in communication and interaction patterns, it is obvious that Fayden rejects a traditional and restricted definition of *culture* that renders it devoid of its dynamic, ideological and political dimensions. Usually, *culture* is considered synonymous with *ethnic culture*. Instead, Fayden treats *culture* as "the representation of lived experiences, material artifacts and practices forged *within the unequal and dialectical relations* that different groups establish in a given society at a particular point in historical time" (Giroux 1987, emphasis added).

This more comprehensive view of culture recognizes the asymmetrical power relations among cultures and is most useful in identifying the subsequent unequal status attributed to member of different ethnic and social groups. In addition, a more comprehensive understanding of culture which is situated into a power relations framework of analysis will enable educators to comprehend why the language and literacy practices of certain groups are viewed as superior to those of low-status groups.

In reality, values placed on language and literacy practices reflect the greater society's socioeconomic and political hierarchy. That is, the language and literacy practices of dominant cultural groups are usually deemed more valuable and desirable than those of groups that are socially, economically, and politically less powerful. Yet a more accurate and academically honest definition of culture reminds us that, despite social preferences and prejudices, the language practices of linguistic-minority and lower-status populations are inherently equal in terms of grammatical rules that govern their realizations to those of higher-status or dominant groups. Such a critical appraisal of language and literacy practices would also help educators distinguish between the intrinsic value and the socially ascribed value of particular practices.

An emphasis on the political and ideological dimensions of culture also challenges the common assumption that the language and literacy practices of lower-status populations magically spring from the earth and are solely the results of an ethnic cultural lifestyle, separate and apart from the sociopolitical and economic realities that impact and shape them. For example, if a particular ethnic group (such as in the case of Native Americans) has (1) been historically stigmatized and perceived or treated as low-status; (2) developed, in the process, antagonistic relations with members of the dominant cultural group in a society; and (3) been prevented (either consciously or unconsciously) from participating in practices that promote the acquisition of language and literacy knowledge and skills valued by the dominant society, the group often develops alternative language and literacy practices that help its members survive. This survival mechanism is not solely a cultural phenomenon; it is also an ideological and political process that should be recognized when discussing the group's practices. The challenge for educators is to understand the ways in which different cultural practices, particularly with respect to literacy events, are sometimes used as a form of resistance to the perceived and real oppressive conditions and how resistance can be used pedagogically as a tool for literacy development.

Fayden conveys this critical macrounderstanding to educators so as to enable them to consider the possible effects of unequal power relations among groups in a society, as well as the possible implications this power asymmetry may have at the classroom level and the adverse effects it can have on learning and teaching. Although Fayden embraces social constructivist learning theory and antiracist multicultural education, she rejects a conventional and "apolitical" social constructivist and multicultural education perspectives that uncritically conceive dominant culture teachers and minority student relations as amicable and tension-free. (It is important to point out that the belief by many educators that education is apolitical or nonpolitical is a fallacy. All education reflects particular ideological positions. However, the tendency exists to label nondominant culture ideological positions as "political" and dominant culture ideological positions as "nonpolitical" or "apolitical.")

In this "ideal" and "apolitical" model, teachers and learners are presented as engaging in harmonious social interactions that permit learners to participate actively in their own learning and ensure that successful teaching and learning can take place. Teachers are expected to cordially and respectfully model desired behavior and language use until the students have internalized these skills and are capable of exhibiting them without assistance. Fayden reminds us that the sociocultural and political reality is more typically one in which teacher and learner are antagonistic toward each other and in which teachers often resist mentoring students perceived as deficient. Furthermore, students often reject the devaluation of their existing language and literacy skills and the imposition of the dominant culture's language and literacy practices. As a result, very little teaching and learning actually takes place even when teachers have the best of intentions. Effective mentorship can only occur when pedagogical spaces are created that enable students to move from object to subject position and become participants in their own learning as Fayden illustrates in chapter 7.

Too often, proponents of conventional social constructivism stop short of discussing the ideological and political dimensions of the theoretical framework. Frequently, in fact, when advocates of this perspective argue that it is necessary to consider the sociocultural context, they refer to the immediate classroom content or to the immediate ethnic community (neighborhood), while disarticulating the classroom context and the ethnic community from the larger social order that influences, shapes, and maintains the asymmetrical distribution of cultural goods. The theoretical net must be cast more broadly since it is also necessary to acknowledge the impact of political and ideological realities on culture formation and maintenance; any discussion of linguistic-minority students' language and literacy practices must take into account the larger sociopolitical context in which these practices have developed and in which teacher and student negotiate the maintenance of primary discourses and the acquisition of the dominant culture secondary discourses. Fayden's multi-level deliberation of Native American students' educational experiences—from the macrosociohistorical context to the microclassroom context—enables the reader to begin to envision the creation and recreation of potentially effective instruction.

Fayden lists and thoughtfully discusses essential antiracist multicultural education and social constructivist pedagogical principles and provides possible applications. In the process, she powerfully illustrates the necessity for educators to free themselves from the blind adoption of so-called effective strategies and programs so that they can begin a critical reflective process which allows them to invent and reinvent teaching methods and materials by always taking into consideration the sociocultural realities that either limit or expand the possibilities of their students' learning. Teachers should keep in mind that educational curricula and instructional methods are social constructions that grow out of and reflect ideologies that often prevent teachers from understanding the pedagogical implications of asymmetrical power relations among different cultural groups. Thus, teachers need to develop ideological perceptiveness that enables them to effectively create, adopt, and modify teaching approaches and strategies that simultaneously respect and challenge learners from diverse and subordinated cultural groups in a variety of learning environments

Fayden reminds us that teachers can maintain the status quo or they can work to the transform the sociocultural reality at the classroom and school level so that the culture at this microlevel does not reflect and reproduce macrolevel inequalities. In this book, Terese Fayden provides a thought-provoking pedagogical framework that is sure to get teachers to think more critically about their pedagogy and to begin to imagine a more humanistic and emancipatory education for all students.

Henry M. Levin

Foreword

As new immigrants stream into the United States, we are faced daily with the dilemma of how to provide an education that builds on and respects their cultures while providing them with the knowledge for full participation in U.S. institutions. This dilemma was not present in the early history of this nation where Native Americans were viewed as primitives who were obligated to embrace "superior" European cultural and religious traditions. Nor were such attempts at conversion done through gentle persuasion with the blunter tools of totalitarian control and military force.

Although the education of Native Americans has changed over time, it is still characterized by deep attitudes of disrespect for Indian culture and the blame of family backgrounds and customs for school failures. Terese Fayden is a teacher who was plunged into this system, assigned to a Kindergarten with a combination of Pueblo Indian and Hispanic children. Students were characterized to school staff as "at-risk" children, behind in basic skills, and particularly in language skills. Teachers had long been indoctrinated with the explanation that poor values in the homes and families of these children or cultural deficits created their deficiencies in educational performance. As a result teachers were imbued with the "if only they were more like us" syndrome for explaining academic failure.

Fayden was puzzled. She noticed that when she got to know these children and observed them closely, they appeared to be "intelligent and knowledgeable," just not in the way that the standardized kindergarten test valued them in labeling them as at-risk.

This is the story of a teacher who responded by undertaking a personal journey in following four Pueblo Indian children in their development of written literacy. In this quest she came to realize that what is considered to be instructional intervention is premised on negative perspectives and interpretations of Indian culture that are often masked in "a pseudo attitude of ethnic tolerance." To the degree that the schools recognize Indian cultures, they view them as a hindrance to educational success of their students. Talk of multiculturalism was ubiquitous, but it took the form of superficial rituals such as "isolated special days, exotic foods, or interesting clothing" rather than any deeper understanding or appreciation of culture.

In contrast, Fayden found that success can be achieved through recognizing and validating the strengths in culture, by seeing student and family culture as a vehicle for educational growth rather than an obstacle to it. Rather than seeing it as a weakness, Fayden treated Pueblo Indian culture as a strength that she could build upon. In following her journey we see that teacher sincerity, awareness, observation, caring, and openness can lead to great insights and breakthroughs for both student and teacher. We can observe not only the flowering of the children, but the corresponding understanding and growth of their teacher. Sadly, little of this potential symbiosis is reflected in the typical curriculum for teacher education.

Fayden's story is an inspiring one of hope, embedded in the poignant detail of her classroom and eliciting possibilities for all who have taught at this level. A reading of this book will provide a powerful countermessage for all teachers who have been told that the family values and culture of their students are obstacles to learning.

Acknowledgments

would like to thank Hank Levin, who has greatly inspired me and whose generosity of time and support stamped indelible thoughts on my mind about the goodness of mankind. Thanks to Kathryn Herr, who was always ready to answer my questions, no matter how frivolous they might have been, and to Dean Birkenkamp and Donaldo Macedo for having faith in my work. My gratitude to Dianne Ewing, whose exceptional thoughtfulness and attention to detail caused the manuscript to be a better one; my appreciation to Kärstin Painter for her insightful editing and preparation of the manuscript, often nothing short of brilliant.

Special thanks go to Paulita Aguilar for her invaluable research. This book would never have been brought to fruition had it not been for the integrity of the people of the Cochiti pueblo. Mary Eunice Romero was kind enough to share her knowledge of village life with me and I was honored when granted permission by the governor and lieutenant governor to do my original language study, which also served as my dissertation. I am truly indebted to the families who trusted me not to take advantage of the knowledge gained by observing their children, my students. Most of all, it was the children themselves who enkindled my spirit to write this book. To Ashley, Jaimee, Cameron, and Lucas: Neyshcha!

—Terese Fayden

Introduction

I am a Kindergarten teacher who worked in a public school on an Indian reservation in the Southwest. The population in my class at the time of this study was roughly 70 percent Pueblo Indian and 30 percent Hispanic. When I first came to the school seven years ago, I was told by much of the administration and staff that the children were academically far below their white middle-class equivalents. The blame for their underachievement was readily placed on the families. It was relayed to me that the parents didn't participate in activities commonly thought of as assisting children in educational pursuits, such as reading to children, helping with schoolwork, and astonishingly, speaking to their children.

The intimation was that these cultures were impoverished because they lacked traits that white America valued (e.g., training children with the resolution of helping them to succeed, preparing children to achieve in a competitive environment, and working exclusively for one's family in order to attain the "American Dream"). There was never any question that middle-class values were the standards to be emulated in school. Subsequently, anything that failed to measure up to these criteria was looked upon as inferior.

Especially concerning the Indian children (I use this term because this is how these people refer to themselves), a picture was painted of parents that rarely engaged their children in extended conversation or spoke with them for pleasure, delight, and especially, instruction. These characteristics, along with the children's low entry-test scores, were the purported reasons for the school's emphasis on remediation efforts to teach the children basic skills and fundamental language capabilities.

Only two generations ago, the children's indigenous vernacular, Keres, was the language commonly spoken in their village. Today, while there is a resurgence in teaching Native language use, daily conversation in the dialect is limited to most of the grandparents and only a few other families. Consequently, most children in the village were growing up with English as a first language. Indians may speak their own form of English, known as Indian English (Leap 1992) in order to retain ties to their community, but this was never recognized by the educators in my school.

The official focus in school was concentrated on the children gaining traditional information, such as the "core" knowledge outlined in books like Hirsch's *Cultural Literacy*. In these types of books, thousands of itemized names and dates are presented with a definite bias toward Eurocentric standards. This approach to learning was a curriculum goal due to the presupposed shortfalls of the children and the school's attempt to have them "catch up" to the level of knowledge that children with more financial resources attain. Thus, the middle-class model set the stage for what was taught, how the children should behave, what meanings should be promulgated, and what values were to be encouraged (or discouraged). Administrators often suggested that the primary responsibility of early-childhood teachers was to educate students in rudimentary knowledge and elementary language expression so that they could counterbalance the years of loss they claimed these children had experienced.

In the beginning of my teaching career, I accepted all this as being true and I expended much effort in order to compensate for the children's supposed limited environment. But over the course of my first few years, I slowly began to see inconsistencies in what I was told and what I observed. For example, when children were engaged in a language experience story, through which the children relayed their experiences while I wrote them down, they had no problems coming up with the content or expression of their adventures. There were many more instances that demonstrated their adeptness, and this was evidenced in all other subject areas as well.

From the beginning of my career at the school, I had questions about literacy differences between my students and their mainstream counterparts. Most journals and books that dealt with young children's writing indicated that Kindergartners usually experimented with print, whereas my students, and the students of other Kindergarten teachers, rarely did. When I questioned the children's dearth of explorations in writing, I was comparing them to those I had read about and concluded that my students were not up to par. In short, I had become a casualty of the prevalent deficit thought that pervaded the educational system for which I worked. I was able to erase these thoughts only when I studied a group of four Indian children at their writing table. There, I was witness to the remarkable unfolding of the children's acquisition of knowledge. What I learned is described in this book through a microanalysis of the children's actions, language, art, and emergent writing.

Although this study lasted five months, there were other factors that were intimately intertwined with the children's education. These issues include the attitudes of deficit thinking, cultural-differences hypotheses, and modes of instruction and curriculum in school systems of poor children. Pedagogy is discussed in the light of Indian and minority education, as it is today and what it can be. The promise of good schooling is portrayed in an examination of multicultural education and social constructivism. Consequently, this book encompasses a macroanalysis of the education of poor children. This is presented in an examination of attitudes, values, and instruction that many underrepresented children are likely to encounter. Indian and other minority children have failed in school for many generations and continue to do so. This book addresses alternative actions that can provide more options for those who are in charge of instructing these children. By confronting disagreeable topics, such as racism and ineffective curriculum, the hope is that children from diverse cultures can receive the education they so richly deserve.

The initial section of chapter 1 addresses methodology. Next, the issue of deficit theory as it applies to this book is considered. When I first came to the conclusion that the elementary school I worked for was suffering from the effects of deficit thinking, I realized that we were congealed in the past. Many of our beliefs were similar to those held in the 1960s—ideas that sprang from much earlier times. The notion of deficit thinking proposes that school systems serving poor children are often driven by the perception of their students as having shortcomings. This helps educators explain their students' persistent failure while ignoring their own. Cultural deprivation assumptions, a direct outcome of deficit thinking, held that because of alleged cultural deficits, families of minorities were to blame for the disparate educational failure of their children. A presumed intellectually depleted climate at home was contiguous with a financially distressed environment. Because of their assumed indifference to education, parents did not transmit values of educational achievement nor provide an instructional atmosphere such as reading to their children, providing an atmosphere conducive to learning, or talking to their children with the intent of teaching. It was presumed that the children's sensory and linguistic settings at home were bereft of any cognitive stimulation that resulted in an impoverishment of language, poor school performance, and a lack of attitudes necessary for academic success. Extended families, such as those found in African American and Indian homes, were said to cause inconsistencies in a child's upbringing that would result in a child's being disorganized and disorderly in school (Pearl 1997).

Accumulated environmental deficit was a spin-off of cultural deprivation. This too held that the culture of the lower socioeconomic class produced an environment that was completely devoid of intellectual stimulation, once again with accusations of a dearth of reading in the home and limited language expression. Impairments that children received were chiefly limited to language deprivation and so this theory generated compensatory education, concentrating on language development. Compensatory education was viewed as a treatment for the cognitive deficiencies of indigent children (Ginsburg 1986). These accusations were common ones in my school and variations of cultural deprivation and accumulated environmental deficit theory were often directed at the students, from Kindergarten through the middle school which our children fed into (both institutions were in close proximity to each other and were treated as one school in regard to staff meetings, problems, solutions, and so on).

Elsewhere (Fayden 1997a), I have investigated the Kindergartners' use of social and private speech and found that their language development was far from wanting. In fact, there was a rich variety of language use while at the same time there was an intellectual striving by the children so their rhetoric would find new applications for communication. When I observed the bounteousness of the children's vocabulary and tended to their sophisticated way of working and playing together, I knew that the school's deficit view of the children was based on much more than the students' cognition. It became almost convenient for the school to blame the children for their failure. In this way, the school's superior status quo was blamelessly preserved and they could rationalize their programs and carry on with their attitudes and curriculum (much the same as they always have). I have chosen to use the terminology *cultural deprivation* chiefly because when referring to accumulated environmental deficits, the children did not fall behind until after the third grade. Yet the belatedness of their "insufficiencies" was not looked upon by the school as its own doing. Rather, they saw the children's early firmly incorporated deficiencies as having a kind of incubation period before they were observed. This overwhelming denial confirms how tenacious schools can be in their unwillingness to take responsibility for their students' failure.

Deficit thinking drove my study. I was originally concerned that my Pueblo Indian students entered school academically behind their middle-class counterparts. (When *Pueblo* is capitalized, it refers to the southwestern group of Indians known as the Pueblo; when it is found in lowercase it refers to the village they live in, a term given to their towns by the conquering Spanish in the 1500s). Initially, I fell prey to the supposition that the children's home conditions were not as advantageous as those of traditional middle-class children. It was this faulty theory that generated this book.

The latter part of chapter 1 addresses the theory of cultural differences. This supposal is controversial: Students seem to improve when culture at home is aligned with culture at school (e.g., see Banks 1999; Mohatt and Erickson 1981). Those arguing against this rationale (e.g., see Pearl 1997) see it as an extension of deficit thinking. They contend that if all children are treated equally in regard to attention, curricula, and expectations, minority children would fare equally as well as those of the white middle class. This does not demean the fact that sociocultural setting has a significant bearing on how children view the world and how they learn about it. Because Pueblo Indians' culture is in contrast (and often opposition) to the mainstream culture, social situatedness becomes an element that plays into learning styles and potential teaching methods. This becomes significant when considering values of communal lifestyle versus the individual. The Pueblo's emphasis on the welfare of the community over individual aspirations should motivate administrators to seek alternative strategies so that their students would be more able to align their backgrounds with school standards, develop an affinity with their education, and thus more readily meet with success, such as fostering cooperative activities. This is because culture most certainly has an effect on the actions of children. For example, although collaboration is seen in many children who are given the opportunity to work together, the Kindergartners' collective upbringing can be seen as having an effect on their spontaneous cooperative actions.

Chapter 2 offers a short history of the village and its people. It briefly describes the cohesiveness of the social group and their concentration on defending their way of life. Pueblo Indians are more fortunate than other Native groups because they have retained much of their original culture and homelands. As educators, we are obligated to understand that the lifestyle of the children, their families, and their community may be different—and that differences do not translate into deficits.

Chapter 3 examines the social construction of knowledge while looking at the Kindergarten foursome at their writing tables. It depicts how the group constructed their knowledge from social interactions. I have traced the children's communal use of the zone of proximal development, that is, how they learned from each other and what modes they chose in order to attain knowledge. They achieved this through collaboration, copying, and deciding on common themes with which to work. All of these motifs are commonly found in their village. I viewed the zone of proximal development from the perspective of peer collaboration rather than the usual unidirectional path of from teacher to child. The goal of this study was to uncover the nescience that surrounds Indian children's cognition. Through this investigation, I hope to educate researchers, school administrators, and teachers on the profound intelligence of Indian and minority children and about forms of education that might prove more successful.

Chapter 4 investigates the participants' pre-history of writing by studying their symbolization in gesture, play, and artwork. The Kindergarten group was found to create their art from part to whole, which indicates that the children may not fit into the Native American stereotype of being primarily holistic thinkers. The children did eventually become writers. Their interest was sparked by the functional use of writing when a school post office was opened. This is described in chapter 5. Here, the children's spelling is compared to Read's seminal study (1971). Differences as well as similarities are noted.

That Indian and minority education has failed is well recognized (Reyhner 1992). In my school alone, most of the children fall far below the fiftieth percentile, year after year, in all subject areas (especially reading and math). The school lacks parent participation and the district high school has a high dropout rate. These factors feed the deficit assumption. Historically low performance has always existed in these groups. That poor and minority children generally receive an inferior education is also well noted (Darling-Hammond 1997; Kozol 1991; Gay 1993). Minority children are exposed to a less challenging course of study than white groups. Thus, they are less likely to receive the opportunity to develop higher-order cognitive skills. Their curriculum is often mundane: one of basic skills. This is also in contrast to the varied and interesting curricula that typical schooled white children receive. "If students are perceived to be 'deficient,' then the educational environment will reflect a no-nonsense back-to-basics drill orientation" (Nieto 1992, 100). Curriculum that minority children are likely to receive is explored in the first part of chapter 6.

These discoveries led me to examine multicultural education—an approach that is outlined in the second half of chapter 6. In the years I have taught in this district, I have heard innumerable racist remarks about Indians. These have ranged from: "Why do we get the riffraff?" (a remark by a teacher in reference to Indian children from the most traditional pueblo coming to our school) to common deficit remarks of ignorance: "The Indian children are wilder," to using a stereotype as a ruse for not hiring qualified Indian educators: "The only thing she can teach is pottery." It's no wonder that Indian staff feel their views go ignored. "They don't listen to us," remarked an Indian teacher after a staff meeting. Three other Indian staff members readily agreed that such lack of respect is real to the Indians; a circumstance they have never been allowed to forget. Multicultural education must be authentic and must confront issues of racism as well as those issues that can minimize prejudice. This can be accomplished only by students and staff seeing participants of all cultures as being essential to the human experience.

Although criticism of attitudes and methods are often aimed at the educators, I want to affirm that many attempts to deal with Indian children are well meaning. As Trueba and Bartolome pointed out, educators of all ethnic backgrounds are unaware that they operate out of the deficit model (1997). One cannot see a clear picture unless one studies the situation. Because most teachers are not involved in research, many of their practices are based on the consensus of what they know even though this may not be necessarily viable for the success of children. There are many caring and experienced teachers and administrators of minority children, in my district as well as others. This book is designed to help those who are struggling to deliver an equitable education to minority children.

Chapter 7 addresses recommendations for teachers instituting an equity pedagogy. It was determined that by applying social constructivist approaches, the strengths of Indian children can be capitalized upon. This improves the prospects for all underrepresented children because, finally, they will be allowed to inquire, solve problems, think critically, and actively engage in authentic work by themselves and in collaboration with others.

1

Background

Studying the Children

wanted to investigate how a group of four Pueblo Indian children enacted literacy during daily writing time. I was curious to see if the values of communal living that they experienced at home would be
brought to school and how these values might be demonstrated. This
undoubtedly would shed light on possible methods that could be implemented or
discarded in order to avoid cultural conflicts and feelings of alienation and,
hopefully, offer insight into ways to help children see their lives meaningfully
represented in a school setting. Throughout the study, when I note values at
home that are repeated in school, I do not intend to state causality. I want to
make clear the similarities between the two. Although the names of those who
were responsible for specific actions were specified, my intention was to portray
the group as an aggregate and to account for the children's actions as a whole
(Gearing and Epstein 1982) so that the four individual children would merge, in
essence, into an assemblage. In accordance with the children's background of
group living—by studying communal interactions I would be more able to un-

9

cover resemblances between shared communication in their Pueblo setting and their actions in the classroom. Thus, individual personalities were not dwelled upon. Rather, group actions were highlighted. I used multiple methods of data collection: (1) Roughly sixty hours of video-recording sessions; (2) Document review; (3) Photographs; (4) Observation; and (5) "Critical friend" (Anderson, Herr, and Nihlen 1994). I had the good fortune to have someone at the pueblo to help me understand life and values from the Indian perspective. She advised me on the indigenous comportment particular to that setting and shared the people's general outlook with me, bolstering my understanding by referring to practices and lore. This helped me to understand Pueblo values and way of life and connect these views to my findings. Of course, I did not rely on her solely to gain my perspective of Native life. Working in a school for many years gave me a tacit understanding of the people and their perspectives. I also interacted with the people, including attending events in the villages such as rabbit hunts, foot races, dances, and "throws." I lived with a family for frequent but brief times in the nearby pueblo. There, I participated in activities such as baking bread with the women, shopping for a feast, helping as families dressed for a dance, and other things one does with friends. The Pueblos value secrecy of their ways as a defense against first Spanish, then Anglo, encroachment. Outsiders must follow the primary rule of refraining from being inquisitive. Many years ago, during my first visit to a pueblo, I had dinner with a family and their friends. The governor of the village happened to be there. After listening to what must have been my incessant inquiries of Indian life, the governor gently told me, "Eat now. Ask questions later." Later never came. Over the years, I have learned to repress my questioning bent and accept what I both see and hear as gifts from the people.

Practitioner Research

The research for this book was specifically practitioner research. I am a Kindergarten teacher and this study was conducted in my classroom. The research evolved out of thoughts and questions I had regarding classroom events. Because I was situated in my own particular place, I possessed implicit understandings that can only be gained by being an insider and by participating in the daily happenings of a school. Practitioner research is not a procedure for substantiating a particular proof but is a view of research that invites an unfolding of knowledge with the specific end of solving problems in order to improve practice and curriculum (Britton 1983). This gave me a practical advantage because new understandings gained could be readily investigated and implemented in my classroom. For example, originally I was concerned that my students were entering school "behind" middle-class white youngsters. Thankfully, I was also examining my own practices. My initial inquiries were not only "Why aren't the Kindergartners investigating writing?" but also "Is there anything more I need to do to help the children attain literacy?" I examined this problem through a comprehensive understanding of a case-study group of four Kindergartners. By examining specific instances, I expected to bring light to a general problem common to teachers of underrepresented children: "Why don't the students fare well in school?" As I discovered the richness of the children's learning, I hoped to illuminate that literacy of diverse children need not be compared to that of their mainstream counterparts, but should be examined through the aggregation of experiences, actions, and values the children actually demonstrated. This included finding the pathways these particular children sought as their natural intelligence developed. This case focused on the particulars of the group studied. In coming to understand it thoroughly, refinement of an understanding may be gained. I hope that this *petite generalization* (Stake 1995) can be applied to those seeking understanding of underrepresented children and that the reader leaves this study with the conception that modifying traditional paradigms of literacy are helpful when one studies children of diverse cultures.

The study involved a group of four Keresan Pueblo Indian children (*Keresan* refers to a particular language grouping of Pueblo Indians), three of whom were ranked at risk, and the fourth, who was ranked between at risk and "normal" based on a standardized Kindergarten test that is given annually, shortly after the children enter our school district. Again, when I weighed their speaking, actions, and work, the children seemed to be intelligent and knowledgeable. This discrepancy fueled my study, and as I examined these children within their writing group, I attempted to develop a more accurate assessment of their literacy. This was achieved by expanding on concepts of intelligence which are commonly determined through established principles of verbal skills to those that included the many fashions through which the children actually communicated, such as gesturing, talking, drawing, creating artwork, dancing, chanting, singing, playing, and writing. When examining these modes, I intended to develop a concept of literacy that authenticated ways of thinking and creating knowledge.

Blaming the Victims

From the time I started teaching Kindergarten at Pueblo Elementary, a school made up of approximately 55 percent Pueblo Indian children and 45 percent Hispanic children, I had been told that the students were behind in basic skills and that they were lagging behind in language development. When discussing the children at staff meetings, the students were frequently spoken of as lacking the parental guidance similar to that of middle-class children. There were many conversations about how the children's families didn't read to them at home, that their parents didn't participate in the parent-teacher organization (PTO) or help with homework, too much money was spent on toys (rather than on books), and so on. In short, it was heavily implied that the families' values did not help children progress and were, in fact, averse to the advancement of their children in school. Deficit thinking was established as the faculty constantly compared our population and their families to mainstream communities, especially during testing, when our students invariably placed well below the norm.

The district administration had a sincere desire for the children to succeed. They implemented what they believed were strong reading and math programs and supported innovative ideas through the awarding of minigrants. Yet the test scores continued to reflect a low level of learning. This, of course, was due to the fact that the school was looking at its students as being of lower rank than middle-class whites. Even the most sophisticated methods of teaching will be rendered ineffective if educators believe their charges to be culturally disadvantaged and in need of modification (Trueba and Bartolome 1997). Operating through deficit assumption has had deleterious effects on minority children through pedagogical attitudes and watered-down curricula.

Literacy procedures for the poor are most often carried out through the "dipstick" method, in which the proverbial brain can be opened up and examined with an instrument (a dipstick) to determine the child's literacy level. If there is not enough literacy inside, it is presumed that more can be added with supplementary formal instruction (Reder 1994). Astonishingly, shortly after I wrote this, a first-grade teacher told me: "If only we could open up their heads with a can opener, we could pour the information in." No credit was given to the students for having a knowledge base or any type of literacy—their culture was completely discounted as irrelevant and unfavorable to the cultivation of academics. Most of the teachers, at one time or another, had voiced their concern as to why the children were not up to par and we continued to investigate methods that would remedy this situation. At school administration proceedings as well as school levels, meeting after meeting was devoted to what could be done to help the children advance, especially in reading and math, so that they could achieve the educational level of middle-class America and prove their worth with their test scores. Primary teachers were frequently told by administration that the children needed "more language" and these teachers frequently complained that the children came into our school already two or three years behind mainstream students. These ridiculous accusations were never challenged.

Cultural Deprivation

At the time, I didn't realize that our particular educational institution was playing into the philosophy of cultural deprivation. This concept supposes that children's upbringing and environment are responsible for their low entry test scores, inadequate language development, and continuing poor performance in school. The model charges the culture and the families with an inability, unwillingness, or ignorance of how to properly stimulate children's cognitive growth, which, in turn, is responsible for their intellectual and linguistic delays. It accuses cultures and families of being unable to produce appropriate skills and attitudes that will help prepare their children for school. Current deficit thought is that poor children enter school "at risk of failure" because they lack the abilities and attitudes of middle-class children. The minority child

> is blamed for his own miseducation. He is said to contain within himself the causes of his inability to read and write well. The shorthand phrase is "cultural deprivation," which, to those in the know, conveys what they allege to be inside information: that the poor child carries a scanty pack of intellectual baggage as he enters school. He doesn't know about books and magazines and newspapers, they say. (No books in the home: the mother fails to subscribe to *Readers' Digest.*) They say that if he talks at all—an unlikely event because slum parents don't talk to their children—he certainly doesn't talk correctly. . . . If you can manage to get him to sit in a chair, they say, he squirms and looks out the window (impulsive ridden, these kids, motoric rather than verbal). In a word he is "disadvantaged" and "socially deprived" they say, and this, of course accounts for his failure (*his* failure, they say) to learn much in school. (Ryan 1971, 4)

Playing Catch-Up

Schools that serve students of diverse populations often create an atmosphere where teachers are placed in the position of helping their students "overcome" their "deprived" background so that they can move on to the intellectual level of their middle-class counterparts who are already proficient in basic skills. The incessant emphasis on catching up transmits the message of cultural shortcomings. Its zeal is as strong, pervasive and similar to the early missionaries who sought to "civilize" the Indians through making them in the image of the white man. The importance of Indian and other underrepresented children succeeding in school cannot be underestimated. However, creating a cultural gap where life and values are dissimilar and not as good as white life is not the way to accomplish it. The thrust of many of these schools is to concentrate on fundamental learning in order to bring up test scores (Bowman 1994) and is often done at the expense of individual motivations, interests, and activities that lead to higher-order thinking skills. This raises the question of access in education for minorities. While schools of diverse cultures are concentrating on the basics (Darling-Hammond 1995), other, more affluent schools are providing a different type of education for their students—one that is rich in problem solving and provides learning within varied curricula (Gay 1993). While helping diverse children to excel in elementary proficiency is certainly a necessary task, the concept of having them parrot other children's performance reveals a subtle form of intolerance by implying that these cultures (usually African American, Hispanic, or Native American) are creating culturally and cognitively deficient children.

Historical Roots of Deficit Thinking

Menchaca described how the roots of deficit thinking applied to the Indians in the early seventeenth century (1997). The theft of Indian land became policy shortly after the arrival of the Pilgrims. Because the British economic appetite for land was insatiable, they would not recognize the Native people as having rightful ownership of their property. Thus, the solution was to relocate and exterminate the Indians. The insidiousness of Pilgrim thinking was that they justified this resettling and annihilation on religious grounds: rationalizing that they were God's chosen people, fashioned to be a superior race. They felt their destiny was to own and populate America with Christians and rescue the Indians from paganism.

Menchaca referred to the work of Nott and Gliddon (1857) when she wrote: "American Indians were viewed to be savages, whose cultural environment had prevented them from cognitively developing in the same manner as Caucasians" (1997, 17). Thus the colonists deflected their unlawfulness by relegating the Indians to an inferior class whose culture, religion, and cognition were deemed defective and immoral. This set the stage for the schooling of Indians and the infamous attempts to estrange them from their own civilization based on the concept of cultural ineptitude.

When the Indian boarding schools were established in the latter part of the nineteenth century, the insinuation was that children raised on reservations were either morally or culturally lacking (Spring 1994). In many ways, this view of Indians has not diminished. Now, as before, this type of narrow-mindedness is evidenced in an appeal to help the children while negating their culture. The difference is that when the boarding schools were established the eradication of culture was an overt and deliberate act, whereas now it is done in an almost unconscious manner, under the guise of helping the children and their families mirror selected attributes of conventional American culture. It is accomplished through the attempted transmission of a myriad of middle-class attitudes such as required nightly storybook reading at home, helping with schoolwork, and attending parental functions. When these obligatory duties are not carried out by family members, their cultural values are blamed for the lack of children's achievement in school.

Deficit Thinking in Various Guises

The communal lifestyle among the Pueblo may prevent families from fulfilling daily school requirements such as reading to their children or helping with homework. In Pueblo life, it is a strong priority to fulfill cooperative responsibility, whether it entails communally baking bread, practicing for a religious dance, attending a village rabbit hunt, or any number of the multitudinous religious and social activities that dominate their lives. The continuation of Pueblo life and their people is the main priority of Pueblo Indians—the way they survive is by participating in these events. The problem is that when we want disparate populations to "be like" those of the mainstream, we are ignoring and trivializing the children's culture. Today, the belief that diverse children are "lacking" is widely accepted: The blame is put on the home life of these students, suggesting insufficiencies in the ways that families raise their children. According to the particular historical time, alleged failings of minorities were said to be inherited through inferior genes, low-rank culture, or incompetent familial socialization (Valencia 1997). Today, the cultural blame is placed on the families' failing to prepare their children for success in school. A common statement that reverberates in the teacher's lounge is: "If only the parents would help their children more (as is seen in many white middle-class families), their young students wouldn't enter school "behind." This belief is common among teachers of minority students who frequently view the home environment as inept and counterproductive to school efforts to educate the children (Miramontes and Commins 1991). For example, when homework tasks are not completed, teachers see the home environment of poor children as inadequate (Commins 1986). Recently, a first-grade teacher in my school complained that a certain child lacked fluency in reading. When I asked her to identify the cause, she replied, "Because the parents won't read to her at home." It would have been an easy task for the teacher to "make up" this need by reading to the child in school but it was even easier to blame the child's family for the failure. As Bernstein sarcastically commented:

> If only parents were interested in the goodies we offer; if only they were like middle-class parents, then we could do our job. Once the problem is seen implicitly in this way, then it becomes appropriate to coin the terms *cultural deprivation, linguistic deprivation,* etc. And then these labels do their own sad work. (1972, 137)

Popular in the 1960s, the cultural-deprivation theory held that because of families' low intellectual standards, limited modes of child-rearing (Hess and Shipman 1965), and the visioning of life with restricted possibilities, minority groups thought concretely and were therefore unable to comprehend the abstract reasoning skills required of school subjects. An outstanding feature of cultural deprivation was lack of motivation; that unlike parents of middle-class children, poor parents failed to provide a provocative atmosphere for their children and didn't spend time naming, clarifying, or providing activities that lent themselves to reflection (Deutsch 1967a). The conviction of paucity was also applied to speech and became the image for linguistic deprivation. Nott and Gliddon (1857 in Menchaca 1997) set the stage for the belief of "high-level" and "low-level" languages by stating that Caucasians spoke intricate languages which was the representation of their superior intellect whereas nonwhites expressed themselves in primitive languages which, in turn, reflected their simple minds. The thought of speaking in inferior styles is still firmly entrenched in the minds of teachers, both Anglo and Native alike. In a course that I attended, given by an illuminating Pueblo man, the professor expounded upon this view when telling the students how middle-class parents ask detailed questions about the child's day while Pueblo parents merely give directives such as "You behave yourself." He ignored the fact that during the forced boarding-school period, Pueblo parents had to be terrified of their children participating in a misdeed because of the severe punishments meted out. The Pueblo, who are keenly aware of their history, may be acting from this reference point. More importantly, however, is the fact that subjugated groups sometimes come to believe the philosophy of the dominant group as a means of survival. Anglo teachers have told the Pueblo for many years that they have deficits, especially linguistic shortcomings, and they have come to believe it. At parent conferences where the teacher is instructed to relay the test results to parents (or guardians), the teacher's records are taken as facts about the student. Often taught that the teacher "knows best," the parents come to believe everything that is told to them. In the Kindergarten tests, the child's answers to questions form a profile of him or her, and this is how the child is labeled at risk. The teacher bandies about words like *behind, lacking, not up to grade level*, and so on. In addition, the very act of a less-educated family member meeting with an "all-knowing" teacher on school grounds hints at a dominator-subjugated relationship. In fact, the entire deficit notion represents rule over the conquered.

Many teachers of Indian children evaluate the children's verbal performance and come to the conclusion that their students suffer from extreme cognitive paucity (John 1972). In part, this may be due to the condensed language used in testing as well as the child being placed in an intimidating situation during formal evaluations (Leacock 1972). Additionally, the teacher may decide on intellectual and linguistic deficits because of the manner in which children express themselves, especially if it differs from her own language use.

A Teacher's Quandary

For several years I accepted the assumption of these children being delayed. The entry and continuing levels were proscribed in the tests that we administered to the children, and our students clearly appeared to be at an impasse. Yet I was puzzled when I was told that the children needed numerous restorative oral-language lessons because their language fell short (compared with the main-stream). My students had abundant vocabularies and seemed to communicate their needs and thoughts in competent ways. The very social nature of life in their village seemed to give the children an affable manner, portrayed by ease and friendliness in conversing with others. All young children benefit from oral-language activities that encourage further language development. I questioned why these well-spoken children needed a type of remedial language program.

Linguistic Deficit

Sociolinguist Basil Bernstein's work was largely responsible for the consigning of the language-deficit concept to conversations about contrarieties of main-stream and minority language ability: He proposed that middle-class children spoke an elaborated language and those of the lower socioeconomic class spoke language that was restricted (1972, 1975). Elaborated speech reflected values of orderliness, steadiness, and command of emotions (Foley 1997). Inherent in this code were features that were contributory to abstract thinking and problem solving, such as being profuse in subordinate clauses, adjectives, and adverbs (Ginsburg 1972). Embellished speech provided access to universal meanings that were not bound by context. In contrast, poor children's language was seen by those who subscribed to deficit theory as "restricted" in the sense that it had features that could lend itself only to concrete thinking. This type of language provided passage only to particularistic meaning, which was bound by context. It was characterized by limited adjectives and adverbs, vernacular statements, and infrequent if-then subordinate clauses. As a result, the common assumption was that the minority child was not able to deal with logical implication. Deficit adherents portrayed diverse families as disordered, impetuous, and lacking in routine. Thus, the families' speech reflected their lifestyle and was restricted in the sense that they didn't offer logical or temporal explanations of their actions to their children. When children's home life and language were seen as having these deficiencies, educators viewed compensatory language in the early years as an antidote for the children's perceived needs.

The idea of an elaborated and restricted code was alive and well in the school where I worked. The charges that our students' language was insufficient and the belief that our students needed compensatory language was based on the presumption that not much speaking took place at home, or, if it did, it was not the expansive language used in middle-class homes. The children's language use was viewed as limited. Thus, the school's attitude was not unlike what was propounded in the heyday of deficit announcements: Lower-class families did not offer the educational language activities that middle-class children enjoyed (Deutsch 1967b). The Pueblo culture's language use was condemned as inadequate and, therefore, fraught with deficiencies. This was in almost ironic contrast to the truth: The Pueblo people live a communal lifestyle. Several levels of language, including social, religious, and political languages, provide them with the means of communication. Effective exchanges with others provide the daily accomplishment of a complex village life. Yet the villagers' language competence was completely discounted.

Cultural Differences in Language Use

Rather than looking at diverse groups' language use at home as wanting, it is preferable to think of it as being different. Heath studied questioning among middle-class whites and lower socioeconomic status (SES) blacks (1981). She found that the middle-class questions at home matched those questions that were asked at school, whereas the black families' questions were a mismatch, resulting in a cultural incongruence between the black children and their white teachers. The white middle-class mothers were often alone in the home with their children so that they looked upon their children as conversational partners. Whereas the Trackton (the black neighborhood) children's mothers were rarely alone with their children, so conversation was not often directed at them. Within the middle-class homes, talk to pre-verbal and verbal preschoolers emphasized questions of the known-answer type (Brown, Palinscar, and Purcell 1986). Adults supplied the entire context, asking questions and then answering them:

> MOTHER *(addressing an eight-week-old infant)*: You want your teddy bear?
> MOTHER: Yes, you want your bear.

White mothers questioned and subsequently paused to hold conversational space for a hypothetical answer. Thereafter, they moved on to the next statement that assumed information from the hypothetical answer:

> MOTHER *(addressing her two-month-old infant)*: You don't know what to make of all those lights, do you? *(Three-second pause.)*
> MOTHER: That's right. I know you don't like them. Let's move over here.

This mode of questioning matches the kind of questioning children encounter in school, where the teachers answer questions to themselves and they count on answers from students to match to those predetermined in the questioner's mind.

The black families' questioning was not of this type. Although different, they were expansive verbal practices. They used analogy, story starting, and accusations. The first two were not used by white families. The black families looked at their children as being capable of recognizing resemblances, comparisons, and differences in things. "What they do ask about and value is metaphorical thinking and narrative exposition" (Brown, Palinscar, and Purcell 1986, 110). The black children were asked questions in school that were mismatched to those of their home environment whereas the white children experienced questioning in school similar to that at home. Thus, it is not unexpected that the white children would fare better in the educational environment.

Deficit Thinking and Genetics

Historically, genetics has been given as the reason for differences in school achievement. Hereditarian investigators proclaimed that whites inherited an intellect superior to that of minorities. Additionally, there was the presumption that this higher *innate* intelligence resulted in the acquisition of high-standing occupations while inferior inborn intelligence concluded in menial work, thus linking genetics with SES (Valencia 1997). Factors such as language differences and equal opportunities were completely overlooked. The celebrated producer of The Stanford Revision and Extension of the Binet-Simon intelligence test, Lewis Terman, described Indians, Mexicans, and African American children as being intellectually slow. He stated: "their dullness seems to be racial, or at least inherent in the family stocks from which they came . . . children of this group should be separated in special classes and given instruction which is concrete and practical" (1916 in Valencia 1997, 61) and "they cannot master abstractions, but they can often be made efficient workers" (Oakes 1985 in Darling-Hammond 1997, 46). To Terman, a man of great influence in educational and political circles, parity in educational possibilities meant that children would have opportunities and instruction proportionate to their *intrinsic* aptitude and that those who were inherently intelligent (white) might achieve high-standing schooling and employment. Thus, underrepresented children were banned from ever engaging in high-status curriculum or positions and were virtually barred from upward mobility.

During this era, testing became the measure for intelligence and determined which track children would be exposed to. This defined their course of study and, consequently, their economic and social opportunities. As early as the third grade in a public elementary school, after being administered IQ tests, I remember children on the academic track were actually discouraged from socializing with those on the vocational track. Almost all of the vocational-track children were from the working-class neighborhood that was on the outskirts of our more affluent one. Thus, class and racial disparities were defined by differences in intelligence (Valencia 1997). Once tested, a child's future was determined by the curriculum that he or she was shuffled into. It isn't very different today. Today, Indian and other underrepresented children are similarly oppressed by testing. Because most of these children's test results are scored on the low end, they, too, are sentenced to an inferior, basic-skills program where there is little opportunity for educational or social mobility. IQ tests are still given to those children who "don't fit" and are recommended for Special Education. In the last several years, I have seen children referred to this program for superficial reasons, such as not paying attention, making trouble for the teacher, and (a common one in this era of medication), not focusing. When consigning them, it is presumed that these children have innate inferior defects (therefore the teacher cannot fix them and is let off the hook) and a low IQ score is generally taken as a license to terminate "regular" education and dispense with high expectations. In the age of inclusion, they are most frequently placed in a class with other, more adept, students where they are neglected and not taught at all.

Children of color have been depicted first as being genetically inferior to whites, and later, when hereditarian views became unpopular, their culture and family life were portrayed as being culturally subordinate. Thoughts of cultural ineptitude are very real today. On February 22, 2001, David Horowitz, author of *Uncivil Wars: The Controversy over Reparations for Slavery,* expounded deficit views toward Indians when he addressed students at Villanova. He suggested an ineffectual, primitive, alienated culture when he challenged the audience to think of a single addition the Indians made to American culture. "What have they done? What have they contributed? Indian culture is nice for museums and around the campfire. Let's bring them into the American culture. Let them take part in *our* economy" (www.cspan.com).

Reasons for Failure in Indian Education

The reasons why Indian education continues to fail is the corrupting influence of deficit adherence:

1. Although masked in a pseudo attitude of ethnic tolerance, many schools continue to keep racism in shrouds. Indian children are looked upon by schools as having deficiencies in culture, familial surroundings, and language. Often, this is inadvertent and may not be apparent to the adherents. After all, most administrators and teachers of Indian children

want them to succeed. Yet they continue to view their charges as lacking the middle-class traits and values that they deem worthy and believe are necessary for school achievement. This spills over to the constant comparison of mainstream children who do well on standardized tests and proves demeaning to the minority children's culture. Perceiving children and families as having deficits is a form of intolerance that can only breed injustice.

2. As a result of these perceived shortcomings, schools charge the children with being at risk of failure. Although pervasively accepted in modern educational circles, the at-risk construct has been attributed by deficit challengers to a resurgence in the belief of cultural deprivation. It is seen as a 1990s retooled construct of this concept (see Swadener and Lubeck 1995; Valencia and Solorzano 1997). The utilization of the at-risk formula preys upon children of color and low-SES backgrounds (Winborne 1991 in Swadener and Lubeck 1995) and predicts likely failure in those to whom it is attributed. Once tested, children are often saddled with a self-fulfilling prophecy that can damage their chances of their teachers having high expectations for them. The lack of a teacher's belief in children can cause powerful damage to budding minds (Polokow in Swadener and Lubeck 1995).

3. Curricula for Indian students are driven to correct the children in jeopardy and their so-called insufficiencies. Generally, this is handled through the delivery of a basic-skills curriculum with emphasis on remedial work and catching up to so-called more fortunate white peers.

4. Cultural inconsistencies between school culture and home culture abound. Because of the school's insistence on traditional methods, the school becomes reluctant to adapt to the culture. Therefore, the culture must adapt to the school. For parents and families of Indians and other minorities, this means leaving their culture at the school entrance gate, something in which they are well versant.

5. There have been many disappointing attempts to generate a multicultural agenda. The schools in my district, as in many schools that serve diverse populations, make sincere efforts to achieve this type of forum. Numerous teachers know that by addressing the children's culture, the students will feel represented in the classroom and will be encouraged to participate. This is important because children from conquered cultures have often failed to succeed in school because they have viewed the school to be a delegate of the dominant white establishment (Spring 1994). Not only is individual culture significant, but also the study of other peoples and their way of life transmits the message of the importance of *all* ways of life. Yet, the results have been discouraging: Multiculturalism is usually presented through isolated special days, exotic foods, or interesting clothing, all of which leads to overly simplified

generalizations that lead to the very stereotypes multiculturalism is designed to eliminate (Derman-Sparks 1993/1994).

The Oppression of Educational Testing

It is common for educators to define and assess literacy in verbal terms. For Kindergarten teachers, this often translates into "How are the children progressing in alphabet, phonetic sounds, emergent reading, and writing?" Generally, if development is proceeding according to white middle-class standards, the children will be labeled as being "on track." If however, students fall below these ideals, usually on standardized tests, they are labeled at risk of failure. All too often, children of minority groups fall within the latter category.

Let us examine how children can be placed at risk. In our district, the Kindergartners are tested with the Early Prevention of School Failure test. The use of this particular instrument attests to the increasing acceptance of the jeopardy model (Swadener and Lubeck 1995). While it is beyond the scope of this book to investigate this test in detail, let me give a few examples. One of the questions asked was "What do you need to dance?" The appropriate answer, according to the administration of this test, is that the child answer "music" or "a partner" or indicates a partner with other appropriate vocabulary. In Pueblo life, of which dance is an integral part, the child often will answer this question with "a dress," "moccasins," or other paraphernalia which they know they need in order to dance in their village. These culturally appropriate answers must be marked incorrect by the test giver because it is not one of the required answers. Other questions, such as asking a child to identify a car as a living or nonliving object becomes another culture-specific response because an automobile, made from elements of the earth, is considered living according to the Pueblo. Once again, the answer must be marked incorrect. Another section of the test is geared to promote deficit thinking: The Goodenough-Harris Draw-a-Person test, which is an adaptation of the 1926 version of Draw a Man (Goodenough 1926). Goodenough was a hereditarian who claimed her test proved that there were innate differences in intelligence between white children and those of color, and this test demonstrated the genetic superiority of whites (Valencia 1997). Yet Havighurst, Gunther, and Pratt found that American Indian children managed better than white children on this test (1946). The evidence pointed to the conclusion that environment affected the performance of children. Today, accomplishment on this test is used to ascertain developmental "readiness" of the child to meet the demands of school. When the country abandoned hereditarian views in favor of cultural-deprivation theory, the test shifted with the philosophy of the time. And so culture was substituted for genetics, although there was never any scientific ground to do so. This pseudoscience that has pervaded deficit theory (Valencia 1997) often provokes school systems to believe in the validity of tests even when it is not present. The premise of this test is that in drawing a person, cognitively gifted children will include particulars, such as appendages, facial features, and so on, while those who are not as cognizant will overlook them. Those who administer the test are unaware that children may draw a person one way in a moment of time and a completely different manner a few minutes or a few days later. Figures 1.1 and 1.2 demonstrate two different depictions of a person made by a five-year-old child, drawn a few minutes apart. The first drawing would rate the child in a low rank. In the second drawing, the child would be rated as intellectually competent. Additionally, because language is minimal, Goodenough may have viewed her test as free from restraints of culture (Valencia 1997): The evidence shows that it is not. Klineberg's observation that Dakota Sioux children drew horses more often than men and, therefore, were not experienced in drawing men; Anastasi's thoughts that black children had little experience with pencil and paper; and Bakare's study, which showed that Nigerian children's performance was positively correlated with SES, indicate that this can be a culturally laden test (Valencia 1997). The point I want to make is this: The use of inadequate testing can cause inadvertent racism because it leads educators to view their charges as having shortages. Especially at the Kindergarten level, where standardized tests are perceived by the staff as determining how well the home environment has prepared the child for school, the reproach is readily placed on the culture and home life as having inadequately equipped the children. Therefore, not only is the child labeled at risk, but also he or she, presumably, is unfortunate enough to be born into a culture that has placed him or her there. Indeed, Thernstrom and Thernstrom remarked that white children are actually "luckier" than minority groups by virtue of the fact that they are born white and have middle-class status, thus more academically suitable backgrounds (2003).

Figure 1.1. Depiction of a person made by a five-year-old child

Figure 1.2. Depiction of a person drawn by the same child minutes later

When we say a diverse child is at risk, we must first apprise how we came to that conclusion. If we have based our evaluation on the norms of mainstream children, we must discard our evaluation and regard it as being imprecise. Because of the Pueblo Indians' seclusive nature (Suina 1992) and their skepticism toward research (Romero 1994), little has been reported on their children. In our school district, which is composed of mainly Pueblo Indian and Hispanic students, scores on standardized tests have traditionally been low. The school where I teach has declared itself a schoolwide Chapter I institution based on low test scores and the determined poverty level of the children. Chapter I is a governmental educational classification—its purpose is to help indigent students deemed in jeopardy of failing.

Native American children and children of other minority cultures have, historically, placed low on standardized tests (Borman 1998; Bray 1999) and frequently do poorly in school language-arts programs (Cleary and Peacock 1998). Yet when they enter Kindergarten, these children, like most other children, have shown themselves to be adept language learners, by virtue of their speaking a language fluently. The ability to learn any language requires intricate conceptual, intellectual aptitudes (Erickson 1986). There is strong evidence that when all children, including those of minority groups, come to school they have succeeded in gaining command over their grammatical system (Gumperz and Hernandez-Chavez 1972). Yet, in an honest effort by schools to have their children catch up to their white middle-class counterparts these abilities are all but ignored. Because Pueblo Indian children have been rarely studied, there has been little understanding of the way they create meaning. Because differences in learning styles, or modes in which the children express themselves, or what they value has not been known, white middle-class standards have been applied to them by default.

Cultural-Differences Theory

Cultural differences between home and school often oppose each other, leading to inaccurate assessments of children's cognitive abilities. If schools are to accurately evaluate their students, they must be aware of these very real distinctions. Different cultures have various ways of making meaning and interpreting situations. For example, Scribner and Cole showed that the Vai were assessed as mentally deficient in general tests of cognitive abilities yet used reasoning skills when called upon to perform a specific cognitive skill appropriate to their culture (1981). When assessing diverse people's competence, applying conventional methods frequently yields preposterous results (Cole and Scribner 1974 in Ginsburg 1986). Thus the Kalahari bushmen quoted by Flavell (1977 in Ginsburg 1986) capably exhibit scientific thinking when they track animals but would not be able to demonstrate proficiency if asked to complete a Piagetian task such as the combining of chemicals.

Similarly, Romero, a Pueblo Indian herself, relays that the learning processes of Pueblo children

> may not be as apparent or may not be perceived as effective learning characteristics in the school environment, an environment that is often alien and unreceptive to culturally diverse learners. In addition, cultural norms and values may influence Pueblo students' performance in the academic environment. (1994, 53)

By focusing on the learning styles and values of the communities, the schools are more likely to be able to work in concert with the children. For example, Pueblo Indian children are taught to gain knowledge from one another. If a child doesn't know the explanation of a problem, other children are expected to help that child. The schools, by advocating competition and frowning on copying (the Anglo system) only serve to alienate Pueblo Indian children because the school's value system is in direct opposition to values the children have learned within their community. If children feel their beliefs have been abandoned in the world of the school, they may experience a sense of isolation or abandonment where maximal learning is unlikely to take place. If the teacher possesses thoughtful acceptance of the children's outlook, she will be more able to interpret their values and incorporate them into the school program. In addition, she will become more qualified to help the children transition these values into responses that will assist in being successful in school and in the future workplace (Soldier 1992).

Historically, as conceptions of cultural differences emerged, explanations of children's cognition began to reflect that learning processes were outgrowths of children's sociocultural situatedness (Cleary and Peacock 1998; Swisher and Dehyle 1992). There seemed to be a large discrepancy between what minority children were able to learn at home and what they were able to learn at school. It became apparent that many of the problems these children were having were due to cultural differences between home culture and school culture, between child and teacher. For instance, black children's language learning follows precise rules of their dialect (Gumperz and Hernandez-Chavez 1972) and has been shown to be just as cognitively complex as standard English (Labov 1970), yet these children traditionally place low in language-arts subject matter. This may be due to the teacher's unwillingness to accept black English as an authentic language (Ginsburg 1972) and, in so doing, become unable to help black children transition to the school's standard English. Teachers usually expect all of their students to respond in ways that mainstream students do: Lorencita, a Navajo student, wasn't able to participate in class because she was unused to the traditional question-answer format—she withdrew from discussions (Wiletto and LeCompte 1998). When instructing children, being consistent with home practices appears to contribute to the student's progress in school. "Warm demanders" was a term given to a group of culturally endorsing teachers who adopted a mien of severity, consistent with the African American style of prodding children to high levels of academic achievement (Irvine and Fraser 1998 in Schmidt 1999). Piestrup (1973 in Cazden 1986) compared black and white teacher responses to black children's dialect and off-task behavior; he found "Black Artful" teachers who responded suitably to aspects of the children's language and culture and provided the most successful reading lessons. The teachers did this by combining black English and verbal play, corresponding to the children's dialect. Piestrup suggested that when instructing children in reading, teachers should build on the student's animated speaking patterns (Au and Kawakami 1994). In a comparable manner, Au and Mason compared teachers— one had a great deal of experience in teaching Hawaiian children and permitted the children to take turns in a joint performance, a participant structure consistent with the children's culture; the other had little experience with children and maintained a traditional participation organization, operating out of the exclusive-rights structure where the teacher chose only one child to speak at a time. When the children were with the experienced teacher, they focused more on reading comprehension in that they discussed the text and also produced more logical inferences about the story. To Au and Mason, this meant that, over time, utilizing participation structures similar to those at home had the possibility of improving reading instruction (1981a). Similarly, accomplishment was low among Athabaskan Native children of Alaska until people from their village began teaching in their school in culturally appropriate ways. The Athabaskans eschewed public reinforcement (either negative or positive) in their child-rearing practices; remaining consistent with those home practices, the Native teachers followed suit in the classroom, allowing the children to achieve success (Barnhardt 1982).

From the Pueblo perspective, there are many differences in learning practices at home and at school. Because these are in opposition to each other they cause feelings of separation in the children when they are in the school environment (Suina 1985). Pueblo children learn through modeling, practicing in private, and group learning: "Due to the emphasis on observation, attention, and focused listening in the early learning years of one's life, Pueblo children learn to internalize their experiences. To the naive educator, this type of learning may be interpreted as reticence, nonparticipation, or "slow" (Romero 1994, 53). Therefore, knowing the learning styles of diverse children can help prevent inaccurate evaluation of their knowledge. Romero's research underscored the differences between Pueblo Indian perspective and that of the mainstream—each of these two societies reflect the values that they esteem, yet these beliefs seem antithetical (1994). Whereas Anglo concepts focus on the individual, the Pueblo concentrates on the community; Pueblos focus on group practices and avoidance of self-promotion, Anglo-led schools focus on competition and self-elevation.

Antipodal incongruities were also found among Warm Springs Indians (Phillips 1972) and their schools. The social rules for speaking at home conflicted with those of speaking at school. In their classrooms, the students were hesitant to speak in front of a group, especially where there was a central figure prodding them, such as the teacher. They were more disposed to participate in group projects where they were able to discuss and direct their own actions. This was reasonable to the children because when at home, they were accustomed to autonomy, such as deciding their activities, determining when they had learned a skill, and when to make their knowledge public. Gaining knowledge at home was in obvious contrast to school, where the teacher was often the sole judge of what was to be done and how well it had been accomplished. The children, so used to speaking and acting with self-governing initiative at home were thus constrained by the authoritarian manner of the teacher and the classroom operations. This change of value systems, participant structures, and the move from independence to dependence caused the children to display reluctance when speaking in front of a group and indifference with regard to directions. Curiously, the elementary-school teachers who attempted to duplicate home-participant structures were later seen in high school as actually hampering the children because they failed to provide them with opportunities of learning how to communicate in those contexts that made children successful in school. These contexts were those that continued to oppose home-participant structures but were the usual, traditional ways schools operate. Phillips suggested that the schools consult with the community concerning their goals for their children

(1972). That is, if the community prefers that their culturally specific speech patterns be preserved, then adaptations of their speech patterns should be made in elementary school. Or, if the community is concerned that their children are provided with the means to successfully compete with non-Indians in high school, then schools can teach the appropriate modes of communication present in the non-Indian world. This formula becomes problematic. If, for example, the community decides that their participation structures should be upheld and that the elementary schools should adapt to them, the children will still be unable to communicate with others, outside of their culture, when they attend high school. Conversely, if the children are taught in non-Indian forms incompatible with their community-participant structures, they might eventually feel cheated of learning cultural formations because of the possible extinction, over time, of their culturally distinct ways of speaking. It may be preferable to view the problem of differences with balance, being culturally sympathetic and also teaching modes consistent with school success.

This disparity is complex and is reflected in what Au and Raphael point out as two views of literacy (2000). One is the autonomous model that defines literacy as a collection of skills and holds that testing results reflect the children's cognitive level in reading and writing. The second, the ideological model maintains that literacy takes place in a sociocultural arena and is circumfused by procedures for socializing inexperienced learners. This view recognizes particular literacies that may already be in place in the community. By ignoring these concepts, the traditionalist view disallows significant practices that may help the student attain expertise in school. The ideological model proposes that results of a standardized test are but one concept of literacy that children are exposed to. Therefore, it includes the autonomous model while expanding it. By recognizing a broader view, we may make accessible the barricade that has typically kept families out. In any event, adapting to cultural differences can be a part of the equation of solving the complex problem of minority school failure. Ogbu noted that cultural differences alone do not govern minority school performance (1995). He contrasted the same minority groups in different school settings and found that they fared differently depending on the specific school they attended. For example, Japanese Buraku students fared poorly in school in Japan compared with the dominant Ippan children, but they performed just as well as the Ippan children in certain American schools. Similarly, West Indians did better in American schools than in British ones. When accommodating differences, schools can seize the opportunity of teaching *every* student new techniques (Nieto 1992). Pearl believes that the differences theory is an extension of deficit thinking because it fails to credit minority students with the capacity to adapt to new situations if given the encouragement that middle-class students receive (1997). If underrepresented children received this support *and* a correspondent curriculum to that of the middle class, they would certainly have the probability of excelling. A case is made for this supposition in this book.

A Short History of the People

The Pueblo

The children in this study are all Pueblo Indian children who live in the same southwestern pueblo. They belong to the Keres branch, one that is united in language and similar culture. There are seven pueblos representing the Keres branch, five of which are served by our district, Sanchez public schools, the other two being geographically farther to the west.

Their village has been in the same location since approximately 1250 A.D. (Mays 1985). Before that time, these people, direct descendants of the ancient Anasazi Indians, occupied land in the Jemez mountains, to the west of their present location, in a town known as Tyuonyi. When a drought and an attack forced the people to move, they chose several homes and, at last, settled where they are today (Scully 1975). The Spanish began coming to the village at the turn of the sixteenth century. In their efforts to proselytize the Pueblos, they employed domineering measures and vicious treatment. Consequently, these Indians joined with other neighboring ones in the Pueblo Revolt of 1680 in order to rid the area of the brutal encroachment of the Spanish. Following the revolt, they deserted their village and fled to the nearby mountains where they established a stronghold (called Cieneguilla) until Spanish reprisals were no longer a threat. The people again took refuge there when the second conquest of the area began in 1692. When they were attacked at Cieneguilla in 1693, they returned to their present-day village and have remained there ever since (Mays 1985). By 1880, the village was composed of about four hundred of these Pueblo Indians and two hundred Spanish people who had formed a settlement there (Eichemeyer 1895). The pueblo had a schoolhouse, which was attended by both the Indian and Spanish children. At that time, all of the Indian people spoke their native Keres language. Many also spoke Spanish. The children's first introduction to English came from their attendance at the pueblo school, which was run by an Anglo woman from Boston, Mrs. Grozier (Eichemeyer 1895).

Today, most of the original Spanish families are gone—only two remain. There are approximately 650 Indian families living in the pueblo. The community is tightly joined in government, religion, and social life. Everyone knows one another and they share many common goals, such as the good of the people, the revitalization of their language, the perpetuation of their culture, and the continuation of their tribe. The children have close ties with each other. At home, the children have had similar upbringings—all are brought up in multigenerational and extended families. Aunties, uncles, cousins, and grandparents are seen on a daily basis and all have a respected input in the child's upbringing. Not only do grandparents exert an influence in the way a child in the family is brought up but their word holds weight in other children's families too—this is because the elders feel responsibility for all of the children (M. Romero, personal communication, October 1997). In this way, the children see life through a kindred lens. Because their life is a communal one, they have "caught on" how to be sociable and get along with others. These children grew up together, participated in religious and recreational events together, went to Head Start together, played (and continue to play) with each other at home and at school, attend language class together, and also attended Kindergarten together. Their parents have had similar affiliations with each other as did their grandparents, and so on. Their sense of community is strong. The pueblo is still a safe place where the children roam freely among people whom they know well. The village is located about thirty-five miles from the nearest city. It is set back about twelve miles from the main highway and is accessible by only one road.

In Pueblo life, there exists a rich social atmosphere in which the people share many mutual events such as weddings, feast days, foot races, dances, and "throws" (an activity in which families toss gifts from their rooftops to people of their community as a means of enacting the concept of sharing). As the whole village mourns for a death, they likewise rejoice at a birth (M. Romero, personal communication, March 1997). All of these activities have rich histories in which most of the people participate, so the people are strongly united by culture. It is not only the "big" events in which the people are linked but also in their everyday activities because they all have a common history and culture. The pervading feeling in the village is "for the good of the people," meaning for the good of the group. In fact, the group may be of more importance than the individual. A child growing up in this community knows his family and knows as his family not only the immediate members but all the people who live in his village. These children may have an advantage over their counterparts who live in other areas because they have a strong sense of who they are and they know where they came from. In addition, and perhaps most important, they know that they belong to the community.

Dance plays a vital part in the culture of all Pueblo Indians. In school, I frequently saw the children break out in a Pueblo dance step. This occurred in class, on the way to the cafeteria, or another such place. When this happened, the other Indian children often followed suit. Dancing is first and foremost a religious event, a way of praying. There are various dances, the most notable one taking place in the summer, in celebration of the patron saint of the pueblo. This is a corn dance: One of its purposes is to pray for rain for the harvest. I have seen all of the children in this study participating in this dance during the pueblo feast day. Dancing is hard work, yet even young children and great grandparents dance. They dress in traditional style: The women wear mantas, black woolen dresses that drape over one shoulder and are bordered with geometric patterns in green, black, white, and red. Under the mantas, they may wear a festive shirt that is trimmed in lace. Wooden headdresses, *tablitas,* with elaborately carved designs, are also worn. The women carry fresh evergreens as symbol of life; some go barefoot and others wear boot-like moccasins. The men wear white kilts, which are also bordered with geometric patterns. At their waists are heavy leather belts adorned with large commercial bells. Their chests are bare and painted, as are their faces. Across their chests, they wear a band of shells diagonally. A few feathers are worn on their heads. One hand carries a gourd rattle and the other carries evergreens and moccasins are worn on the feet. Dressed in this traditional style, the people dance out of one of the two *kivas,* (underground Pueblo religious chambers) in the morning and assemble themselves in a long line, stepping all the while to the beat of the drums and a chorus of male singers (young to old). As the Keres teacher, who is a drummer, informed me, the beat of the drums actually tells the dancers which steps to take. They dance in unison, moving to the center of the plaza, and an aura seems to fill the air as the steps, bells, shells, rattles, drum, and song all meet in perfect concord, so that it becomes a spiritual event for many, not only the villagers. The villagers continue their dancing for about forty-five minutes, when they are relieved by a second group that proceeds out of the other kiva. The two groups alternate all day, stopping only for a brief lunch, and then continuing until sunset. Of those that are not dancing (sometimes up to three hundred people will dance), almost the entire village will watch from various vantage points.

Participation is the most basic social statement a Pueblo can make. When a Pueblo decides to sing, dance, drum, or watch, he or she substantiates a commitment to being a Pueblo and contributes to the cohesiveness of the group (Sweet 1985). The villagers and the tourists make for an audience of more than one thousand people. Almost everyone, including the tourists, is suspended in long moments of rapt attention. Although tourists are invited, the dance is never a performance for them—there are some dances that are reserved for Pueblo eyes only and, at that time, the village may be closed to outsiders.

The attempted subjugation by the dominant society (M. Romero, personal communication, March 1997) and the U.S. government's dam on community property served as major contributors to the endangerment of the native Keres language in the pueblo. The dam was built in 1969 for a large city seventy miles away to prevent flooding of a local river. Exudate from the dam destroyed sacred locations and agricultural lands of the pueblo. Families found themselves without means of support, and ceremonies specific to the hallowed land were terminated. Communal activities, such as cleaning irrigation ditches for the benefit of planting, and farming itself, ceased. A large chunk of pueblo life ended. With it, so did the language that accompanied these activities. As traditional activities eroded, so did the language.

A 1992 survey at the pueblo showed that native-language fluency existed only with those villagers who were thirty-five years of age or older; with comprehension dropping with age (Benjamin, Pecos, and Romero 1997; Laresse 2002). Most of the grandparents still speak the language, although they usually reserve their everyday Native conversations for others of their age (personal communication 1997), thereby accommodating the younger, English-speaking generations. Almost all of the children, and all of the children in this study, speak English as a first language, as did most of their parents. A resurgence of the desire to revive the language exists in the pueblo. This enterprise is evidenced in several layers (Benjamin, Pecos, and Romero 1997):

1. Community—Through the revival of events and ceremonies that bring its members together, it is thought that language learning will have an opportunity to thrive.
2. The teaching of the language in the schools—Native teachers see the Pueblo students for forty-five minutes a day, Monday through Friday. During this time, the teachers engage the students in the Keres language. This is accomplished through immersion. Classes are also continued in the pueblo summer-school program.
3. Nesting—Babies and toddlers are involved in a day care situation where Keres only is spoken (Laresse 2002).
4. Mentorships—Pairing of people who are experienced and inexperienced in culture and language continues to be promulgated.

5. Bringing multigenerations together to be reengaged, children will be provided with consistent contact with fluent members. Adolescents will be paired with elders assisting them in work chores and, in exchange, the elders will teach them language and cultural information.

The present Kindergarten classes will continue, as will all succeeding Kindergarten programs, to be conducted in the children's Indian language. They will also continue to be taught Keres as they progress through the grades. The children take a great interest in learning the language. In the regular Kindergarten class, they spontaneously sing songs in their language, use words, greet each other, and call each other by their Indian names. The people have a long history of oral tradition—elders were storytellers and transmitters of cultural information. Because of this, the people have a history of learning through listening. Storytelling, too, is now an endangered part of pueblo life (J. Suina, personal communication, 1996).

Some of the original structures in the pueblo still exist, but many of the people live in newer single-family and mobile homes. There is a central plaza in which the dances and communal events take place and a Catholic mission church that dates after the Pueblo Revolt, the original church having been burned by the people in an effort to revolt against their dominators.

The people share the ancient and revered Indian religion and most have been baptized and had their first communion in the Catholic church. Most villagers practice the two religions simultaneously. The private Indian religion has been hidden from the public so their ways may be preserved. Some people practice only the Indian faith, and very few practice only Catholicism. Numerous families are involved in the pueblos' traditional arts, which include pottery, jewelry making, sewing, and drum making. Originally, these were not regarded as separate forms of "art," but were an integral part of the lives of the people. For example, pottery was and is still used for cooking and carrying water. As the dominant society exerts its influence on the people, and as the people have moved from a primarily agricultural community to one where jobs are sought in nearby cities, original ideas have been transformed and the struggle between the traditional and the new prevails.

The Surroundings

The Hispanic children who attend our school live in two nearby areas. Many live in a small village about one mile from the school. This small hamlet consists of the Catholic church, of which most people are members, and two main stores; one a small grocery and the other a five and dime. The people who reside in this community also live in single-family or mobile homes. The other area, which is strictly residential and also not on the reservation, consists mainly of Hispanics but includes some Pueblo Indian families, all of whom are members of another nearby pueblo. In both of these communities, most of the families have lived here for many generations, originally having come from Mexico. Only two generations ago, Spanish was the only language spoken. Currently, almost all of the children speak English as a first language. For most of the children, Spanish is a language spoken only by a handful of their parents and most of their grandparents. Many of the customs that were carried over from Mexico such as the Posada, a practice in danger of dwindling, wherein the events surrounding the birth of Christ are reenacted at Christmastime. There is a third community about one-half mile from the pueblo. This is on the reservation and the land has been deeded by the pueblo to this small settlement. It is predominantly made up of Anglos, many of whom comprise a small art and retirement community. The few children that live there also attend our school.

About nine miles from the pueblo is another Indian pueblo, most of whose children go to another nearby school, which is also in our school district. This pueblo shares the same culture with the one whose children were studied and a few of their children attend our school.

The Participants

DAVID is a handsome stocky boy who was five-and-a-half-years old at the inception of the study. His father was from the village where the children live and his mother was from a nearby pueblo. He was a child who always sought to do the right thing. He was extremely well behaved and always listened to and followed instructions and rules. He got upset if another child did not comport himself or herself properly. If he witnessed that type of behavior, he gently castigated the child by telling him the requisite behavior. A very caring child, he demonstrated concern when anyone was spoken to in a rough manner or was otherwise abused by a peer. David loved to draw and his favorite artistic topic was the construction of paper monsters, which he repeated over and over again. He had a placid temperament that gave him the unusual ability to sit and work for an extended period of time. He made friends easily and attracted other children as he was always cheerful and agreeable.

MARTIN is a boy who was five-and-a-half-years old when this study began. Both of his parents were from the pueblo where the children resided. His mother was valedictorian at the local Sanchez high school. Both she and her husband took an extreme interest in the child, reading to him at home and helping him with other reading and writing activities. He learned easily and was extremely curious and creative. He was always thoughtful of the welfare of others: His aunt relayed to me that when they were in the car he had noticed a woman walking and was concerned that she needed a ride. Martin wanted his drawings to have a realistic look and frequently referred to books when puzzled about how to make a particular drawing. He was very physically active and enjoyed drawing media characters like Power Rangers. He delighted in engaging in comical antics and possessed the uncanny ability to elicit laughter from adults as well as other children.

KAREN was five-years-and-eight-months old at the start of this study. She had an older brother and sister and a younger brother. Karen's greatest pleasure was in making massive three-dimensional representations. She took the position of being a little mother and reflected this attitude at school as well as at home, according to her mother (the school nurse). She delighted in taking care of her little brother and looked out for him all of the time. If anything was ever amiss, she would be the one to right the situation. If someone was the brunt of another child's mistreatment, Karen would be the one to mediate and smooth over the situation. She, naturally, fit into the position of leader and initiated activities that many children would follow.

BETSY is a girl who was five-years-and-nine-months old at the beginning of the study. She lived with her mom, dad, and four older brothers. The family was so happy that they finally had a girl that she was nicknamed "Sister." Betsy was very persevering: Once she decided on a project, she would spend long periods of time completing it until it was to her liking. After the onset of our class post office, Betsy became very drawn to writing letters. She constantly asked me for spellings of family member names such as mom, dad, brother, grandma, grandpa, and so on. Her mom told me this interest remained with her as she and her brother wrote to their nearby grandparents during the summer, even going to the extent of mailing it in the pueblo post office. Betsy always wanted to help children and was alert to those who needed help. Additionally, she always sought me out to inquire if I needed help with anything and frequently volunteered her services to me.

The children were both intelligent and kindhearted. They provided guidance and support to each other and were especially eager to help when one of the group needed assistance. In the same vein, they were quick to lean on others or directly ask for help when they themselves needed it. Their enjoyment of others was unmistakable. They laughed, joked, and pursued intellectual undertakings. They rarely complained but, rather, almost always were enthusiastic about entering into any interesting activity presented to them. Their life at home was a very social one, where accommodating others for the good of the group was the norm. Perhaps as a result of this, they demonstrated a certain finesse in social situations with adults as well as other children. They were able to deftly enter into various forms of conversations and did so without reticence. As will be seen in this book, they were able to make tremendous cognitive strides when in situations that afforded them intellectual challenges.

When looking at American Indians, there is a certain camp that romanticizes them, lumping them together and putting them on a spiritual pedestal where they are viewed as communing, inevitably to the sound of a drumbeat, with Mother Nature. It seems that mainstream society, especially in the Southwest where many Indians live, takes the best of Indian life while ignoring many of the realities that Natives experience. One can go into a shop in these areas and be welcomed by the calming effects of Indian flute music while shopping for indigenous American items. Recently, a new highway was built between Santa Fe and its northern regions and it has been decorated with beautifully painted Native symbols. While one can argue that society is celebrating the best of Native art, this type of "celebration" can become exploitative. There is nothing wrong with creating an ambient cultural atmosphere for commercial purposes, but when capitalizing upon that particular culture, there is a certain ethical responsibility that should be considered (such as adopting actions or, at the very least, an attitude that would better the exploited group). I know of several Indian families that live without running water and lack electricity. No one in our rich country should live without basic amenities such as these. Indian history bespeaks of an outlook of oneness with the community and with nature. Their culture invites cooperation and a sense of togetherness. We can all learn from these values without hyperbolizing the culture. Diametrically, Indians should not be viewed as having insurmountable social problems, commonly conceived with a view of low intellectual atmosphere, lack of hope, and rampant alcoholism. As with any people, it is incumbent upon us to view them simply as members of the human community with all of our greatness and foils, our good and our evil.

American Indians suffered abuse at the hands of the white man: having their land stolen, being ripped from the protection of their homes and placed in alien boarding schools against their will, having clothespins clipped upon their tongues for speaking their Native language, and always being assigned the role of the most invisible culture in America. We are morally obliged to do all we can to help them so these underrepresented people achieve the safety, security, and the quest for happiness that are inherent rights of humanhood. A great part of this equalization entails access to a quality education. This book aims in its own small way to contribute to this ideal.

The Social Construction of Knowledge

Social Origins of Cognition,

Language, and Literacy

*W*hen young children are engaged in the graphic process they express themselves in a variety of ways—by scribbling, gesturing, drawing, constructing artwork, and sometimes, through emergent writing. When they are engaged in this together, in a classroom setting, they talk, laugh, joke, help each other, and perform a myriad of social and intellectual activities. From their first day in school, and almost every day thereafter, the children in my Kindergarten class were given a variety of paper and writing implements and asked to write. No agenda was set before them and they were free to express themselves through the materials in any way that they desired. Without questioning, they engaged in animated conversation and drew pictures that ranged from dinosaurs to Ninja Turtles to pictures of themselves and their families. The writing of words was seen infrequently. The children sat, four at a table, and were free to explore the graphic mediums as they socialized during the roughly fifty minutes of daily writing time. For a long time, I was puzzled by the quality of writing that my students produced. They rarely involved themselves with explorations in writing—they almost always preferred drawings that contained little print. When print was used by the children, it was a rare event that was restricted to one or a few words that were well known and had been repeated time after time, with very little exploration of new vocabulary or terminology. Kindergartners think drawing is more enjoyable than writing (Baghban 1992), but researchers of young children invariably report that during writing time, as the children drew, they were frequently writing and reflected this by *spontaneously* engaging in invented spellings (Aubrey 1987; Brock and Green 1992).

The research that originally detailed invented spelling used white middle- and upper-class preschool children as subjects (see Read 1971); other investigations that detailed the ingenuity of these significations depended upon accounts of comparable children (see Bissex 1980; Chomsky 1971). Spelling in young children was seen from a Piagetian perspective. That is, this process was global and so, from this viewpoint, it was expected that not only would all literate children go through invented spelling in similar ways but also they would construct these methods as they sought to equilibrate their cognitive disequilibrium.

The Social Fabric of Learning

The sociocognitive view maintains that children have distinct ways of creating literacy, and it is embedded within their sociocultural history. Because my Indian students led communal lives, in regular cooperation with extended families and other members of their village, it stood to reason that they might reflect their learning in dissimilar ways than their middle-class counterparts who generally live with a nuclear family. Children construct knowledge within their social settings and learn through social interaction. This is later re-created and internalized and becomes part of the thought processes (Vygotsky 1978). This suggests that primary learning for young children in school comes not through direct teaching, but with social and intellectual interactions both with the teacher and the children's social allies. Thus, when children are engaged in writing groups and are continually exposed to interaction with their peers, we can expect contacts such as exchanges of information, helping, teaching, and learning. These activities have been shown among mainstream children (Aubrey 1987; Rowe 1993) and children of diverse cultures (Dyson 1993) and have contributed to literacy (Ballenger 1993), although this knowledge may be represented in various ways, according to the children's social development. Unique literacies are rooted in families' cultural practices: Jehovah's Witnesses place importance on scriptural analysis so that they involve their children in biblical text in an environment of Bible-study groups (Teale 1986). Because of particular black inner-city families' cultural orientation to read sociohistorical texts, their children, seeing them used in the home, become cognizant of books and magazines that are related to African American culture. Literacy in these African American homes also includes learning the names of family members that are inscribed on the front pages of Bibles (Taylor and Dorsey-Gaines 1988).

Pueblo oral literacy is represented by the ability to speak the Native language. Those that are said to be the most knowledgeable are those who know "old" registers. Knowledge in Pueblo society is given in increments. When one is judged ready to learn a concept, he is given that particular learning—it is possible for two people of the same age to be literate in different degrees. There are also special words and prayers specific to one's position in the village. For example, a medicine man is given the particular language that he needs in order to perform his duties. With new knowledge come new words and more complex voices in much the same way that a scientist has possession of language appropriate to his field of expertise. Storytelling was used as a means of transmitting Pueblo culture and moral values of the people, while also entertaining the villagers. Through these experiences, children learned about the history and values of their people, thus gaining significant wisdom. The unique attribute of knowing old, specialized words carries with it knowledge of culture, so that those who know these words and their uses therefore know ancestral customs—ones that must be preserved in order for the tribe to endure. Therefore, the verbal literacy of the Pueblo is associated with the inextricable combination of language and cultural knowledge for the benefit of preserving customs and the survival of the tribe.

Benjamin, Pecos, and Romero explain that in an oral society such as the one the children come from, the means of attaining knowledge is through participation in ceremonial affairs (1997). These events embody intense conversation, opportunities to ask questions, and the chance to listen to older, more experienced mentors explain the complexity of meaning in these cultural happenings. Over a period of time, and with the commitment of attending these functions where thoughts are shared, feelings are verbalized, and clarification is given, the learner becomes more fluent in the underlying cultural symbolism and the language that is enmeshed within it. While partaking in rituals contributes knowledge to the participant, the participant likewise contributes to the larger society by the very act of joining in, learning the language and the culture in order to ultimately share it with others. Pueblo literacy, then, serves as a tool for the continuation of basic values and the perpetuation of the tribe. Because nothing is written, cultural knowledge is transmitted through talking, listening, and participating. Ultimately, the one who learns later teaches others.

Cognitive acts have been shown to vary among cultures (Scribner and Cole 1981) because perception reflects historical and cultural orientation (Turiel 1989). Thought is social interplay that has evolved internally so that children's inner introspection eventually contains what they have transformed and internalized from their social lives (Vygotsky 1978). Thus, the ability to use language, which originates socially, becomes the voice for internal cognitive processes where the child can be viewed as its active constructor. Children build their language base through interaction with others. Within these exchanges, learning is intersubjective and social (Halliday 1971). In the early stages of development, children learn language from their caregivers who share the same culture and, therefore, children's speech becomes embedded within their own cultural framework, within the context of the meanings that exist there. So when children learn language, they learn to make themselves understood through a social as well as a linguistic system. The specific sociolinguistic setting that children experience provides the basis for their language. Heath demonstrated how the magnitude of sociocultural setting affected language and literacy learning of working-class and mainstream Anglo and black preschool children in the Piedmont Carolinas region (1983). She studied three communities that were united by traditions, family history, and, in the case of the townspeople, by power. By dissecting the linguistic behavior regularly rendered in each kind of home, it was identified how children learned habits that provided indicators for success or failure in reading and writing in school. At first glance, deficit thinkers may feel that this validates the cultural-deprivation theory in that certain practices provide success in school whereas others do not. Instead of castigating the culture for failing to provide specific attributes, it is helpful to learn what structures exist in the home. Knowledge of sociolinguistic style can inform the educator about what modifications could be made in order to enhance student learning. Schools can look to the children's settings to discern how their students' learning has been scaffolded at home. This will give them indications of the unique talents their students possess. Rather than disregarding a people's values and gifts in the hope of educating children according to old models, educators must learn to build on those gifts that are inherent within the community. In an effort to establish a new paradigm of children's literacy for myself, I knew the prime consideration was to take into account *what the children were actually doing*. Also, I knew that it was limiting to define their literacy strictly in verbocentric terms because my Kindergartners were expressing themselves in more plentiful ways—through art, music, dance, play, language, and, ultimately, writing. If one examines research across these disciplines, one can see that children form hypotheses that require thinking in all areas. According to sociohistorical orientation, thinking could be evidenced in many different ways:

> It is crucial . . . to allow for the development of varied ways of thought in schools. Nowhere is this injunction of greater importance than in the classrooms of Indian children, who bring with them a rich oral and visual tradition, an asset seldom understood or developed in the school years. (John 1972, 341)

The forms of literacy found in the Indian village where the particpants of this study live are both multimodal and multidimensional. There, people are involved in making drums, jewelry, pottery, painting, sewing, drawing, dancing, composing songs, and drumming. Every child weaves knowledge from the broad threads of his existence through reason of his ethnic heritage, culture, family, gender, class, language, religious beliefs, and political orientation. The possibilities for creating wisdom depend upon the manners with which schools respond to children's endeavors in applying these manifold backdrops for meaning making (O'Loughlin 1990 in Dyson 1993).

The Kindergartners and Their Writing Time

Traditionally, schools have been confined to the fundamental ideology that achievement in the language arts constitutes literacy. They assess children's literacy with standardized testing and by observing their accomplishments in reading and writing. Even for a young child, composing a building in the block area or creating a work of art does not usually get the approbation by teachers that composing a written work does, however elemental that writing may be. Many schools pay lip service to Gardner's (1980) multiple intelligences, but the ones that are favored by traditional educators are those having to do with reading, writing, or mathematical abilities. Art and music are often relegated to extracurricular realms. I realized that I was doing a disservice to the children by comparing the Pueblo Kindergartners to mainstream Kindergartners. I knew that I needed to look at them through a wider lens—one that would focus upon what they were accomplishing instead of what they were not. So, sensing that something special was going on during writing time, and knowing that the children were extremely intelligent, I set out to discover what it was that they were accomplishing as they talked and socialized and worked within this group. I suspected that this foursome was quite involved with learning and that, perhaps, they gained literacy through avenues different from their white, middle-class counterparts. Writing time in my class started out as an activity where the children sat and explored the graphic medium using markers and crayons. The children were free to talk and socialize with each other. Although it started out as a fifteen- to twenty-minute activity, the children themselves extended it to almost an hour. They regulated their actions through involving themselves in meaningful work. They usually remained at their tables, involved in their work, but were free to move about the room as desired. In the beginning, the children were only exposed to pencils, markers, crayons, and paper, but they became keenly interested in using other materials as I introduced them—staplers, tape, glue, construction paper, and craft materials. I provided them with what they sought.

Mastering Knowledge and Skill

What all children probably have in common during writing time is that their voices are articulated as they express meaning in their work. All of these meanings are grounded in the children's situatedness within their sociocultural settings—that which they bring to school and that which they learn within the school community. Learning meaning and becoming literate involves interacting with others in a social environment, through speech and action and also through text and print. Within these places, children learn to negotiate between their own desires and thoughts and those of others. Needing others to help them construct their reality, they negotiate between their culture and that of the school despite the fact that school is a contrived culture. In fact, the process of becoming literate is a process of negotiation—that which the child thinks is so at that point in time, and that which particular cultures tells them *is*. From a sociocultural view, literacy learning is a phenomenon that meshes social and cultural interchanges from both home and school (Schmidt 1995).

For young children, drawing and creating artwork offers more of an opportunity for cultural expression than writing, whereas in writing the children must eventually learn, at least in the beginning, the rigid constraints of language, where there is only one way to write the letter R or spell *dog* (Dyson 1989). In drawing, children have the impulse to copy the pictorial representations of their culture (Winner 1989). Expressing oneself through meaning is prevalent in children's graphic representations. Because of the interrelationships of children's drawings and writings, and because these are frequently surrounded by talk and other social events, in order to fully understand their meaning and their place in the literacy of children, it is necessary to look at the setting and activity surrounding the texts. When one looks at a child's text, which consists of seemingly random dots all over the page, one could not possibly extract the child's meaning unless one heard the child say to his friend as he drew, "It's raining!"

Teachers and administrators have often reduced the concept of literacy in young students to their ability to read and write. Because many observers (see Dyson 1983; Gallas 1992; Rowe 1993) have noted that young children inextricably combine art, gesturing, playing, talking, writing, and so on, there is a more generous way of interpreting literacy behaviors—one that takes into account that young children construct knowledge across these modes. When children are engaged in any activity, they are involved in learning how to create meaning. Thus, literacy can be interpreted as multimodal.

Writing Group

In the writing group situation, because I made a conscious effort to remain a minimal presence, the children came to rely on their friends. They did this by collaborating, copying, and creating common topics with which they all wanted to work. The children used these three features to promote literacy situations for themselves. From the beginning of my teaching career seven years ago, I had recognized writing time as a delight for children. They actually enjoyed it as much as any play activity. I knew this because, year after year, when I picked up my students from the bus they ran to me and asked, in one form or another, "Can we have writing time?" I had always thought that, like playtime, they were best left with little interference from me—they wanted to explore autonomy while working. The urge for independence is one of the vital forces in children, as in all humankind. Of course, I was always there for facilitation the children needed, whether it was sought directly or indirectly. In addition, I wanted to promote a coactive discourse among the children. As a believer in the children's ability to be active constructors of their own knowledge, I felt that children talking among themselves would yield beneficial effects. Rather than thinking of education as transference, I preferred to promote it as transaction. The way to achieve this was through expansive opportunities for dialogue and problem solving in a climate of mutual activities (Chang-Wells and Wells 1993). When children collaborate without the involvement of a teacher, a great deal of learning can take place. This occurs when students help one another in the performances of joint activities (Chang-Wells and Wells 1993). I was able to create a setting in which the children were encouraged to appropriate different mediational means (i.e., social language) than the ones they otherwise would employ if they were in a typical teaching/learning environment in which the teacher directs the discourse in traditional ways (Wertsch, Tulviste, and Hagstrom 1993). When working with young children, talk in nonstructured, nonschool-like ways should be an accepted part of the curriculum. The concept of learning through peer interaction has implications in the ways children learn through reciprocal speech acts:

> If we believe Vygotsky's theory of internalization from inter- to intrapsychological processes, then peer interactions assume special importance in school because of the asymmetry of teacher-pupil relationships. Children never give directions to teachers, and rarely ask questions except for procedures and permissions. The only context in which children can reverse interactional roles with the same intellectual content, giving directions as well as following them, and asking questions as well as answering them, is with their peers. (Cazden 1986, 449)

In an atmosphere such as working with peers, one would expect Vygotsky's zone of proximal development (hereafter known as the Zone or Zoped), where children learn to do things (with more experienced people) that ordinarily they could not do by themselves, to flourish. In peer interactions, the common understanding of the transfer of knowledge from a more experienced peer to a less experienced one must be expanded because there are several forms of peer collaboration. Some forms include peer tutoring, collaborative problem solving, and cooperative learning (Damon and Phelps 1987 in Forman and McPhail 1993). Other forms that the participants demonstrated were observing others, copying, suggesting, discussing, and reflecting one another's work. This chapter is intended to establish the forms of peer interaction the Kindergarten group's collaborative actions took. As I examined the children, I observed that through working together they created ways of learning. Children share and help one another in many other communities, and this is typical of what I find as a teacher in this area. This can only serve to speak of the universal nature of cooperation. When middle-class suburban children were exposed to cooperative learning, a sense of community was developed in the classroom (Soloman, Watson, Battistich, Schaps, and Delucchi 1996). Dyson (1993) found her young African American participants collaborating in writing group, as did Rowe (1993) with her Anglo pre-preschoolers. In fact, one would likely find fellowship and imitation demonstrated in many children. The motifs of collaboration, copying, and theme making were so interrelated that the reader will find examples of one of these topics as I am describing another. Yet in all three of these subject matters, the children demonstrated their desire to continually educate themselves and others.

Communal Activities at Home

The children's sociohistorical orientation is compatible with working and playing with cooperation. At home, village life is inextricably connected to working and collaborating with others. When women bake bread, they bake communally, with other women, family, and friends. The process is a long one and is accomplished outdoors. The bread is baked in large clay furnaces, dubbed *hornos*. Prior to a village event, such as a feast day, many of the women can be found performing this activity together. Rarely do women bake alone. Most often, they enlist the help of others. There are many other communal activities, such as foot races, where the villagers watch from the plaza while the participants race one another. Dances, which I have mentioned, also involve the community. Religious, political, legal, economic, instructional, and recreational facets of Pueblo life are all accomplished through collective events. People learn *through* working, playing, and talking with others. The community is used to living and working in communal fashion in order to accomplish their activities.

Working Together in School

School is a cultural institution and its primary purpose is augmenting the literacy of children. This can include children leaning from one another. Fassler found that diverse English as a Second Language (ESL) Kindergartners utilized the resources of their classmates in informal peer interactions (1998). The children increased their strategies for obtaining knowledge while they investigated and facilitated each other's oral expression. As children talk and socialize with their peers, they involve themselves in learning—they master unique ways of working with others by being in various situations, such as writing-group time. Working in alliance with peers within writing-group time is a direct outgrowth of social participation. When young children are seated together in writing groups, they naturally gravitate to talking and sharing their enterprises. As they participate with others, they generate joint stories about their drawings (Dyson 1993), suggest ideas to others concerning their work (Labbo 1996), reflect upon their work in response to peer questions and critiques (Copple 1981), and create shared texts. Children who are in environments where talk is encouraged are given to join together, and as a result, the children learn interdependence among themselves (as opposed to dependence on the teacher) and come to view themselves as both capable teachers and learners. As young children work together, they acquire literacy by sharing knowledge. Haitian preschoolers combined forces during writing time, and the children became teachers and learners to each other (Ballenger 1993). White, Mexican, and black preschoolers demonstrated that when young children are together at writing tables, they frequently partake in mutually supportive, literacy-related interchanges (Labbo 1996). As children are engaged in drawing and writing groups, collaborations flourish. This may be explained by the fact that working together provides social camaraderie and an atmosphere where propositions burgeon. In a writing group, this leads to joint constructions of works of art and stories of various types, including those that depend on common home experiences. Collaboration itself is learning because when children participate in discussion, they are actually gaining knowledge as they verbalize and clarify ideas so that they can share them with others (Wray and Medwell 1990). When Kewley investigated a group of middle-class white and Native American fifth graders, she found that their cooperative problem solving led to more flexible thinking, multiple solutions, and a clearer understanding of the steps leading up to those solutions. Peer collaboration among urban minority students was found to lead to the advancement of critical-thinking strategies (Samaha and DeLisi 2000). Cooperation and joint action within the peer group were found to be the favored style of writing among older Chicano students. This was because the students were able to express common feelings while reinforcing cultural values from home. When cultural values are promulgated by the school, the children are more able to convert their failure into success (Trueba 1993). Dialogue helps children critique and reflect upon their work, and new ideas can be generated. Discussion and demonstrations help children produce ideas for subjects that can later be adjusted, extended, or refitted as they construct their own texts (Rowe 1993).

The Kindergartners created individual texts that, in great part, reflected shared interaction because they were influenced by the others at the writing table. Often, the children participated in social interaction by working in similar genres, such as producing similar drawings at the writing table. This was because as children see and talk about one another's work, they adapt another's ideas and incorporate them as their own: a form of copying. Children copy items of interest such as making hearts, bracelets, kites, rainbows, and snowflakes (DuCharme 1991).

Collaboration in the Writing Group

These Kindergartners collaborated within their writing group just as do other children when in a writing-group situation. Collaboration has been demonstrated in various Kindergarten- and primary-writing groups, with children of mainstream and diverse cultures (Lamme and Childers 1983). By allowing the children to work together in an environment they sought, I promoted the attendant conditions in which their working together was likely to take place. Cooperation is an important means of operating in the children's village. The Kindergarten program allowed for the matching of ways of socializing and working both at home and school. Vygotsky's concept of the Zone focused on a child's learning with an adult or an older peer (1978). As I watched the children, I saw that this concept was expanded to peers of the same age who were engaged in joint social surroundings. This places the Zone in an environment where children engage in collaborative activity choosing their knowledge from a dynamic sociocultural context, a "collective" Zoped (Moll and Whitmore 1993). The children learned from each other as they sought each other out as a means of obtaining the knowledge they needed at a particular moment. While the children worked, the room was usually abuzz with talk, laughter, singing, chanting, acting, and playing. The participants demonstrated collaboration in several ways: by making joint stories about their drawings; verbally suggesting a change in someone else's work; physically altering another's work; and accepting these suggestions or alterations (i.e., allowing these modifications to occur, resulting in a change of text from its original production). This give-and-take among the children made for a general, *comfortable* feeling of kinship that transferred to their work—one's work was open for comment, change, and sharing. Engaging in conversation is tantamount to engaging in collaborative activity. It is collaborative: because of the methodical succession of speaking and listening; because the meanings are related to all those that proceed and follow; and because participants consent on the phenomena and events to which significance is applied in a shared situation (Wells 1981b).

Joint Story Making

The children collaborated to make joint stories. As they drew they talked and as they talked they created stories about their drawings. The drawings sparked their conversation and their conversation fueled their drawings, so reciprocity existed between the two modes. Talk centered on the children's work and sparked additions. This was exemplified in the following episode in which David and Martin's talk and work spurred them onto similar creations:

1   DAVID: I'm putting rain. *(He drew dots for rain.)*
2   KAREN TO DAVID: You're putting rain.
3   DAVID: For my grass.
4   MARTIN TO DAVID *(looking at David's drawing)*: So the trees can grow too?

In the beginning of the episode, David declared that he was making rain. This act of drawing a symbol and stating that he had done so set the stage for the scene that the children entered. In sociodramatic play, it is complementary to "I'll be the daddy and you be the mommy." It occurred when there had been little or no previous discussion about that particular project and there was a need, at that time, to communicate what one's work was. This is a type of initiation (Barnes and Todd 1977); it served to draw others into the conversation. Martin was moved to enter the story making not only because of David's opening remark but because there was a response to his remark (when Karen rejoined) and David's subsequent one, which advanced the remark to a conversation. Conversations entice others to join in because they are prime sources of socialization. From babyhood, children are included in family discussions that accompany everyday actions—by this age, the children are used to conversing and easily use it as an essential part of communicating and making meaning. When Martin questioned David's remark, he indicated that he was a willing partner in the joint story making.

5   DAVID TO MARTIN: That already growed and it growed apples.
6   MARTIN TO DAVID: I'm growing apples, too. *(Martin drew a tree with apples.)*
7   DAVID TO MARTIN: It's raining hard now. *(David drew the rain in strokes rather than the dots he had made before. He drew the strokes coming out of the clouds that he was drawing. He held his work up.)*

8 MARTIN TO DAVID *(as he finished drawing the tree)*: I growed some trees. I'm gonna put some rain now.

David's dialogue concerning the action ("it growed apples" and "it's raining hard now") within his drawing influenced Martin to integrate it into his own work. By doing so, Martin was able to continue with the mutual account. Later on in the episode, David repeated this same move, with the same results:

9 DAVID *(as he put his hand on his drawing)*: Lookit the grass changed; it growed and growed and growed.
10 MARTIN TO DAVID: I'm gonna make my grass grow too. *(Martin lengthened the grass with upward strokes.)*

The story continued:

11 DAVID TO MARTIN *(as David spoke, he drew upward strokes of grass)*: Make it grow higher and higher and higher . . . growing, growing, growing, growing, and something happened! It's starting to rain hard! *(He drew more grass.)* My grass growed and growed. *(Martin nodded his head as he looked at David's work.)*
12 MARTIN: Let me see your work. *(Martin took the work out of David's hand and looked at it.)* Wow, it growed. It went high, high.

David and Martin's use of repetitive words (*growed, high*) supported the coherence of the evolving story (Dyson 1993). The repetitions and pronominalizations used were part of the collaborative syntactic and lexical dialogue (Halliday and Hasan 1976).

Not only did David and Martin create but also they built on those creations, re-creating their works (they didn't amend—they added to), with further drawing (another apple tree, more rain, higher grass, a change in type of rain). There was much excitement as David and Martin lived through the joint action of their narrative and drawings. There was a unity in their manner as they cooperated with each other to describe and draw the rainy scene. In this episode the children's talk drove them to create further works (e.g., "Make it grow higher") and the works actually drove their talk (e.g., "My grass growed and growed"). There was an interplay between drawing and speech that ignited each other. Drawings became living tableaus where shared story making made actions happen. The drawings would not have looked like they did had it not been for the collaboration between the two boys. Each child took turns and each turn revealed reference to the antecedent statement. There was general agreement on the referents and, consequently, their language communicated a collective tone.

Collaboration through Altering the Work

Sometimes the collaboration consisted of unsolicited recommendations. A child would volunteer suggestions to another's work. The child to whom the proposition was directed usually took the advice. Guidance was given with the hope of improving another's creation or to invite someone to continue with joint storytelling. In the following two episodes, one child gives unsought suggestions to another:

> DAVID TO MARTIN: Make him different colors. *(Martin subsequently made his Power Rangers various colors.)*
> DAVID TO MARTIN: Make it [the grass] grow higher and higher." *(David and Martin both made higher grass.)*

As contrasted with black Kindergarten participants of low socioeconomic status, who did not initially welcome unsolicited help (Allen and Carr 1989), these children gladly received unsolicited counsel. Perhaps it was because the Kindergartners in the former study did not know each other at home, whereas my participants did. Knowing someone well makes it easier to receive advice. In any event, it must be noted that these children often became involved in another's work. The cultural timbre in school became one of assisting, caring, and seeing that one "did his best." The children had mutual trust in each other so that they could use and try out the various ideas of another, ultimately incorporating it into their own repertoires. Thus, it was evident that the children constructed their knowledge from the sociocultural base that they created in school, one that had many similarities to that of home.

At other times, the collaboration consisted of physically adjusting another's work. The child who was doing the adjusting did so unbidden. It was intended as an act of help—either to achieve an improved version of the work or to help the child achieve a skill he was unable to do. In the following two episodes, the children physically adjusted another child's work. It was unasked for, yet the child doing the adjusting acted in this manner because he or she thought it would improve the other's work and knew the advice, most likely, would be welcomed:

1   DAVID TO MARTIN: I put windows on yours [an airplane], OK? *(David had drawn windows on Martin's airplane.)*
2   *(Martin murmured "Mmmm" to David, signifying that it was indeed all right to do so.)*

In another episode:

BETSY TO DAVID: I folded your kite. *(Betsy had folded David's kite.)*

Frequently, the adjustment was solicited. One child would directly ask another to aid in an action she did not have the knowledge to do alone. Sometimes the request was indirect, as in the following event:

1 MARTIN *(put his face in hand as he sat)*: I did it wrong.
2 BETSY TO MARTIN *(going to Martin, carrying an open marker)*: Just do like this *(as she altered his drawing)*.
3 BETSY TO MARTIN: How 'bout his legs?
4 MARTIN TO BETSY: I'm gonna make him legs. *(Martin drew a leg.)*
5 DAVID TO MARTIN *(as he leaned over to look at Martin's drawing)*: No, he's supposed to have two legs.
6 MARTIN: Oh, I messed up again. *(He drew another leg.)*
7 DAVID TO MARTIN *(as he again leaned over toward Martin's work)*: The Blue Ranger is supposed to have a triangle like this. *(David moved his fingers on Martin's work, showing him how to make it.)*
8 MARTIN TO DAVID: I know, I forgot.
9 DAVID TO MARTIN *(as David drew on Martin's work)*: Remember, you're supposed to draw this part black.
10 MARTIN TO DAVID: Yeah.

In this episode, Martin appealed for help through his statements of need. In lines 1, 6, and 8, Martin lamented that he had neglected something, either by doing it wrong, messing up, or forgetting. Thus, he alerted the group to his necessity for recommendations. Each time he summoned them, they were quick to respond. In lines 2 and 9, the children responded by physically adjusting Martin's drawing. Lines 3, 5, 7, and 9 offered suggestions for change. Martin was very receptive to the children's suggestions and alterations (the addition of two legs for each Power Ranger, a triangular form, the adjustment Betsy made, and the black markings), so his text changed from what it would have been. When he had all the advice and assistance he needed, he was able to draw two more Power Rangers, completing the work alone. In this way, the aid of his peers through collaboration helped Martin achieve the text he sought. Martin created the atmosphere for help to arrive. He continued to ask for help as the work progressed. The Zoped was gradually attained by a collective progression of suggestions, interjections, and requests. The text actually became an aggregate. The construction of knowledge can be seen in the construction of text. Each new piece was assembled upon the original. As each element was added, with mediated assistance, the construction improved. That is, it looked more like what the child wanted it to represent (in this instance, the desired Power Ranger). Martin used cultural resources as tools to develop his own learning. When he finally was able to draw the Power Rangers by himself, he was able to carry what he had learned in the social intermental plane, transforming it to the intramental area by, ultimately, drawing his own Power Rangers.

At other times, the request was direct. The child would ask for help outright. The child wanted to gain knowledge that she did not have and, by asking, hoped to acquire. In the following episodes, the children asked in a straightforward manner how to make a particular object:

MARTIN TO BETSY: Howdja make that, Betsy?
BETSY TO DAVID: How do you make a Easter egg? *(David left the table to get paper. Karen responded by telling Betsy how to make her egg.)* [Note: the article *an* is not used in this region.]

When Karen told Betsy how to make the egg, she freely substituted herself for the person who was sought because that person was not present. In a group situation, the sought-out person did not have to be the helper. The supporter could be anyone who knew someone needed help. This type of substitution occurred frequently. At first glance, it may appear that a failed message was delivered or that rudeness was exhibited because the person entreated left the table before coming to the aid of the one who solicited help. Rather, the one who was requested was preoccupied with another activity. It was evident that one of the other children would heed the needs of the child who appealed for help. If the sought-out individual was otherwise involved, one could still rely on the group. This, of course, has its parallel in communal life where one depends on the group. Working in group unison pervades the villagers' lives: They go on rabbit hunts together. When a man catches a rabbit, he throws it to the group of waiting women and whoever catches it gets to keep it. Although it is used as food, the man who gets the rabbit does not "save" it for family members. The rabbit becomes community property, so to speak. When the parties stop for lunch, they take out their food and everything is shared. Although rabbits are a desirable source of food, the point of the hunt is to engage in a communal outing where fellowship is solidified. This and other community activities presuppose group planning and group participation. Because these actions are achieved together, members come to rely upon one another for the successful completion of any event. In this way, the children's sociocultural history was in accordance with their behavior at school. In fact, the children's behavior may have indicated the carrying of their history into the classroom. The group environment became what the children made it. Values such as sharing, helping, and cooperating became the context in which the children worked.

Copying

The children learned by copying each other. They would copy an aspect of a work or the whole work, adapting it to suit their needs. They seemed to copy what they needed to know. For example, if a child used scissors in a particular way, such as cut-out forms on paper, and another child wanted to learn how to make those particular cuts, he or she would copy the cutting. If a child needed to learn how to make an Easter egg, he would copy the egg of another child. If one wanted to learn how to staple, he or she would copy the movements of the child who was stapling in order to learn how to do it. Ideas, too, were frequently copied, such as when Martin copied David's ideas about making an apple tree or putting rain on the grass. Here, the Zoped took on new dimensions—the child observed and attended to what others had done. At the same time, the child constructed knowledge from these observations, acted upon them (copied them), and finally, was able to incorporate them into his repertoire, using them independently. Once the children began their creations, interest was sparked in one another's work. Copying was a frequent occurrence.

One day the children raided the cooking shelf and found paper plates and muffin cups:

1   MARTIN: I'm gonna make something. *(He glued the base of a muffin cup to the center of a paper plate and attached two paper strips to the end of the plate so that they looked like streamers. He placed it on his head, the muffin cup touching his hair, and said the following to Betsy, Karen, and David.)* Hey look, hey look, hey look! *(He elicited laughter from the group. David made the same creation and put it on his head too, which also evoked laughter.)*

2   MARTIN TO DAVID: You copied! *(Martin giggled.)*

Martin used repetitions (e.g., "Hey look, hey look, hey look"), which was utilized to attract others to his work. David was attracted to Martin's work and the laughter that it evoked, so he made a duplicate of it.

3   DAVID *(Waving his paper plate with attached strips back and forth)*: This is a alien ship . . . landing. *(As he spoke, he slid his work onto the table.)*

4   DAVID TO BETSY: Lookit: a alien ship! Betsy then announced: I'm gonna make a alien ship.

5   BETSY *(Looking at Karen's assemblage of materials)*: Naah, I'm not gonna make it.

David's movement of sliding his spaceship in front of Betsy served as enticement to Betsy to copy, although she subsequently changed her mind (because she became interested in the materials Karen had collected).

6　KAREN: You guys know what I'm gonna make?

7　DAVID: What?

8　KAREN: Something that can shake like for music. *(She put some small Mylar squares on her paper plate. Betsy left the table and came back with a plate full of the Mylar squares. Betsy copied Karen step for step as Karen made her music shaker.)*

9　KAREN TO BETSY: Are you copying?

10　BETSY TO KAREN: I'm not copying.

(Martin started to make cuts on his original paper plate "hat," imitating David's cut-outs. David had been cutting and coloring his earlier copy of Martin's work.)

11　DAVID TO MARTIN *(as Martin picked up the scissors)*: Martin, are you going to make the same thing?

12　MARTIN TO DAVID: No, but I'm gonna make something like a eye.

During this writing event, there were three comments by the children on their peers' copying. There was never any intimation that it was inappropriate to do so. In the first, where David copied Martin's hat, Martin observed David's reproduction but said it laughingly. In the second, Betsy replied to Karen's question, "Are you copying?" by saying, "I'm not copying" (although she was); Martin replied to David's "Are you going to make the same thing?" by denying it and calling it "a eye" possibly because that's what it looked like to him. It may be that the children do not see their work as an imitation. After all, copying often takes place in village life. For example, when one is learning a dance, one watches other, more experienced participants in order to learn the steps. It has been documented that learning in village life entails observation of others (Romero 1994) and, therefore, watching and copying are expected norms. In school, the children have not yet advanced to grades where they are taught that copying is not an accepted Anglo mode of learning. There were never any negative connotations mentioned about copying in class. When the children worked, they were busy drawing, cutting, stapling, gluing, and, when copying, are involved in their own particular variation of the work. Frequently, when charged with copying, they seem to be taken by surprise when informed that their work is not all their own doing. Yet, it is interesting to note that Betsy later relayed that she intended to copy David's work that is detailed below. The episode continued:

Betsy opened her paper plates, which were then stapled only at one end, and let the Mylar pieces pour out.

13 KAREN TO BETSY: What are you doing? You can make a mouth out of it. *(Betsy opened the two plates, except where they were stapled at one end, and moved them like a mouth, opening and closing the plates. Then she drew eyes and a nose on it.)*

14 BETSY TO MARTIN *(she held up her "mouth," opening and closing it, and said, as she directed her "mouth" and gaze at Martin, in mock rough voice)*: I'm gonna eat you, Martin!

Betsy copied Karen's idea of making a mouth out of her work. Copying one's ideas was really a form of adopting one's suggestion. Copying involved not only imitating another's work but also incorporating the ideas of another.

15 BETSY TO DAVID *(Betsy put down her "mouth" and cut the fluted part of a paper plate as she had seen David do)*: I'm gonna copy you now.

16 DAVID TO BETSY: Are you going to make the same thing that I made? *(Betsy moved her head to indicate the negative as she looked down at her cutting.)*

17 DAVID TO BETSY: It's gonna be a different one? *(Betsy nodded her head in the affirmative as she finished her cutting.)*

When Betsy said she intended to copy David's work, she didn't mean that she was going to duplicate it. She meant that she was going to copy *an aspect* of his work, that aspect being the cut-outs on the paper plate. Copying part of a work involves critical thinking—one must decide what configuration of another's work one needs in order to create what it is they intend to make.

18 BETSY TO DAVID: How do you make pants?

19 DAVID TO BETSY: Wait, I'll show you, Betsy; let me draw . . . *(David showed her by drawing a pair of pants. He gave it to Betsy to cut out. She tore them up and made her own, ones that looked like the pants David made for her.)*

Having learned how to make pants from David, Betsy destroyed David's template so that she could make them herself. Thus, she incorporated the knowledge she learned from David's model and used it for her own purposes.

Betsy completed her work and named it a "cheerleader." After I called for cleanup, Karen quickly made another creation, which she first called a "star," then called it "a angel." It resembled Betsy's cheerleader.

In this session there was a great deal of copying. David was attracted to Martin's work, or the laughter that it evoked, and made a duplicate of Martin's work. Betsy stated she would copy David's alien ship, but changed her mind and copied Karen's work by making a music shaker. Betsy copied Karen's idea and made a mouth. Martin copied David's cut-outs when he made his eye; Betsy copied David's cuts from a paper plate and also copied his pants. Karen copied Betsy's cheerleader. Betsy, Karen, and Martin all copied the cut-outs from David, whose work originally was a copy of Martin's. So we see reciprocity of copying one from another in which the results are original creations whose initial ideas belonged to someone else. The children learned by copying. Copying from peers lead to learning new ways of knowing. All of the children constructed their literacy when they copied from one another: David learned new ways of social interaction by eliciting laughter; they all increased their fine-motor development by cutting; and, chiefly, they became experienced in new ways of representation. Learning took place in a multilayered dimension, learning from one or another in the group and, in turn, giving knowledge back to one or another in the group. The children were able to create works that they ordinarily would not have created alone. When copying, they attained this knowledge first through observation. They observed, conferred with others, took action, and then incorporated their new knowledge into their work, making it their own. The children learned by observing other's work and by determining what piece they wanted to copy—this lead to the learning of new concepts and skills. There was a mutuality present in all the learning so that transfer of knowledge from one person to another, back and forth, moved not only vertically, but more often, horizontally. During horizontal interchanges, a student can often extract beneficial information from others who are not generally more capable, and some members of the group can be more able at some moment during peer interaction (Hatano 1993). The children were invested in one another's work, creating a confluence of learning that resulted in an aggregated Zoped.

Theme Making

As the Kindergartners worked in their group, they invented their own themes. Their social interchanges exercised an influence on their topic selection (Brock and Green 1992). Theme making occurred when the entire group of four children chose a particular topic to work on. It began as one child expressed his or her ideas to another child and, subsequently, the group "caught on." It occurred when certain materials were used—these materials sparked ideas that spread to the group; it occurred when one child saw another making something that was of interest and proceeded to make it, and others also found it engaging; and it occurred when a combination of these events took place. What made theme making distinct from copying was that a theme was adopted by the entire group and was usually sustained throughout the entire writing period. The children intertwined their thoughts and works together in a *gestalt* as they decided on themes.

Often materials sparked the idea for theme making. On the day the group chose to make Easter bunnies, I had merely placed some pipe cleaners on each table. Each child was quiet for a moment as they looked at the pipe cleaners, manipulated them, and formulated ideas for their potential use. Karen slid her fingers alongside them as if feeling the texture; thereupon she made Vs with them and twirled them around each other. Martin stood up from his chair, manipulated them, moved them back and forth in his fingers, bent and straightened them, placed them lengthwise on the front of his head, just above his forehead, as though he was trying them on. Betsy looked down at the pipe cleaners and copied Martin—she too put them on her forehead and said to herself, "What I should make?" She called Martin ("Martin, look!") so he would see the pipe cleaners on her forehead. The pipe cleaners kindled the idea of bunnies, just as string often sparked the idea of making kites. David also handled them, moving them as he looked down at them. Suddenly, he made bunny ears with them, holding them both up in the air: "Lookit, look at my Easter bunny." Martin immediately said he wanted to make a bunny, Betsy told David she was making a bunny, and Karen soon joined in. Thus, the theme for the day was established. The children obtained materials as they thought of what they needed—tissue paper, cotton balls, markers, and so on. If one child had an idea, it caught on as the theme developed. Three of the children, David, Karen, and Betsy, worked at the writing table whereas Martin went to the library corner in order to get a book about bunnies. When he found one, he stayed there, drawing his picture. Each child made a bunny, but each one was made quite differently. Although each was distinct, there were certain resemblances between the bunnies drawn by Betsy, Karen, and David, who had been sitting together while fabricating their constructions (see figures 3.1 through 3.3). The three children used the original pipe-cleaner ears that had inspired the theme. Each child *drew* the face in similarly. All three made whiskers; David and Betsy had whiskers coming from the nose whereas Karen had whiskers on the mouth. David and Karen made eyes in the same way: a dot surrounded by a circle. Both Karen and Betsy used pipe-cleaner arms and tissue-paper clothing. Betsy used cotton balls to stuff her bunny, whereas Martin used them to cover his bunny (see figure 3.4). Martin made his bunny quite unlike the others, having drawn his entire work, save for the gluing of the cotton balls. He spent much of the time away from the group looking for his picture, insisting that he needed one in order to make his work. Martin's was not like the others because he wasn't physically at the table with the group for most of the time. Therefore, he didn't have the opportunity to copy the details of his work. As for the three children who sat next to each other, theme making involved a good deal of copying from one another so that they were involved in the commerce of ideas—how to make ears, faces, and clothing. As in all of their thematic undertakings, there was a great deal of replication from one to another. One child would copy a particular aspect while another child copied a different aspect so that, although all the works were unique, there were many similarities. Here, all four works exhibited the same thematic topic.

Action was the incentive for other themes. For example, the following episode demonstrated how the children created an airplane theme. Betsy was absent on this day.

Figure 3.1. David's bunny

1   *(Martin folded his paper to the shape of an airplane and flew it, causing it to land on the table several times.)*

2   DAVID TO MARTIN *(he picked up the airplane and flew it back to Martin)*: Is that how you fly this airplane?

3   *(David went back to his drawing.)*

4   *(Martin flew his plane past the children many times. He loudly voiced the sounds of airplanes taking off and landing.)*

5   *(Both David and Karen drew pictures while Martin was doing this.)*

6   MARTIN: I'm gonna draw people in this airplane. *(He started to draw people. Karen and David continued with their drawings. Martin looked at David.)* I'm gonna draw people, draw people.

7   DAVID *(He immediately stood up)*: I'm gonna make a airplane. Howdja make that?

8   *(Martin left the table to get paper.)*

9   KAREN TO DAVID: You have to fold the paper, look, go like this. Go like this, watch. *(She made the folds on a piece of paper.)*

10   DAVID TO KAREN *(He watched Karen and copied her. After several attempts, he mastered the fold)*: There, now I got it. *(He then stapled the folded airplane, drew a person looking out of the window, and flew it.)*

11 *(Martin returned to the table.)*

12 DAVID TO MARTIN: If you don't staple your work it will fall apart right away. *(He pointed to his stapled work.)* Like I did it, look.

13 *(Martin picked up the stapler and stapled his airplane.)*

14 KAREN *(She stood up after she finished making her version of an airplane.)*: Look at mine! *(Karen said this in a triumphant voice.)*

15 DAVID: I'm gonna make that too . . . I'm gonna make the same thing as Karen's. *(He went to get paper. Karen stood up and tried to fly her airplane. It didn't fly too far.)*

16 MARTIN TO KAREN: Go like this with your arm . . . like this. *(He showed Karen how to fly her plane. She tried it and was successful.)*

17 DAVID *(when he returned to the table and looked at Karen's work)*: It's a rocket ship! A rocket ship! . . . I'm making a rocket ship too. *(David made a work similar to Karen's work.)*

Martin's introduction, throwing the plane on the table, did not capture the interest of Karen or David. They kept right on drawing (line 5). Yet, when Martin employed repetitions in his speech (line 5, line 6), David became interested (line 7). Repetitions were used to attract others to one's work. When Karen heard that David needed help, she entered the arena by offering it. Giving and receiving help became a dominant factor when the children created their themes. Once again, a child *stood in* for the one sought: Karen substituted herself for Martin (line 9).

Therefore, David learned to make an airplane by copying what Karen taught him (line 10). When Martin returned to the table, David offered advice to Martin ("If you don't staple your work it will fall apart right away") (line 12), and Mar-

Figure 3.2. Karen's bunny

Figure 3.3. Betsy's bunny

tin acted on David's warning (line 13). Martin taught Karen how to fly her plane (line 16). David's copy of Karen's rocket ship was an almost exact duplicate. All airplanes showed a likeness of construction and design; all displayed windows, exhibited personages in their windows, and those figures were all drawn in stick-figure fashion. Each child took on the register of teacher, asking the learner to observe what was modeled (lines 9 and 12). In each case, the learner followed what the teacher modeled, a learning style consistent with Pueblo ways of knowing (Romero 1994). Each learner physically tried out and adopted what was taught.

Unlike the Easter bunny episode, where the theme was established early on and the children decided what they would make, concurrent with that theme, this theme unfolded as the children gained expertise in making airplanes. By the end of the writing session, the children had helped each other learn many skills: David learned how to make airplanes; Martin learned how make them more durable by stapling them; Karen learned how to make them and fly them.

When the children involved themselves in theme making, there was usually a mutual hubbub of copying—one copied a part of the work from one child and then another child and, in turn, parts of the child's own work served as examples for others. Frequently, when a child finished one work, others were created (whatever the theme happened to be). Not only were the children learning from one another but the works themselves became symbiotic—they unfolded as assisted works because they were done in concert with others.

The children also created a ghost theme. These ghosts were predominantly made from straws, tissues, and yarn. The children created one after another as they mastered the art of taping, tying string, centering objects on straws, fine-tuning their motor skills as they pasted hair and created faces, and so on. Although they all used similar materials, once again, each work was unique and manifested its own creativity. Theme making, with these children, did not involve mundane reproductions but innovative permutations. As they created these ghosts, they sang *Caspar the Ghost* and chanted en masse the poem they had learned during Halloween, *The Five Little Ghosts*. They danced around the room with their ghosts—this exemplified the use of many modes of literacy, involving the creation of three-dimensional works, singing, chanting, and dancing. Multimodal literacy was demonstrated especially during theme making because the children, having similar creations, involved themselves in expressing them. When the children made paper-bag puppets, they performed an impromptu puppet show and spontaneously created a dance, where they hopped, stepped, and skipped with puppets in tow. They tended to combine the disciplines of art, music, and dance as natural ingredients of literacy.

Moving through the Zone

The Kindergartners demonstrated that they learned by collaborating, copying, and theme making. As they sought to gain knowledge, they turned to those they knew would help them. From others, they learned those facets of knowledge that they would never have understood had they been working alone—they moved to higher intellectual understandings. By working together in a social atmosphere, they constructed a communal awareness that surpassed each of their individual awarenesses. Subsequent to the collaboration, each took away a sizable portion of this communal awareness as his or her own knowledge (Wray and Medwell 1990). Therefore, learning in the Zoped occurred through a joint construction of meaning. This was promoted by the various activities that were inherent in the writing group. The children actively pursued the cultural means to help in their own development (Moll and Whitmore 1993).

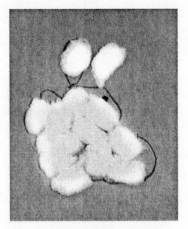

Figure 3.4. Martin's bunny

When peer collaboration is evaluated for its effectiveness, motivation should be taken into account (Tudge 1990; Forman and McPhail 1993). There is certainly no doubt that the children were highly motivated to solve their problems and knew they could do so collectively, with the aid of the group. During horizontal arrangements, participants' motivations to unveil their ideas are strong because no autocratic "right" answers are expected to come instantly (Hatano 1993). Darling-Hammond observed that when children are engaged in group situations, each zone extends from the youngster's present level of ability to a level urging more understanding which the child can shortly attain with the help of others (1997). Within the Kindergartners' peer collaborations, the varied overlapping of zones interacted to provide serviceable understandings and pathways to others in the group so that the surroundings became a place of constantly moving thoughts, suggestions, and ideas. This was the setting for evolutionary thought where concepts were often floating in the air, so to speak, ready to be picked up by anyone in the group who needed the information. These interactions occurred through speech, gesture, and activity. When ideas were presented, the children had the options of selection, modification, or rejection, all in a noncompetitive, nonthreatening space. Conversation within the context of collective activities became learning because an audience was provided so that the speaker could try out ideas, think out loud, and receive feedback. Moll and Whitmore's concept of the Zoped as being "collective" means that it is erroneous to think of the Zone as a solitary property of the child but, rather, of the child involved in collaborative activity within particular social (dialogue) climates (1993). The importance is in discerning the social dealings that went on within the writing group, the socioculture of the group.

The children learned by actively interacting with one another within that social place. The Kindergartners depended on multiple sources of knowledge that gave them more options to construct additional knowledge with others. Manifold input makes possible communities in which each child makes notable offerings to the incipient perception of all of its members (Palinscar, Brown, and Campione 1993). The Kindergarten group created a dynamic atmosphere where, through reciprocal trust and dependence on each other, they were able to question, advise, suggest, intervene, direct, observe, and create ideas with which to work. There was no passivity involved—the children actively pursued knowledge by choosing the mediational and cultural means necessary to assist in their own development.

4

The Children's Pre-History
of Writing

F undamental to Vygotsky's work is that in order to understand human mental functioning one must always look at the history of its development.
This is why, when investigating the development of writing in the child,
we must examine its evolution—the history of gesture, dramatic play, drawing,
and speech (Vygotsky 1978). Children learn to make meaning through these
components, and when they do so, they become equipped with the knowledge of
how to represent. When we investigate these avenues, we are able to appreciate
the importance of what we can refer to as the early stages of writing. When the
Kindergartners were engaged in activities during writing time, they became able
to more fully develop their symbolic repertoires. It was important to set the environment for the unfolding of symbolizing. The children's expansion of this ability was a natural process—nothing needed to be taught. The children needed
only the freedom to express themselves and the materials with which to act. In
this chapter, I will follow the children's progress of signifying throughout the

modes of gesturing, dramatic play, creating artwork, and early writing. Following this advancement entails the process of looking at the formation of symbols that emanate from the child rather than investigating the marks that we may read into the child's text. My aim is to show the growing ability of the children to symbolize.

Gesturing and Dramatic Play

In play, if a child can perform the same gesture to an imaginary object as she can to the real object, the imaginary object becomes a symbol for the real one and the appropriate gestures are what give the meaning. This is first-order symbolism because the substituted article directly denotes the real one (Vygotsky 1978). Let us examine how the children signified materiality:

> KAREN TO ME: Miss Terese, I'm going to take a picture of you. *(She held a muffin cup up to her face, elbows bent. She squinted and then made a clicking sound. At the same time, she moved her finger as though pressing the button.)*

In this example, Karen's muffin cup referred to a camera. Her gestures accurately portrayed that she was photographing because she used the same motions with her imaginary camera that she would have used with a real one. Speech was also needed to delineate her symbol.

On a particular day, I placed a bunch of coiled gift ribbons on the table. Each of the three children (Karen was absent) took some of the ribbons.

> *(David placed ribbons on his ear lobe, mimicking an earring. Martin did the same thing. Betsy put ribbons on both sides of her head.)*
> BETSY TO THE GROUP: My curly hair. My curly hair. *(She moved her head from side to side, making the ribbons bounce back and forth. David put ribbons on both sides of his head. He rocked from side to side so that his ribbons also jiggled.)*
> DAVID TO THE GROUP: My curly hair. My curly hair.

The children signified curly hair with the ribbons. The curly hair was defined by the gestures of oscillating movements—back and forth, to and fro. These movements caused the ribbons to swing and sway, just as curly hair would. Initially, both David and Martin put the ribbons on their ears but didn't use any speech. Their manipulations were unable to come to fruition by gesture alone. Gestures needed speech to define the activity. Betsy's symbol was accompanied by language and, thus, perceived. While the muffin cup did not particularly resemble a camera, the ribbons did have a likeness to curly hair.

Although Vygotsky theorized that it was the gesture that transformed the object, he pointed out that as children develop, they begin to discern characteristics in the imaginary object that correspond with the real one (1978). The Kindergartners usually displayed this feature by choosing a property whose attributes were similar to the referent. The children were involved in using various materials for artwork that gave them many options to design representation. For example, a pom pom became a powder puff and bits of straws became bullets. Appropriate gesture was the driving factor: The pom pom was used to pat the face as though makeup was being applied; the cut-up straws were thrown to serve as bullets. The pom pom, the straws, and (in the former examples) the muffin cup and the coiled ribbons became signs for the real objects and were able to replace them. Because of this, children's symbolic play can be understood as a very complex system of speaking through gestures that communicated and indicated the meaning of playthings.

(David was cutting straws. As he cut the straws, he placed them one by one into a film container.)
DAVID: I'm cutting some meat loaf.
BETSY TO DAVID: OK. *(David's hand slipped and his straws fell out of the container.)*
DAVID: My meatloaf fell out!

This is an example of second-order symbolism because the "object acquires a sign function with a developmental history of its own that is now independent of the child's gesture" (Vygotsky 1978, 110). This is how dramatic play and writing are linked—they are both forms of second-order symbolism (Dyson 1982). This will be discussed in detail in chapter 5.

Drawing and Artwork

When the children gained access to scissors, staplers, tape, and craft goods, they frequently replaced drawings with productions constructed from paper and assorted materials. The children's work was important for their cognitive development because, with each created artistic endeavor, they acquired additional instrumentality for symbol making. Each representation was also an opportunity for creative problem solving. Fabricating a three-dimensional work lent itself to learning abstraction, whether making designs or fashioning other objects such as jewelry, ghosts, masks, and a myriad of other creations. The symbol was capable of change as one meaning was replaced with another. For example, when Karen's "queen's hat," a tall and grand looking hat that she had made, was standing up on the table, she threw a paper in the cylindrical portion and remarked, "It's a trash can!"

This change of perception was not uncommon—the children often modified the naming of a work after it appeared as something other than what they had originally planned. These changes were the manifestations of enterprising minds, continually seeking meaning in all that they noticed. The Kindergartners' natural predisposition to symbolize was constantly energized by fresh observations, so that newly fashioned works were continually visualized. Representation was often in the form of complex symbolization where, in this example (see figure 4.1), the row of buttons represented singing children, the one button at the top center was the priest, and the creation itself was described as: "The priest for the chorus . . . these kids [the row of buttons] made a concert" by Karen, who described her work as a church concert where the children sang in a chorus led by the priest [the lone larger button on top]. This was an actual event in Karen's life. Often there was a story with their work. For example, Betsy told me, "The mama's going to put the nest in there so she can sit on it." The "nest" was a wad of corkscrew ribbons glued to her paper.

> We see that when a child unburdens his repository of memory in drawing, he does so in the mode of speech—telling a story. A major feature of this mode is a certain degree of abstraction, which any verbal representation necessarily entails. Thus we see that drawing is graphic speech that arises on the basis of verbal speech. (Vygotsky 1978, 112–13)

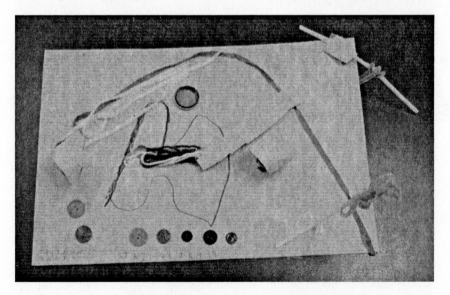

Figure 4.1. Karen's depiction of church event

Developmental psychologists have often viewed symbolism in children's drawing from only two schools of thought—the cognitive and affective (Gardner 1980; Rosenblatt and Winner 1989). The cognitive school approaches children's

symbol making in their drawings to discover how a child is developing intellectually. Those who view child art as an index of mental process have been influenced in great part by Piaget, who viewed children's drawings as an indication
of their intellectual semblance (1963). This has set the stage for viewing children's drawings as a step-like progression of adding more detail and expertise
with the ultimate outcome being visual realism (Golomb 2002). Ignored here is
evidence that this kind of realism is not a universally accepted goal in art and
that few people reach it without proper training.

Psychologists (and others attempting to analyze children's art from a psychological perspective) have looked at children's drawings and found "deficiencies." "Tadpole" drawings, drawings in which legs and, to a lesser degree, arms
emanate from a central circle (the head), have signified to some that the child
has poor perception, and thus can view things only globally (Piaget 1963) or the
child has poor memory of body parts (Freeman 1980 in Rosenblatt and Winner
1989). When tadpoles or "globals" (the head only, the earliest form of human
representation) or stick figures are seen in five-year-olds, school personnel (administrators, teachers, aides) have been indoctrinated to attribute these types of
drawings to intellectual immaturity, chiefly because of the pervasive acceptance
of the proposition that children's drawings are indicators of cognitive growth.
Equating individual drawings with intellectual accomplishment has been largely
promulgated through the use of the Goodenough-Harris Draw-a-Person test
(Harris 1963).

While particularizing aspects of drawing could bespeak of well-developed
perception, attempting to interpret single drawings and relate them to intellectual
development is erroneous, misleading, and damaging to those children who are
labeled as having undeveloped cognition. In the school system where this study
took place, this test is used as part of an assessment used to determine the at-risk
status of the child. Children who draw the tadpoles, globals, or stick-figure con-
figurations are given a low score. As they add details such as torso, arms with
hands, legs with feet, and fingers, they are given more points. Maximum points
accrue as more details such as hair, eyebrows, eyelashes, and so on, are evidenced. However, children have distinct aims when they draw and it is this in-
ducement that is often seen in their final product. In these instances, children's
goals drive their productions.

Betsy decided to make a book and announced this by stating: "I'm gonna
make a book." She put four papers together and folded them down the middle,
which resulted in the book having sixteen pages. Her aim was to make a book
according to her conception of one. If each page were examined, we could determine that the motive of making a book was predominant in her mind. She had
no story line, characters were not embellished, background was unimportant.
She simply wanted to make a generic book. She wanted to utilize all the pages

because she knew that there weren't empty pages in books. All the pages depicted globals, other cursory figures, or tadpole drawings. Figures in the book imparted sketchy depictions of humans. It was evident that her intention was not to portray any attribute concerning persons but merely to draw figures that symbolized humans. It is apparent that Betsy's plan was only to depict a representation of a book, not a story. This necessitated filling the pages with *any personage*. On one of the pages, she merely scribbled. She did not draw with any regard for narration, characterization, or plot. Her goal was to make a book and that is what she accomplished. To adults, a book embodies a story or relays information. But Betsy conveyed her model of a book, its archetype, so to speak.

To produce an archetype requires that one represents only the general qualities of the symbol. Because she was making only the form of a book, her drawings were incidental, they relayed only that pages had a message of some sort. Her drawings served as symbols of drawings in a book. This gave her good reason to illustrate abbreviated versions of people, which are viewed as global or tadpole figures. These were a kind of condensed notation (Golomb 1981), which is precisely what Betsy needed to enact. The drawings did not represent a limited intellect but were sacrificed, so to speak, in order to fulfill the distinct objective of denoting a book. Betsy drew figures on all pages. She merely wanted to represent the pages with the characteristic elements of what is in a book. Because children initially create globals and tadpoles as representational figures of all humans, and because Betsy wanted to display only the prototype of a human, she selected first-known representations of one. She returned to previous forms,

Figure 4.2. Betsy's generic symbol of a person

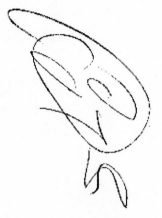

Figure 4.3. Betsy's second symbol of a generic person

those that represented the figuration of *anyone*. Shown here are her pages seven and eight (figures 4.2 and 4.3). This revisiting of beginning figures leads to an understanding that children build on representational knowledge, keeping early forms in a reservoir, where they can retrieve knowledge when it is needed. When an earlier form is chosen, it should not be looked upon as *reverting* but, rather, as an active cognitive process of selection and employment.

In contrast to the drawings in Betsy's book was another drawing (figure 4.4), which was created on Career Day. In this drawing, Betsy communicated her desire to be a nurse, so the embodiment of a nurse was her focal point. The nurse was composed of a head, shoulders, body, arms, hands, fingers, and legs. The hands were highlighted with dark marks. One hand had five fingers and the other hand had six. The principal consideration was the portrayal of a nurse whose hands were very important for her work. Betsy drew a uniform, complete with hat, tunic, and pants, with the appropriate stereotypical nursing emblems on the hat and tunic. These days, nurses do not wear caps such as the cap drawn by Betsy. We can conclude that the child had the prototype of a nurse in her mind, perhaps from the media's typical model of a nurse, which is often portrayed with a nurse's cap, frequently with a red cross on it. The face had a smile and she depicted a full nose, complete with a nostril and eyes that included eyelashes. This drawing's detail was completely antipodal to the figures in her book, which had no distinguishing features, yet the drawings were made within days of each other. Betsy drew those features that were important to accomplish her representation. When she made her book, her overriding concern was to depict her understanding of a book so that the drawings inside the pages were only there to symbolize what appears in every book (to her). When she drew a nurse, she

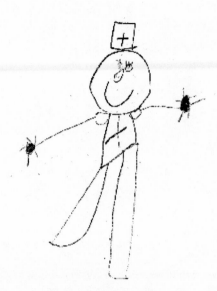

Figure 4.4. Betsy's characterization of a nurse

symbolized her understanding of a particular person (a nurse). Therefore, attributing cognitive functioning by looking at one drawing cannot be valid. This is consistent with both Golomb's (2002) and Cox's (1993) explanations that children draw according to intention, mood, and their evaluation of the nature of the task. For example, those that exclude arms will draw arms if the figure is playing ball, draw a torso if the figure is pregnant, and draw ears if the person is wearing earrings (Golomb 2002). If any of the drawings in Betsy's book were evaluated by the standards in the Goodenough-Harris Draw-a-Person test, she would have received a minimal score for her "primitive" drawings and a much higher score if her nurse drawing were to be evaluated. Yet, they were both symbols of what the child wanted to create. Therefore, what first may appear as disparities in drawings ultimately represents a reflection of the child's driving motive. This phenomenon was exemplified often.

David's focus was on learning to make an airplane. After expending much energy on this, he drew a window with stick figures in it. He represented that airplanes transported people. His intention was not to portray anyone in particular. Therefore, he drew generic people, delineated by stick figures. On the same day, he drew Power Rangers and their children, all of whom had a head, torso, arms, and legs or feet. Here, he was being specific, so he added detail that explained who the characters were. A month later, he drew a map with a man about to follow its path. The man, who represented any man, was drawn in tadpole style. Once again, because his intention was nonspecific, he drew a nonspecific man. The man was incidental to the map, which was drawn in great detail. Three weeks later, David drew a picture of the school's principal. Here, the importance was placed on a specific person. Her dress formed the torso and she was drawn with great detail: hat, facial features with eyelashes, and clothing. He was quite specific because he wanted to portray a particular person. Another drawing depicted two Power Rangers. One could see proper torsos, arms, fingers, legs, and a detailed face in each one. David and the other children were capable of many types of drawing, depending on their intentions.

The same variation can be seen in Karen's drawings. On the same day, she drew a tadpole with arms and legs emanating from the head and a figure with a torso, face with hair, and arms with fingers. In the former, the figure was added as a decoration because the main message was telling her mom that she loved her. In the latter, she was depicting herself, which accounts for more detail. A week later, Karen drew a global that consisted of only the face. This was a message of affection to me. Indeed, one would not need more than a happy face, just as adults draw, when one wants to convey a happy attitude to another. It is evident that when these children drew, they conveyed their motivations through their work. It must be kept in mind that we cannot always glean the child's intent, especially not when we only view the drawing. The child's level of intelligence cannot be determined from the history of his or her drawing in general. These children drew what is regarded as early representation not because they were unable to designate with a specific amount of detail, but because they didn't want to draw particulars when they were forming symbols for generic people. Therefore, the child's symbol in drawing is largely dependent upon his or her motive.

Lastly, figures 4.5a, 4.5b, 4.6a, and 4.6b depict two Kindergarten children's drawings when they were administered the Goodenough-Harris Draw-a-Person test. The first of the two was taken in September (figures 4.5a and 4.6a) and the second was taken in April (figures 4.5b and 4.6b). According to the test, the children's early depictions were more "advanced" than their later portrayals. When the director of testing looked at these tests, she expressed consternation that the April depictions were "less advanced" than the ones drawn in September.

I explained my work on children's drawings to her, citing instances where children drew differently within the span of a few days. Yet the common supposition that, as children advance in age, they will add more detail to their drawings, and thus must move on only to a higher (more intelligent) level of drawing remains firmly entrenched in the minds of those who administer the exam. The Goodenough-Harris Draw-a-Person test trains school personnel to view Kindergarten children who draw globals, tadpoles, or stick figures as being intellectually indigent and "behind." The director ignored my explanation and repeated her statement, wondering why the children placed lower at the end of this pre-

**Figures 4.5a and 4.5b. People drawn by the same child
using the Goodenough-Harris Draw-a-Person test.
Pre-test (left) and post-test (right).**

**Figures 4.6a and 4.6b. People drawn by the same child using the
Goodenough-Harris Draw-a-Person test (different child from the one who
drew figures above). Pre-test (left) and post-test (right).**

sent school year. She suggested that the children need more instruction in how to draw people. The persistence in ignoring vital information, the adherence to disregarding truth about minority children, and the bowing to the authority of the test contribute to underrepresented children appearing as though they have deficits when they do not. This occurs more often in schools of underrepresented children, where belief in the test goes largely unquestioned. In more affluent schools, these tests are but one form of assessment. There, portfolios, performance exhibitions, and the like help the teacher understand the varied ways in which children develop. Unhappily, the supreme authority of the test remains with those who are involved in teaching minority children. Examining children's art from a psychological perspective can develop into a hunt for finding deficits. Assessing development from this perspective can be detrimental and self-defeating.

The cognitive school approaches children's symbol making in their drawings as a means to discover how a child is developing intellectually (Piaget 1963). The affective approach examines the type of symbols the child uses in his or her drawing and combines this with known factors concerning the child's life, then makes a determination on the child's psychological state (Gardner 1980). Psychopathology has been attributed to observations of children's work, attributing symbols that may not have been intended: persistent use of black or dark colors (Altschuler and Hardwick 1947 in Rosenblatt and Winner 1989); scowling people or a lack of happy faces; and hesitant marks—"The secure, well adjusted child will happily scribble freely across the available space. In contrast, the insecure child will make timid, barely visible, broken strokes in the lower corner of the paper" (Lasky and Mukerji 1990, 7). Levick studied children's drawings in order to determine the individual's emotional health (1998). Although she stated that it was important not to judge one work alone, she argued that there were warning signs that indicated something was psychologically awry. One of these supposedly dangerous symptoms included a child who drew a repeated consistent form that was produced again and again. She cited a child who continually made an open gaping mouth, sometimes labeled as monsters. Contrarily, Montessori believed that repetition was necessary when a child was attempting to perfect a certain form (1995). Or the child may repeat because he derives pleasure from the object.

David seemed to me to be a happy, well-adjusted child, yet he continually drew what he called monsters. David called the large cut-out paper forms big monsters and the small triangular forms (they were leftover scraps from the cut-outs) small monsters. The mouths were indicated by a straight line with a zig-zag on top of it, demonstrating sharp teeth. He was entranced by the fact that folding a paper and cutting it produced these extravagant forms. Another common warning sign that was supposed to indicate ill emotional health was the drawing of forms of an earlier level (Levick 1998). Gardner argues that viewing child art only through the cognitive or affective lens is a limited approach because it cannot account for the abundance of circumstances that are involved in the production of each symbolic product (1980).

Children's Artistic Development

The course of child art generally moves toward a broadening intricacy of representation with age (Golomb 2002). Although children advance through these stages, they never retire from them (Korzenik 1977) so these steps can be thought of as discoveries of ways of graphic representation rather than fixed levels. There are times when children revert to using even their earliest marks on paper. An eight-year-old may use gesture when making zoom lines on a racing car or when making fire coming out of a dragon's mouth, and even an adult may use stick figures (Wolf and Perry 1989). In art, children continue to use early forms, rather than simply discarding primitive conceptions while spiraling upward, as they do when learning how to read. This eliminates the view that children's artistic endeavors have, as their endpoint, visual realism. When we shed this idea, we are more apt to see their art as a search for equivalences that stand for the object (Golomb 2002). As children gain more expertise, they naturally learn to distinguish features. In this way, they become more adept at representing the specific items that they want to. Thus, we can regard child art as an exercise in symbolism, often with a search for clearer depiction. The following section traces samples of the Kindergartner's concurrent use of the many levels of artistic progression. This will shed light on what kind of storehouse the children had at their disposal, the use of which could help them expand to more intricate representations.

How Children Develop Representation

Scribbling presages drawing and writing. Random scribbles begin to be used at the age of about one year and they move into more controlled scribbles by the age of about two years. Scribbles frequently elicit an afterthought of representative interpretation beginning when adults question children about the meaning of their work. One cannot understand the significance of many early scribbles by observing the text alone—one must view the child's speech and gestures that accompany the scribble because they are an often inherent part of it (Korzenik 1977). This is because early scribbles are not really drawings at all. They are gestural signs fixed on paper (Vygotsky 1978). Much of scribbling has been shown to be primitive trials in representation, although the dependence is on gestural rather than pictorial depiction. Golomb distinguished between prerepresentation in scribbling as motor actions on a medium and representation in pictorial design as intentional actions, postulating that only deliberate performance constituted true representation (2002). This is because a motor movement elicits a form that accompanies the action but it is not an image that is intended to be similar to an object. Representation is a purposeful mental act that is established when the artist aims for a likeness that coincides with some portion of his or her life. In order for a work of art to be representative, the artist must have devised a means of reproducing the referent. A child may be pretending, motioning a heli-copter coming in for landing, using dramatic motions, speech, and gestures to indicate this, and completing the landing with a slash or scribble of pencil mark on paper. He may move his brush in circular motions to indicate an airplane (Matthews 1984 in Winner 1989) or imitate a rabbit by making hopping motions with his pencil in hand, resulting in dots on the paper (Vygotsky 1978). Al-though these children were not representing the airplane or the rabbit by striving to reproduce them through pictorial design, they were indicating qualities of the referents through their motor-sensory movements. By looking at the accompany-ing gesture and verbalizations, a true glimpse into the child's motives can be gained. The child's accompanying manner (speech, gesture, etc.) sustain the meaning (Cox 1993), making scribbles a forerunner of graphic representation. In true pictorial symbolization, the illustration itself signifies the meaning.

Children become users of symbolizing between the ages of one to three as shown by their having made a set of linguistic and gestural rules. Children uti-lize a highly advanced visual-spatial symbol system: They have the ability to slip in and out of representation, for example, making "cheese" from a yellow block and visually defining patterns such as seeing the shape of a Y in a tree branch (Wolf and Perry 1989). The following is an example of the Kindergart-ner's use of gestural representation:

(David and Martin were pretending to be camping. They embellished on this theme, talking about telling ghost stories by the campfire at night. This brought up the subject of blood and Martin asked David to draw a picture of blood.)
DAVID TO MARTIN: I'm gonna draw myself blood. *(He reached for a red marker and put his hand on his forehead)*: Ugh! He got me in the forehead! *(He bent backward and "falling down," drew a red scribble on the paper.)*

When David symbolized blood, he carried his gesture over into his work. It was an extension of his speech. This type of scribble depended upon material action. Children from varied ethnic and mainstream environments use these physical, rather than illustrated, signals. Dyson showed how one of her ethni-cally diverse Kindergarten participants combined speech with the act of gesture and blatant motor-sensory accompaniments as he was drawing (1986). These features dominated the drawing, proscribing what should be drawn. As the child loudly declared a "countdown," he wrote the numbers on the paper. Similarly,

Gardner, Wolf, and Smith exemplified this concept in his examples of drawing in a middle-class, white preschool child, Max (1982). Max's drawings were an extension of his dramatic play—when he finished his outdoor playing of Batman and Robin, he came into the house, picked up a marker, and continued the game on paper, drawing marks to symbolize exploits of these characters.

Gradually, by about the age of three, the gestural scribble is followed by a pictorial one. After having made a gestural scribble, the child recognizes it as something he or she knows, and then names it (Brittain 1979). Or the child may be asked what his or her work was and sees a resemblance to a real object, and *reads off* a response (Golomb 2002). Basically, the children now can envision a relationship between their notations on the paper and the phenomena in their encounters (Brittain 1979). Although children may not contrive to make a specific likeness, they are able to read meaning into it when completed. The children were, thus, able to infuse representation into their work. This allowed them to become more adept at symbolizing. Although they did not have the intention that Golomb spoke of when she defined true representation, they still had the task of finding a symbol for a referent.

Differences in drawing and writing appear at this point. Scribbles are circular. Writing appears as marks that have linearity and horizontal orientation (Dyson 1982). One of the drawings displays Karen's scribbles. The work had two cut-out sections where she had originally intended to make a kite. Karen became interested in something else and when she again picked up this paper, she began by making stabbing actions with the marker. Next, she switched to scribbling as she accompanied it with babbling tongue movements ("BADAD-ABADADA"). When she finished her work, she told me, "That's where we went to see fireworks." Indeed, the finished picture could pass very well for fireworks. There is much movement in the work and it is permeated with bright colors. Round shapes indicated motion (Gardner, Wolf, and Smith 1982). The bottom right contained faux cursive writing, indicating Karen's distinction of writing from scribbling. It is linear in structure and follows a horizontal arrangement that appears as fluid and authentic as the real thing. Karen probably named her work after she drew it. She hadn't spoken of any plan before creating it. When she discovered her work had similarities to fireworks, she was able to link her marks with her experience. Thus, she graphically represented an actual adventure, although not intentionally.

At four years of age or thereabouts, the child begins to depict his or her representation pictorially. He or she *deliberately* represents something in his or her environment or imagination. Here, with the loss of gesture, the graphic portrayals begin to designate the objects independently and become first-order symbols. That is, they directly depict objects or events (Vygotsky 1978). One characteristic of this stage is demonstrated when several referents are drawn and they seem to be placed arbitrarily on the page, with no seeming relation to each other (Brittain 1979). The human figure is usually depicted as a head with legs or a head with arms and legs. The child draws with X-ray vision, that is, drawing something as seen when it really cannot be such. Cox claimed these transparencies were of two types: purposeful and accidental (1993). When it is of the first type, the child wants to convey what she knows. That is, if a child drew a purse, he or she would draw not only the outside of it but also its contents. The unintentional includes frontal vision: In drawing a profile of a person, the child draws both eyes and a complete mouth. Cox found transparency drawings of human figures to be infrequent in children whose average age was five years and six months (1993). Out of 330 drawings, she found only six such drawings. Characteristics of x-ray drawings provide evidence that children do not strive for authenticity. Rather, they "are much more symbolists than naturalists . . . rather they try more to name and designate rather than represent" (Vygotsky 1978, 112). Letters and letter-like symbols appear. Children begin to write names and solicit names of familiar objects (Dyson 1982). It is at this stage that drawing and writing can be seen as clearly differentiated.

In my classroom, we had recently studied plant life and had stressed the importance of a plant's growing roots. Each child had grown his own bulb in a glass jar. The roots were clearly visible and very dramatic because they grew rapidly every day. True to X-ray vision, David drew flowers with their roots. Each flower had its corresponding root, and the roots remained visible. X-ray drawings and taking license with nature were common because the children's intentions were not to literally duplicate nature, but to symbolize it. Transparencies are often used to depict what one knows. David was demonstrating his knowledge of plant roots.

At approximately five years of age, the child moves to the preschematic stage. Objects are no longer "flying" on the page, but are more grounded. In fact, the beginnings of a definite ground line and skyline appear. Many of the characteristics of the last stage are still present, such as the frequent frontal view and X-ray vision. The child is interested in representing a visual similarity (Winner 1989) rather than showing the actual visual qualities of the referent. This produces a kind of shorthand symbolic notation of a drawing: Only general qualities of the referent are drawn; objects are drawn generically: A person is drawn the same way no matter who he or she may be and only the most important characteristics are drawn. The child may use simple geometric figures (circle, square, rectangle, dots, lines) to depict his objects of attention and then join these together with lines of some kind (Wolf and Perry 1989). The human figure is now endowed with a body that has arms and legs coming out of it. The general, rather than the specific, qualities are shown—a cylinder may be shown as a closed circle. In my classroom, Martin used elementary geometric forms. The upper section displayed circles and circles within circles. Under those marks were a series of triangles connected with a series of lines.

Karen depicted a good example of a visual equivalent. It is a portrait of Karen's family: "Dad, Mom, Brother and me." Here, Karen drew nonspecific faces—they all had the same heads, eyes, and noses. All eyes were drawn with a dot of some kind. The only differences were the father's teeth and Karen's arms. Once again, we are reminded that children's drawings display the driving motive—in a family portrait, the child needed only to generalize her family. To Karen, the addition of arms, legs, bodies, and so on would not have added more to the understanding of *who* constituted her family. Her drawing demonstrated a visual likeness of its members. In short, she accomplished what she set out to do; she showed us who made up her family.

David demonstrated an example of X-ray drawing when he drew the underground roots of flowers as visible. Although it is said that children between the ages of five and six continue to draw with X-ray vision and a frontal view (Brittain 1979), the children in my study seemed to be in a transitory stage between frontal and lateral views. In animal drawings, mixed views are popular (Golomb 2002). Martin drew a bunny rabbit. Overall, the rabbit gave the impression of being turned toward the side. One eye was visible, yet the complete mouth was depicted. The anterior profile of a rabbit's face does appear to be somewhat ovoid-shaped as represented in Martin's rabbit. What is presumed to be the ear closest to the observer is larger, while the ear that is meant to be farther away is somewhat smaller. This gives the feeling that the smaller ear is farther behind the larger one. There is one foreleg and only the paw of the other one. Drawing only one hind leg gave the impression of a lateral view.

Let us now examine Martin's "Rudolph the Red-Nosed Reindeer." There was one eye as is manifested in a true lateral view. The front foreleg was longer than the other legs, giving the feeling that the other legs were farther behind. The posterior hind leg was drawn thinner so that it, too, gave the sense of being behind the other leg. This follows through to the antlers, where the anterior one was longer than the left, once again giving the sensation that the left was somewhat farther away. Betsy did an elephant drawing that also gave different outlooks: The two back legs were made shorter than the others; one eye portrays a profile, while the full mouth reveals a frontal view. The children were clearly beginning to think about linear perspective. These moves may be related to planning. In true X-ray vision, the child impulsively draws the object or his experience, just like he or she draws without plan. As the child moves forward and uses speech to plan his or her work, the child begins to think more about it. Drawing only one eye or shorter back legs to portray a lateral view means the child was no longer drawing impetuously, but was deliberating. Naming work at the beginning also entails reflecting on it. This means that the child's developmental history of drawing may run parallel to speech development and is, therefore, dependent on the move to the intrapersonal realm. Vygotsky postulated that children initially draw from memory and they draw not what they see, but what they know (1978). Martin has clearly moved from this early stage. Remember that Martin relinquished his memory of a rabbit in favor of consulting a book in order to depict one (see chapter 3, page 56). This was in spite of the fact that rabbits are frequently found in the area and are part of the children's culture. But as regularly as Martin saw rabbits, he still wanted to refer to a model in a book. He did not want to rely on memory; rather, he wanted to deliberate on his work. Figure 4.7 depicts Martin's attempts to perfect his work—a move to assessing and appraising. Contemplating one's work is an important cognitive function because it entails reflective planning.

In summary, as was seen in the above descriptions of artwork, the Kindergartners advanced to higher levels of drawing while maintaining earlier graphic markings. It is not accidental that this phenomenon was also found with levels of speech (see Fayden 1997a). Hetzer determined that the fundamental channel of symbolization in children was their speech (1926 in Vygotsky 1978). All other sign systems evolve from speech so that the move toward naming a work of art indicates the powerful impact of speech in the development of drawing. As children progress along the road to written language, they depend on earlier discovered concepts of symbol making to help them understand new ways of representation. Thus speech, gesture, dramatic play, and drawing can be seen as distinct junctures in the unitary course of the evolution of written language (Vygotsky 1978). Creating art, especially three-dimensional types, lent itself to learning new ways of symbolizing, which, in turn, provided the necessary history so that the children were able to eventually gain the tools for writing. This does not mean that the only merit to artwork is that it serves as a building block for writing. Because *"every* form of representation neglects some aspect of the world" (Eisner 1982, 49), each form evokes a particular type of conception and only exposure to varied forms will bring about a range of cognitive functions. All the forms of representation contribute to learning how to find meaning. Therefore, educators must not view literacy as a narrow path of reading and writing skills, but as a complex network of interconnected disciplines, each one adding thickness to the child's developing mind. It is akin to a large multigenerational extended family whose members are interrelated and where each one makes significant contributions to the welfare of the child.

Art in Parts

The Kindergartners most often created their art in separate parts and, subsequently, connected these parts to make a whole. For example, instead of fashioning a figure and later adding hands, feet, shoes, a hat, and so on, the children created all the parts separately and then combined them. This was a frequent occurrence. A few examples will offer insight to this process.

Betsy made her cheerleader in many parts. She started out by drawing and then cutting out the head. Next, she made a skirt from a muffin cup. Then she asked David, "How do you make pants?" (see chapter 3, page 54). After he showed her, she drew a pair of her own and cut them out. Subsequently, she made the arms and the shoes and, when finished making all these segments, glued them together.

Martin fashioned a man first by making the face—he cut straws and then taped them on a muffin cup to represent the ears on the face. He drew and cut out the shirt, the arms, the pants, and the shoes all separately. Then, he glued them on as he proceeded down the model.

David formed a fish first by drawing an eye on the face and then drawing and cutting out a mouth He drew and cut out the fins and the tail. Then, he glued the parts on the fish's body.

Betsy created a robot first by drawing a square and cutting it out. This served as the body. She made the head and glued it to the body. Next, she made the legs by drawing them and cutting them out. She took film-cartridge tops and taped them to the bottom of the legs, making shoes. When the legs were complete, she glued them to the body. Afterward, she made arms with hands and fingers and spent much time cutting out the fingers. Only then did she attach the arms to the body. She created the eyes and nose by gluing buttons to the face, and made a smiling face. She created hair and glued it to the head. It took her two days to make the robot, and she persisted until she was finished. As the children created their artwork, they continually involved themselves in undertakings that moved from part to whole.

Karen's flag was made in two separate parts; the pole and the flag itself. Martin's gun was made in several parts, the barrel, the trigger, and the stock, and then taped together. David and Betsy's airplanes both had independent tails that they drew and then glued on. Karen also made a large man in parts. First, she stapled many pieces of paper together, in spite of the fact that she could have selected one long piece of paper from our paper roll. Thereafter, she made a face and wrote her name and "To Mom" on her work. She drew arms and hands, cut separately, and glued them together and then onto the body. Subsequently, she drew legs with feet, cut them out, and glued them to her work. Karen and Betsy danced as they carried the man to another area of the room where it required both of them to "stand him up."

Golomb (1981) found that, in an early representation, children prepare individual parts of dough in an arrangement. This is composed of a head, facial features, sometimes with a body, arms, and legs. They are laid out in proper order but are not connected. Then, they are assembled into the graphic model, with each portion being placed in proper order. Scottish children also worked from part to whole when they broke off pieces of clay and molded appendages that they then attached to their model. In contrast, Inuit children constructed clay models from whole to part, carving features into a cylindrical block with a modeling tool. This technique was consistent with the Inuit traditional carvings of bone and stone (Cox 1993). Art in the Kindergartner's culture is especially renowned for the creation of pottery, most notably, the storyteller dolls. These depict a storyteller with listening children sitting around her. Although this pottery appears to be one piece, it has several component parts. Each listening child is a disconnected segment that is later added on. The narrator's skirt, a flap, is made separately and then attached to the sitting figure. Her (or, occasionally, his) hair is often made independently and later fixed upon the head, much as one would secure a wig. In addition, the *chongo,* a traditional bun at the back of the head, is also made apart from the main hair and later affixed to it. The yarn that binds the chongo is also produced separately and then placed around it. If the traditional headband is used, it, too, is made in a detached form and is later placed on the head.

The process of other Pueblo pottery, such as bowls, is a long one and is composed of a series of procedures, done separately and added on incrementally. Rather than taking a wad of clay and hollowing it out, Inuit style (Barry 1984), Pueblo potters use the coil method. Bowls are built by adding separate coils of clay to a base. First, the base is formed by molding clay into a saucer or a tin pie plate. Long spiral coils are rolled between the hands or by placing the clay on the floor and rolling the clay against the hands. The first coil is placed on the lip of the base. Other coils are added until the desired height is achieved (Bunzel 1929/72). This assemblage of parts is also found in traditional jewelry *heishe* (shell) making, drum making, and most other Pueblo art forms. All entail a series of separate steps that comprise a long process. Accordingly, Pueblo art is not created from whole to part but, rather, from part to whole. Thus, as Inuit children mimic their elders in the creation of their art (Cox 1993), Pueblo children similarly imitate their art from what they witness in their village. This is discussed below, when questions of learning styles arise.

In the children's bunny-making episode (discussed on page 56), each bunny was also made in parts. Let us examine speech and action in Karen's construction to determine if there was a relation between her planning and constructing art in components:

Karen first tried to make a bunny by cutting out some green tissue paper. She abandoned it, took a piece of turquoise construction paper, and cut out two circles. She placed them on top of each other, stuffed them in the middle with cotton balls, and stapled them together. She held it up and said, "Miss Terese, look at my stomach." Because she made the two circles, it may be presumed that she knew what she was making before she made it. She probably abandoned the green tissue paper for the construction paper because the tissue paper was not sturdy enough to stuff and staple. She drew a small circle in the middle of the "stomach" and while doing so, said to Betsy, "Now I'm making the belly button."

Her speech and drawing existed together. Karen cut lavender paper and drew a face on it. Talking to herself, she said, "Then you staple it and then you tape it," and stapled it to the body. She taped the ears on. In these instances, she evidenced planning because the speech came before the action of placing the

Figure 4.7. Martin's endeavors to draw a rabbit (in order of attempt) and his finished product

face and ears. She said to Betsy, "I'm gonna make some clothes." She made a shirt and taped it over the body. To herself, she said "arms," cut a pipe cleaner, and taped the pipe-cleaner arms to the body. Last, she asked for another pipe cleaner, getting it from Betsy. She folded it and taped the pink pipe-cleaner base on the back.

Karen had not stated her intention before she worked. She used speech to guide her through many of the elements of her enterprise: the belly button, stapling the head, taping the ears, making the shirt, constructing arms, and asking for the final pipe cleaner. Her speech described bite-sized segments, those small enough to make her work possible. Although she hadn't originally described detailed plans, as she worked, it became clear what she would make. That is when she began to emit speech that detailed her steps ("then you staple it and then you tape it"; "I'm gonna make some clothes"; "arms").

Therefore, art in parts seemed to be executed so that the child could construct his work in manageable portions. In all of these examples, the children created works that involved complex procedures. For this particular event, Karen first used speech to explain, and then to guide, her work. In this way, her speech was utilized to plan many of the portions of her work. This indicates analytic, rather than holistic, thinking. Therefore, the stereotypical image of the Indian child as a holistic thinker should be challenged. This is further discussed in chapter 7, in the section on learning styles. Educators should not limit their view of the children to any particular category but must make available to *all* children the rich array of teaching styles that cater to many modes of learning. Accordingly, Indian and minority children can have a rich assemblage to choose from when constructing their knowledge.

The Emergence of Writing

Using a Variety of Approaches

This chapter describes the Kindergartners' emergence into writing. As will be demonstrated, it was accomplished through their involvement with a combination of various methods, using a functional approach combined with very distinct lessons on sound/letter correspondences. Saint-Laurent and Giasson also found that by combining features of emergent literacy with phonological awareness tasks, their "at-risk" (their word), French-speaking, low-SES Kindergartners increased their use of invented spelling (2001). This also held true for minority students in Australia who became engaged in the Schoolwide Early Language and Literacy (SWELL) program (Center, Freeman, and Robertson 1998), a combination of literature and phonics. These findings are important because they give credence to the idea that programs for young children don't have to follow an either/or curriculum. In whole-language programs, phonics is often neglected (Reyhner 2001). Conversely, those who hold dear to phonological agendas often skimp on authentic literature. By combining the two methods, we can allow the children to benefit from both worlds. Watt found that urban, public-school Kindergartners who were trained in invented spelling during writing time made substantially greater gains in letter identification, matching rhyme, blending sounds, and segmenting sounds than children who were not treated to the writing intervention (2001). These findings suggest that children focus on sounds in words when using invented spelling. When low-income inner-city Kindergartners were exposed to phoneme awareness intervention, their invented spellings were found to be developmentally superior to those of the control group who did not have phoneme intervention (Tangel and Blachman 1992). With regard to Kindergartners who live in poverty, Hecht and Close found that the relationship between phonemic awareness and spelling were bidirectional (2002): The act of spelling influenced growth in phonemic awareness and phonemic awareness contributed to growth in spelling.

The School Post Office

Keeping in mind that writing should be used for real purposes, and discovering that I was running out of supplies, I wrote a grant for a K–6 post office. I thought the children would enjoy learning how to write letters, especially to brothers, sisters, and other friends and family. We received our award and, suddenly, I had the money I needed to replace the Kindergartner's rapidly dwindling supplies. I purchased many types of stationery, a myriad of paper, markers, pens, tape, glue sticks, envelopes, play postal stamps, and so on. I also purchased play postal boxes for all grades in the elementary school with the grant money.

Every day, I demonstrated letter writing on a large sheet of chart paper and the class decided to whom we would write. We learned about the formalities of letter writing—letters communicated a message; they should have a current date, a salutation, a body (which I told them could be words or pictures), and a closing. I introduced them to words such as *Dear, From, To,* and so on. All of a sudden, they exhibited a keen interest in knowing how to spell words like *mom, dad, Grandma, sister, brother, auntie, uncle,* as well as their friends' names. A fever of writing caught on in the Kindergarten class and at the school as the children wrote to each other and participated in weekly mail delivery. The children were very excited about the stationery and the only requirement to use it was that one had to write a letter. This letter could be expressed merely by a drawing but had to indicate on the envelope to whom it was addressed.

At first, the children wrote to their families; later, as we started a pickup and delivery service at school, they began to write and receive letters from friends and relatives in other classes. The children were fervently involved in writing and reading letters. This post office promoted emergent writing because it gave the children a purpose for writing. They had a reason to write—to communicate with family and friends in a novel and fun way. The pure functionality of it made sense to the children—they enjoyed writing in order to send a message to a loved one. Letter writing fueled further writing in the class—it never diminished. In fact, when I met with Betsy's mother the following school year, she told me that Betsy and her brother had written to their grandparents during the summer, going to the extent of mailing their letters in the pueblo post office, even though the grandparents lived nearby in the village. When writing was expressed as a form of personal communication, the Kindergartners' interest was provoked. There were many letters, and questions about letters and words, as the post-office concept spread throughout the school. The children wrote their letters during writing time and combined writing and making their other usual artistic productions. Letter writing provided a springboard for the children's interest in other types of writing. It set the stage for further writing in the classroom. As the children engaged themselves in letter writing, they learned about many facets of reading and writing. Because they were allowed to develop their interests, they were able to choose those aspects of learning that were important to them. This encouraged the children to take an active part in their learning. When we honor children's choices, they gain confidence in their actions and view themselves as capable decision makers (Fayden 1997b).

Betsy read me her as-yet incomplete letter, "Dear Mom, I love You." Betsy asked, "How do you spell *from*?" I went up to the dry-erase board where *from* was written. I showed her the word. Karen showed Betsy the paper on which she herself had written it. I wrote it on a piece of paper for her. She cut the word out of the paper. I asked her what the word spelled. She didn't know. I told her it spelled *from*. She then covered the M and asked me what it said. I told her "*fro*." Next, she covered the O and asked what that word said. I told her "*fr*." Lastly, she covered the R and asked what the word said. I made the F sound. She again read me her letter: "Dear Mom, I love You."

Next, I turned my attention to Karen. Betsy again asked, "What does this say?" holding up the word *from*. I was busy helping Karen and could not answer her immediately. (The children knew that if I was busy working with someone, they needed to wait.) Betsy picked up the paper that had *from* written on it and sounded it out, saying, "F . . . Fr..Fro..From!" A little later, she came up to me and read me her completed letter, which had the word *from* in it. This incident demonstrated how the children directed their own learning. Betsy was interested in the various sounds that made up the word and proceeded to first seek the information and then apply the information by sounding out the word. She solved her problem by herself. It is important that teachers have confidence in the intelligence of their students and allow them time to come up with their own answer to a problem. This gives them ownership of their learning.

David said, "I'm writing *mom* and I know how to spell it." He said out loud, "I love you, mom," and wrote I, with a drawing of a heart to represent love and U (because U has the sound of the word *you*), and, lastly, the word *mom*. Clearly, David thought of himself as a writer. David's writing of the letter U in this manner is an example of self-taught phonetic knowledge in that the child hears the sound of the name of the letter, abstracts that sound, and applies it to a word with the same sound. There is evidence that this is an early but progressive characteristic of writing development (Dyson 1991).

Karen left a cut-out of her work with the scraps on the table. She had written the word *to* and then decided that she didn't need it. Betsy saw the paper on the table and asked me, "Does this say *to*?" This is an example of emergent reading. When she began writing *to* on her envelopes for our post office, she had no difficulty remembering how to write it. Now, when it was removed from letter writing, she was able to recognize it and read it in an isolated form.

Karen got a piece of stationery and asked, "How do you spell *dear*?"

David responded, "D-O-A-N."

Karen repeated that and wrote it. To me, it was not important that Karen was "supposed" to spell the word correctly because I knew she would see it spelled correctly many times. In fact, she saw it on someone else's letter the next day and then spelled it correctly. What was important was not to diminish David's confidence in thinking of himself as a speller. As the children continued with their writing, they became teachers of this medium just as they had with their artwork. The following two vignettes emphasize this point:

KAREN TO BETSY *(She gave a stack of papers to her.)*: Here, Betsy, your notes came in.

BETSY TO KAREN: Do I have to write on it?

KAREN TO BETSY: Yes, you have to write your name, your address. *(Betsy started to write on the paper.)*

KAREN TO BETSY: Your phone number, too.

BETSY TO KAREN: A phone number, too? *(She poised the marker on the paper.)* A phone number on top?

KAREN TO BETSY: Yeah.

KAREN TO BETSY: This is what I mean: Spell your name. *(Karen wrote on the back of her own paper.)* Like this, see? *(She wrote her first and last names and her phone number on her own paper. She pointed to her own writing as she said her name and phone number. Betsy wrote on her own paper. Karen crumpled up her work and went to throw it away.)* I asked her for it and asked what she had made. She said, "My name and phone number," as she showed me.

BETSY TO ME: Oh mine is like this, teacher. *(She continued writing.)* My phone number is like that.

So the children involved themselves in literacy events by inventing them. Karen and Betsy had a conversation about writing; Karen showed a writing sample to Betsy so that she could learn what to do. When Karen had finished "teaching" Betsy how to write the note, she had no more use for the model and threw it away.

The following is another event in which the children acted as teachers:

(Martin wrote mon.*)*

MARTIN TO GROUP: This is how you spell *daddy*. *(He held his paper up so the other children could see.)*

BETSY TO MARTIN: That's not *dad*. *(Martin amended his work and wrote* mom.*)*

DAVID TO MARTIN *(as he leaned over to Martin's paper, pointing at it)*: Yeah, that's not *dad* and that's not *dad*.

MARTIN *(Nodding his head in the affirmative)*: Um hum um hum.

BETSY TO MARTIN *(shaking her head no):* Uh uh.

DAVID TO ME: Huh, teacher, that's not how you spell *dad*?

DAVID TO MARTIN: That's not how you write *dad*.

DAVID TO MARTIN: I'll show you. *(David wrote the word* dad *backward on Martin's paper.)*

KAREN TO MARTIN *(Karen wrote the word* dad *on a piece of paper)*: Here, Martin, that spells *dad*. D-A-D.

This is how writing emerged. Martin had seen *mom* and *dad* written many times, especially in the children's letters. He may have come to learn that one of either word may be *mom* or *dad*. He may have thought *mom* was *dad* and *dad* was *mom*. When he made an attempt to write *dad*, he mistakenly wrote *mon*; he was very close to the correct spelling of *mom*, although he had the wrong word. When told he had spelled the word incorrectly, he amended his spelling and spelled *mom* correctly, thus having the correct spelling of the wrong word. Although the children informed him that the word was spelled incorrectly, they were striving for him to get a correct understanding. Martin allowed David to write on his paper in order to learn the correct spelling. Karen may have recognized that David wrote the word backward. In any event, she too wanted Martin to spell the word correctly, so she wrote it for him. There was a collective effort by the group to help Martin.

After the children's inexhaustible *I love you*s, they became interested in writing other words (though they never lost interest in writing *I love you*). The children requested the spellings of names, words, and sentences that, at first, I wrote for them. Later, when they gained more expertise, I assigned the responsibility of writing themselves. When a child asks how to spell a word, it is the embodiment of emergent writing—these questions are manifestations of what we seek to accomplish—curiosity about writing. Copying has value only when the request originates from the child. Otherwise, it becomes a meaningless drill that is not inspired by the child's motivations. If the request for a name, word, or sentence emanates from the child's interest, learning is likely to take place. For example, when Betsy wrote a letter to the school coach, she sought from me the sentence: *We did exercise at the gym* (which I wrote for her). Many erudite behaviors took place as she copied this sentence: She gained an understanding of the separation of words—she originally attached the D to the word *we,* then crossed it out and made a hyphen—showing that the next word was definitely to be delineated and separated. She also separated the rest of the words with hyphens. An interest in punctuation along with the knowledge that written words must be separated are regarded as reading strategies (Clay 1985). Consequently, as Betsy wrote, she was not merely copying, she was very much aware of what the words said. As a result, she was reading new words with one-to-one correspondence. She said each word in a low voice as she wrote it. One must understand one-to-one correspondence in order to be able to read. Many of us have seen young children "reading" as they say the words that they have come to memorize, but they may recite or point to the word(s) ahead or behind the intended word as they say it. While acting in this manner is important, those children have not yet caught on to certain mechanics of reading. A milestone is accomplished when the child knows which word reads what, even if they may not yet be able to read the word out of context.

Everyday there were more requests: *Teacher, spell* coach. *Teacher, how do you spell* Mrs. Deeds (the principal)? *Teacher, how do you spell* Gloria (the guidance counselor)? *Teacher, how do you spell* how do you spell?

I think the favorite message was *I love you* simply because they loved so much and they knew how to write that favored phrase. They knew that it was a universal message and, as they saw friends write it, they would say things such as, "Hey, I know what that spells." It was the preferred phrase of all the children. Writing this, and other asked-for words, made for purposeful and gratifying writing and elucidated to the children that writing was a way of communication; one could speak to an audience from the heart through writing.

Symbolization in Writing

"Children's understanding of the symbol system of drawing (of using lines and curves to represent objects) may serve as a transition to their initial understanding of the symbol system of writing (of using lines and curves of letters to represent the names of objects)" (Dyson 1986, 380). The shift from drawing to writing involves the movement from first-order symbolization, graphically denoting objects, to second-order symbolization, composing written signs for the spoken representations of words, and then back to first-order symbolization, graphically denoting meaning. At first, the child uses writing as a first-order symbol as she did when drawing. Hence, contrary to what is widely believed, initial written characters symbolize the object or occurrence directly—not the spoken pronouncement (Dyson 1986). Next, the child attains second-order symbolism, "which involves the creation of written signs for the spoken symbols of words. For this, the child must make a basic discovery—namely that one can draw not only things but also speech" (Vygotsky 1978, 115). Eventually, the child must return to a first-order symbol. Speech as an intermediary is no longer necessary and the written words come to denote the meanings themselves. Thus, written language becomes direct symbolism, as is spoken language. As children progress along the road to written language, they depend upon earlier, familiar concepts of symbol making to help them understand new ways of representation. Thus, speech, gesture, dramatic play, and artwork can be seen as different moments in the fundamentally united course of written language development (Vygotsky 1978). Let us examine some early writings of the children to determine how speaking, playing, and drawing (their previous symbol making) influenced their incipient writing.

Betsy drew and cut out bills of money. She created them in various numerical denominations, all with a generic face. Here, writing is a first-order symbol, while the graphics (the drawing of faces and the writing of numbers) denote the object: money. This is compatible with Vygotsky's hypothesis that early writings do not stand for oral utterances. On the contrary, they denote objects and events (1978). As discussed in the section on drawing, when generating symbols of generic objects, only the essential features need be abstracted and recorded. A general symbol is a concise representation of the real. Betsy, therefore, depicted only those qualities which depicted real currency to her and to her peers—the image of a face and the quantity of money. This type of symbol making was similar to the time she drew globals and tadpole figures in her book (see chapter 4). In her book, she drew concise figures to represent *any person*. The same holds true for her global faces on the bills. The important point, because we are referring to writing, is that she wrote *any numbers*, which were universal representations of denominations. This provides a window for us to view Betsy's evolution of drawing into writing: She learned how to symbolize a generic person in drawing. This is how she denoted the nonspecific. As she moved into writing, she used the same technique for depicting a generic quality: She *wrote* generic symbols that were evidenced in the *any* numerals. For example, if she were depicting, specifically, the purchase of a doll that cost $10, she would probably draw a bill with the numeral 10 on it. In this case, she was simply making nonspecific, generic money, so the amounts on the denominations were not important. After Betsy made her money, she and the other children played with it, pretending they were buying and selling various commodities. Therefore, Betsy (and the others) made links between accustomed symbol-making activities, such as playing, talking, drawing, and now, writing (McLane 1990).

Writing as a Social Activity

Karen drew an attendance form. Her intention was to duplicate the real form, on which each child's name was listed on the left, followed by a grid indicating the five days of the week. She began to write the class roster. Karen asked Betsy how she spelled her name and Betsy wrote her name on a piece of paper for Karen to use as a model (note the interchange of roles). Betsy said the letters aloud as Karen wrote each letter of Betsy's name. By doing so, Betsy became a collaborator in Karen's work. Karen then proceeded to the other writing tables in order to ask each child the spelling of his or her name, which she promptly wrote down as they told her. When the children relayed their names to Karen, they authenticated her work. An important factor needed for children to produce new symbols is social interchange (Dyson 1991). This is because children need an audience to confirm and, often, to contribute to their meaning making. Karen used writing as a resource for promulgating social relationships. When Karen finished recording many of the names in the class, Betsy was amazed at the length of the list and asked Karen if she had "spelled all these?" Karen replied that she had. As Betsy looked down the list, she asked Karen where her [Betsy's] name was. They looked together and found Betsy's name. Next, Betsy, with some help from Karen, read the roster out loud. Betsy inquired if the list of names was for a birthday invitation, to which Karen replied, "No, it's an attendance sheet." Alliances between the symbol maker and audience(s) yield discussion between persons and societies concerning the function and quality of a text. Therefore, social associations can be achieved in and around written texts. There is a further benefit to this dialogue: Vygotsky contended that in order to write, children need to use language as an object of reflection, which both girls certainly demonstrated (1962). Betsy became the recipient that Karen needed—a platform upon which Karen was able to elucidate her work. The two girls, therefore, created a literacy event by dialoguing and deliberating on Karen's text.

Composing Words

As the children's interests turned to writing, I began to stress phonics in ways that I had never considered before. My philosophy had been one of whole language and, in the past, I shied away from teaching those aspects of phonics that were isolated from a literary text. As the children's writing surfaced, one problem frequently recurred: When the children sought to compose new words, they complained that they didn't know how to formulate them. I wanted the children to become independent users of sound/letter correspondences. Clearly, trusting that the children would learn these equivalencies solely within context proved to be insufficient. Therefore, I decided to use phonics activities in order to increase the children's competence in this field. Everyday, as the class gathered for circle time, we played auditory games such as identifying the initial sounds in words. We did this with miniature toys (see Lakeshore 2004). I would place a toy, such as a dinosaur, in my hand and would say, "I see something that begins with a D," using the sound. All of the children would raise their hands to tell me that it was a dinosaur. The chosen child would get to hold the toy while the game continued. The result was that each child retained a toy at the end of the game. Although I "gave" the answer by holding the object and giving the initial sound, the children were able to learn the concept that words of objects have initial sounds. The game progressed to the point where I didn't give the answer. Rather, I would hold up the object and the children would tell me the beginning sound. Later, I placed three photos (i.e., a cat, a rabbit, the sun) on a pocket chart and said, "I am thinking of a word that begins with an S-sound," and they would have to find the sun. In this way, the children learned to detect the sound as well as its psychological reverse, to detect the object that began with the sound. Along with these activities, I created phonics learning centers. This consisted of various hands-on sound/letter correspondence activities. For example, one exercise consisted of a grid that had several consonants printed at the top, such as B, H, F, G, and so on. Along with this, there were several pictures of objects that started with the sound of one of the letters, such as a bat, a goat, a hammer, a fish, and the like. The child was to match the object or picture to the initial letter by placing it under the proper corresponding site on the grid. There were other activities, where the children worked on ending and medial sounds. Daily, I had the children orally segment three-letter phonetic words such as hat, log, bun, and so on. When the children demonstrated command over the sound/letter associations, many activities became available for them to choose from, all of them designed to increase the Kindergartners' independence in composing. One center consisted of small boxes with pictures of phonetic words, a pencil, and lined papers. The children's jobs were to try to spell the words (e.g., if the picture was a hat, the child's job was to write the word *hat*). This entailed sounding out the word and writing those sounds. Initially, I sat with the children and assisted them. Because they had rarely explored spelling, they needed to be taught explicitly how to combine letters to make words. For example:

ME: What is this a picture of?
CHILD: A hat.
ME: H-aa-t. *(I segmented the sounds and, while doing so, I held an imaginary cleaver with which I cut the word as I segmented it.)*
CHILD: H-aa-t. *(The child segmented the sounds, using his own imaginary cleaver.)*
ME: What is the first sound?

CHILD *(using the sound)*: H. *(I wrote the letter* H *on a piece of paper. The child did the same.)*

ME *(sounding)*: H-aa-t. Aa. *(The child also sounded out the "aa" sound. I wrote the letter* A *on the piece of paper next to the letter* H. *The child did the same.)*

ME *(sounding): T. (Child sounded* T. *I wrote the letter* T *and the child did the same.)* We wrote hat *(sounding and pointing to corresponding letter).* H-aa-t. Hat. *(Child repeated my sounding, pointing, and saying the word.)*

ME: Now you try another one.

The child took a picture of a mop, orally segmented the word using the "cleaver," and wrote the letter M. She repeated the segmenting and wrote the letter O. The same held true for the remaining letter of the word. The child often wrote the correct letter, but I did not correct her if she didn't. The Kindergartners needed to go through this type of lesson several times. After a short while, they were writing the letters they heard and, consequently, began to write three-letter phonetic words with confidence and without asking me how to spell them. After the children were able to accomplish this, I opened another center that consisted of several laminated squares folded in book-like fashion. Once again using the example of a hat, the front of the book had a picture of a hat on the front cover. The word *hat* was written on the inside. The child would say "hat," write it by sounding it out, and open the book in order to check his spelling. The children most often attempted the spelling first because they were motivated to meet the challenge. Sometimes, a child would open the book first and then spell the word. I allowed the children to set their own pace. When the children were capably writing three-letter phonetic words, I opened other centers designed to teach various combinations of letters. For example, there were pictures of objects and their words began with digraphs and blends. Moustafa claims that children are not able to segment words but, on the contrary, naturally segment onsets and rimes (1997). Yet Moustafa's work depended upon the children having a repository of words at their disposal. In those instances, the children are able to read unknown words by making analogies between the words that are known and those that are unknown. The Kindergartner's knowledge was just emerging, so they didn't have the experience needed to make those comparisons. Specific coaching on segmenting words according to letter/phoneme correspondence was successful because it helped the children determine which sounds they needed in order to write desired words.

Reading and writing activities were often combined. For example, the children played the "action game" where they read three-letter phonetic verbs to one another by sounding them out. The words included verbs such as run, hop, jog, and so on. Then, they acted out the words by running, hopping, jogging, and so on. In this way, they constructed the words together. I also set up a center with pictures of more complex objects, many of them multisyllabic and not necessarily phonetic. I put these pictures in a craft box that consisted of twenty-six tiny drawers. A letter of the alphabet was written on each drawer. Inside the drawers were tiny, laminated pictures that began with the letter appearing on the drawer. There were also lined writing pads and pencils. The goal was not to have the children spell all the words correctly but to become confident in sounding out and writing any word they might want to spell, therefore, becoming more fluent writers. By doing this work, the children were able to gain experience in invented spelling. I will relay some of the children's word lists as they were written. (Unclear attempts are indicated by U.W. [unknown word]).

Betsy's word list included: cando (candle), cat, cor (car), and cerit (carrot). She was unsure if the words that began with C are written with C or K because she wrote the letter K inside the letter C in both *candle* and *cat*. It is evident that she has command over three-letter phonetic words and is attempting to write words with two syllables.

David's word list included : batub (bathtub), sh (U.W.), bag, budfly (butterfly), bat, bulon (balloon), ans (ants), ax (apple), alugadr (alligator), hrt (heart), han (hand), hat, hors (horse), rug, rak (rake), and reng (ring). Every child in the group advanced rapidly and an analysis of their spellings will be described in detail later. I did not correct the children; however, they often compared and discussed their spellings with one another. The Kindergartners rapidly gained expertise in composing words and there were fewer appeals to me to spell words for them.

As the children engaged themselves in what we called word work (working at centers with words), they invented spellings. This was an unusual occurrence because I had never before witnessed extensive explorations in writing with my Kindergarten students. I attributed much of the writing to the fact that the children found delight in the post office, which provided a communicative aspect to writing. After working with words, they gained the ability to write them through phonetic "sounding out." This was, in great part, achieved through the increased exercises in decontextualized phonics. It gave the children the ability to make informed estimates when selecting sounds for drafting words. Children are natural workers (Montessori 1995), so it was not surprising to see them deeply engaged in the word centers. We continued with our usual literature-based program, and it was not unusual to see the children sounding out words when coming to words they didn't recognize in books. Additionally, in activities such as shared reading or modeled writing, I continued to emphasize phonetic correspondences within context, always promoting the meaning of the text. The Kindergarten program, thus, became a more balanced one, with the benefits of whole-language activities combined with decontextualized phonics at the word centers.

Yet it is not only the instruction that matters: My subjects were deeply engaged in social activity when they sat at their word workstations. They enjoyed constant peer interaction and social reflection on their own work as well as the work of others. Canella found that middle-class Kindergarten children fared better on the Richgels test of invented spelling if they were subject to group activities that enjoined children to explore writing and reflect on their work with each other (1991). Dyson took a similar stance concerning her African American Kindergartners (1991). She demonstrated that they learned concepts about print and writing when engaged in social interactions that invite questioning and deliberating on others' work. Invented spelling marks a conceptual landmark in that the child has formed hypotheses concerning the alphabetic system, that words must appear different if they are to be read, and that letters symbolize sounds in words. Spanish-speaking Argentinean children were shown to develop these theories (Ferreiro and Teberosky 1982), as were Mexican children and English-speaking children from both suburban and urban areas who were black and white, of middle- and low-SES (Kamii, Long, Manning, and Manning 1990).

But because the children were working at their word centers in a decontextualized atmosphere, their inherent search for significance infused meaning into their work. Figure 5.1 makes this quest evident. Karen drew pictures next to many of her invented words: hart (heart), hand, hat, hors (horse), mop, melbox (mailbox), men, and mrmad (mermaid). She also sought to individualize her list by elaborating the letters, so that the Hs were drawn as arches and the M words were double inscribed. As necessary as I felt composing isolated words were, as we continued with shared reading, I always invited the children to note specific features of words within the context of authentic literature. Additionally, I felt compelled to have their learning placed in an environment where the words would crystallize in ideas and meaning. Therefore, I encouraged the children to write their thoughts in sentences. They needed the same type of coaching they required to learn how to compose words. During modeled writing, the children learned how to create sentences orally. After several of my examples, the children began to contribute:

"I went to the mall with my mom."

"My dog's name is Blackie."

"I played house with my sister."

When the children were able to relay sentences orally, I instructed them individually in sentence writing.

ME: What sentence do you want to write today?
CHILD (often): I don't know.
ME: What did you do after school yesterday? (or some such prompt)
CHILD: I played with my sister.

Figure 5.1. Karen's word list

ME: Let's write, *I played with my sister.* "I-played-with-my-sis-ter." (The concentration was not on segmenting sounds in words but in separating words as units. Again, we used the imaginary cleaver.)

CHILD (often repeating the segmentation): I-played-with-my-sis-ter.

ME: *(Child would write* I *as he repeated it.)*

ME: Played. *(Child said "played," sounded out "played," and wrote it as it was sounded, etc.)*

In this way, the children began to write sentences. Accordingly, I requested that the children write at least one sentence per day. It was the last month of school and the post office had been closed for the teachers to wind down their activities and review the year's curriculum, so the children were not writing many letters to their friends. Instead, they wrote sentences that pertained to their lives, their feelings, what they were doing, what they liked, and their wishes. This is exemplified in the following sample of sentences:

I play whit my lito sistr,

My sistr is hape kus I play wit her. (Notice that *with* is spelled two different

ways; these two sentences were written by the same child.)

My mom is tacing me ad my bruth to the woovese (upside down M)

I lik yonukons

My mom wus hape wen I wus danse

I wish that it wussumr

(On the death of an aunt, in this region, an aunt is designated as *auntie.*): I

mis my ante so much

My bruvr nis toome.

I am butfol

In this way, the disconnected phonics lessons and word centers led to meaningful expression and adoption of voice in writing. There must be a balance in teaching methods. Unlike their Anglo counterparts (see Chomsky 1971), these children had not spontaneously engaged in invented spelling. They had to be explicitly instructed in this format. Whole-language methods, which contextualized phonics teaching within the environment of real literature, had a limited effect on the children's phonetic knowledge. The children had to study phonics independently so that they could systematically focus on the sound/letter correspondences. Here, they needed the support of the teacher who guided them through various activities designed to teach these associations. When this was accomplished, the children were instructed in the mechanics of composing a word and, later, writing sentences. This was achieved through individual instruction but was fortified with learning centers, where the children had choice, freedom, and the social interaction to reconstruct and practice what had been introduced by the teacher. In the relation between teacher and child, there was no simple pouring of knowledge from a more knowledgeable leader to an inexperienced proselyte. The child moved through the Zoped, with the teacher, through a dyactic mentoring: Let us take the earlier example of a child learning to write the word *hat.* Knowledge was conveyed through the couplet of teacher and child. Both the teacher (me) and the child worked together as a duet. At first, the child was carried through the task of writing the word *hat*. The child and I both said the word *hat*, sounded it out, and wrote those sounds, until we both had the word *hat* written down. At each step, the child had only one part to carry out and was guided through questions and gestures (the cleaver). Gradually, more and more of the steps were handed over to the child until the child shared the same organizational plan as the previously more knowledgeable teacher. In the final step, the members of the pair, who began as unequal partners, became equal (Litowitz 1993). The one who originally knew less became, like the one who knew more, able to take responsibility for composing words and sentences. This has exciting ramifications for teachers. If a teacher *allows* and *trusts* a child to take control of his or her learning, while at the same time giving up dictatorship, a teacher can begin to view his or her role with the child as one of partnership, with the important goal of the child becoming an independent learner. The dyactic process allows us to view the child's learning pattern as one that needs to acquire, from a more experienced confrere, the organizational exemplar, rather than the information itself.

The Kindergarten Group's Spellings

In his seminal work on young children's spelling, Read described that some *privileged* (Read's word) preschool, Kindergarten, and first-grade children instinctively created their words based on tacit knowledge of articulatory characteristics (1971). As I investigated his subject's ingenious spellings, I was curious to know if my Kindergartners shared any of the hypotheses of the children in Read's study. There were some basic differences in data collection. Read intervened with his participants by asking them to produce words based on his dictation. For the older first-grade children, Read not only read words aloud but additionally used photographs of objects, which he asked the children to spell. I collected the Kindergartners' work and explored its characteristics later, so there was no intervention nor question/answer feedback. Read's children were primarily preschoolers, under five years of age. To a lesser degree, he also investigated the spellings of older children, those in Kindergarten and first grade. When he did so, I have made appropriate comparisons. Read's work was of special interest to me because his study has set the standard of what is known as invented spelling—a driving force behind this study. Because the Kindergartners eventually produced a substantial amount of emergent writing, I welcomed the unexpected opportunity to uncover resemblances and/or differences between Read's groups and mine. This investigation sheds light on how inexperienced spellers, such as my participants, theorize about their writing. In contrast, Read described his subjects as experienced spellers because they frequently explored writing at home at an early age. As early as three-and-a-half, before his subjects learned to read, they started writing. Each child first learned the letters of the alphabet.

Then through movable toys, such as alphabet blocks, the children began to spell words and moved to the production of written messages, including stories, letters, and poems. In order to glean the comparison between Read's subjects and mine, I followed Read's original format. (Broad) phonetic transcriptions will appear in square brackets; phonological representations, in slashes. The children's spellings, largely invented, will be entirely uppercase; standard spellings and individual letters will be lowercase and placed in parentheses.

Vowels

Pertaining to lax vowels (as in *bit, bet, rat, pot*), Read's participants formed lax vowels on the basis of tacit understanding of phonetic relationships. Each lax vowel was represented by its corresponding tense form. The children matched the lax vowel with the tense on the basis of points of articulation. The phonetic correspondence of tense-lax complements is as follows:

	Tense	Lax	Tense	Lax	Tense	Lax
Symbol	[īy]	[i]	[ēy]	[e]	[āy]	[a]
Spelling	serēne	divīnity	cāme	extrēmity	līne	phōnic

With these correspondences in mind, Read's participants, who based their spellings largely on their unconscious understanding of the language, regularly paired the lax vowels with the tense vowels on the basis of phonetic relationships: fish was FES, fell was spelled FALL, got was GIT (for further understanding of these developmentally historical complements, see Lehiste 2002).

The Kindergarten subject group, for the most part, adapted their experiences from the word centers and most frequently spelled these vowels correctly (phonetically). Here is a sample of their use of these sounds:

[i]	[e]	[a]
PRASTiS (practice)	FREN (friend)	HOT (hopped)
BASGIT (basket)	WET (went)	BOL (ball)
PUPCIN (pumpkin)	EX (the letter X)	CHOCLIT (chocolate)
WIT (with)	AMEREKA (America)	GOT (got)
GEV (give)		

Occasionally, but not often, the children exhibited similarities of the preschoolers. Thus, the Kindergarten subjects depended more upon their newfound knowledge of sound/letter correspondences than upon their articulatory features.

However, the Kindergartners' spellings concurred with Read's children by presenting spellings of words having sounds of tense vowels (those in *rake, feed, side,* and *boat*), by referring to their alphabetic names. My participants wrote the following:

MI (my)   LIX (likes)   SNAK (snake)
ET (eat)   BECH (beach)   WINDO (second syllable of window)

Read explained that older first-grade children who have learned conventional spellings of lax vowels sometimes spelled a tense vowel with the letter they had formerly associated with the corresponding lax form. Here, the children strove to retain phonetic alliance while virtually ignoring the obvious association between the letter names and the tense vowels that they originally started with. I saw no evidence of this with my Kindergartners. They began and continued to represent the tense vowels with their corresponding letter names.

Read's participants' spellings of tense vowels did not adhere to conventional strategies such as doubling the vowels or adding a silent E. Often my Kindergarten group doubled vowels, although the second vowel was often incorrect because they lacked experience with reading words. Once again, the children depended upon their phonetic school knowledge. This was because, as part of our word centers, the children read double- and single-vowel words, matching both types of words with pictures and composing both types of words when writing. They knew that when they saw two vowels, the first one "said" its name and the second one was silent. They had been explicitly taught this rule. Much of this transferred to their spelling of words that had double vowel alphabetic names. Although there are many exceptions to this principle, it was a good beginning. Some examples of my students' use of double vowels and/or silent E follow:

LIEK (like)   LIIK (like)   TEECHER (teacher)
BNEE (bunny)   MEE (me)   BAYBEE (baby)
NAIM (name)   MIE (my)   BRUHARE (silent E in brother)
HAPEE (happy)   OOVIR (over)   PUZLE (silent E in puzzle)
GLOOB (globe)   VEAIREE (second syllable in very)

My Kindergarten subjects displayed concurrent use of single and double vowels, but when using a double vowel, they almost always exhibited the first vowel having the letter name that was heard. The act of doubling a vowel exhibits their intention to follow the precept they had been taught.

In reference to the back rounded vowels of *boot, boat,* and *bought,* Read's participants chose backness as the dimension to be represented. They spelled those sounds with an O. For example, *soon* was spelled SOWN, *goat* was spelled GOWT, and *all* was spelled OL. Vowels with back glides [w] as in *boot* [ūw] and *boat* [ōw] were often spelled OW, as can be seen in the previous examples. Read hypothesized his subjects distinguished a vocalic segment from a glide because the children could have represented the [ōw] with one letter, O. The Kindergartners consistently chose to designate these sounds with the letter O. However, they didn't demonstrate a preference for representing these sounds with the OW spelling, which suggests that they depended more upon their knowledge that the sound of an alphabetic letter was represented by its symbol, or when its sound was heard, it was represented, by two vowels, at least for the words that sounded like [ōw]. It must be noted that learning the names of letters was fairly new information to many of the Kindergartners. The sounds [ōw] were as follows:

WINDOU (window)   SNOMANS (snowmans)
SNOY (snow)   HOLOWEN (Halloween)
GAWN (going)   GAOING (going)   GOWN (going)
EOVR (over, the E and O probably being unintentionally reversed)

In these sounds, the Kindergartners continued to represent the alphabetic sound of the letter, although not entirely correctly. They didn't depict backward glides by spelling OW. Of the two OW spellings above, the children were representing the sound of the letter W so they were depicting *wing* in *going* and *ween* in *Halloween.* This was gleaned from the child's spelling of *Halloween* the day before. It was then spelled HLWN so that the child had the concept of the last syllable of the word being *ween.* There were two spellings of the sound [ūw] and they were spelled in the traditional sense, SOON, POOL. For the sound in *bought,* the children wrote only three words: *mall, because,* and *called.* They were designated as follows:

MAL (mall)   BECUS (because)   BECOOS (because)   KOD (called)

Mall was once spelled MAL and the other spelled correctly, MALL. The first spelling of *because* displays a phonetic attempt. The second spelling denotes a choice of backwardness as does the spelling of *called.*

Reducing

It was evident that phonetic lessons and their accompanying work had an overwhelming impact on the Kindergartner's spellings. When the vowel had the sound in *bit*, Read's younger participants reduced with an E for the reasons already discussed. My Kindergartners sometimes had this in common with them:

CHOK*E*T (chocolate)

APP*E*L (apple)

AMER*E*KA (America)

When the spelling of the vowel in *bit* developed to I in Read's older children, the reduced vowel was also spelled with an I. My Kindergartners also evinced reducing with an I:

EDAESO*IS* (Edaphosaurus)   CAR*IT* (carrot)

STIGSOR*IS* (Stegosaurus)   PUPC*IN* (pumpkin)

And sometimes the Kindergarten group reduced with other sound/letter attempts:

SGSRW*US* (Stegosaurus)   TABOL (table)

PCEP*ON* (pumpkin)   ERZONU (Arizona)

In the previous example, we see that the Kindergartners did not consistently reduce using the same manner of spelling that Read's older group did. At times, they reduced using the letter E, more frequently with the letter I. At other times, they did so by designating a vowel that was not necessarily phonetically correct. This was because they were experimenting with multisyllabic words. Read stated that reduction reveals "what the children know and what they don't yet know" (10). As the child struggles to make sense of words, words that contain more than one syllable present a particular challenge. The Kindergartners stressed each syllable when "sounding out" and attempting to write. Thus, the unstressed vowel received a stress that was not normal. This caused a certain distortion that may be the reason for the variety of vowels found in the previous examples.

Affrication

The letters [t] and [d] before [r] are slowly released as "shh" and are said to be affricated. The /t/ and /sh/ are the constituents of /ch/ (Merriam 1973). Read discovered his subjects' invented spellings for these affricates: CH (for tr) and JR (for dr). Those representations had a phonetic basis: The sounds are articulated in the same place as the letters we spell [t] and [d], but in the manner of palatal affricates [č] and /□/ that conventional spelling represents as *ch* and *j*, *respectively*. In other words, the children perceived affrication. We know that Read extended his participants to first graders. Those children who were making average progress consistently represented the affricates in this way. The following are representations of my Kindergarten group:

CHRAST (traced)

CHRAYN (train)

CHRAC (truck)

CHREESU (Teresa, the name of our aide)

TRESU (Teresa, written later by the same child possibly after seeing the
    name spelled)

JRESS (dress, note the double S)

The children perceived the affricates. In order to spell these sounds with standard spellings, the child would need to gain experience in using these words or be told directly, as in the instance of the second spelling of *Teresa*. The affricate in *Teresa* was, subsequently, spelled in a more conventional form; that is, the sound of *tr* was represented with standard letters after the child was told or saw the spelling of her name. Note that the double vowel is absent in the second spelling. Most likely, the child was concentrating on the initial sound, which took most of the effort. Interestingly, the ending of both versions of *Teresa* was spelled with a U. The children learned that this sound (as spelled in hut) was designated with a U, thus the spelling. Once again, the children precisely followed the sound/letter correspondences they had learned in the word centers.

Flaps

When [t] and [d] appear between vowels, they progress as a stroke of the tip of the tongue that touches the teeth ridge (Merriam 1973). This is a voiced sound and its timbre is closer to the /d/. This is the reason that Read's preschool participants wrote D in words like LADER (ladder) and PREDE (pretty). However, by the time his older first-grade children reached the age of six, they ceased representing the flap. My Kindergartners primarily, but not always, ignored the D in their spellings:

SADURDIA (Saturday)	BYTYFL (beautiful)
SISDR (sister)	SISTR (sister, same child who wrote SISDR)
DODR (daughter)	DOTR (daughter, later by the same child)
LTTE (little)	LTL (little)
ETR (Easter)	

The Kindergartners' early writings were represented by the D and, later, by the T. Read affirmed that his three-and-a-half-year-olds followed this same pattern (1971). His subjects were reading by five years of age and were given words to spell, upon request, by their families. Therefore, they came to learn spelling through experience. Because the Kindergartners were not early spellers, it seems that they advanced rather rapidly. This may present evidence that decontextualized phonetic lessons influence late spellers to the extent that they base their abstractions on their knowledge of phonics lessons.

Both my subjects as well as Read's first graders discovered the phonological relation between the voiced flap and the corresponding voiceless stop. They both adopted the abstract form in their spelling as a result. This is important because, although my participants were inexperienced spellers, they were able to compensate for this by adroitly using what they had come to learn. Not only did they not have deficits but were able to become as adept as Read's advantaged subjects.

When children use these abstractions in most instances, we can come to the conclusion that spelling is "rule governed"; that is, words do not need to be learned one by one but, rather, can be learned as principles (Read 1971). This has important implications for the ineffectiveness of basic skills programs, where spellings are laboriously taught one at a time. Schools, textbooks, administrators, teachers, and parents regard the weekly spelling test as a requisite instrument for children's learning. Far from helping children learn lexical representations that conform to standard spelling, the use of habitual spelling tests hampers minority students from developing mindful abstractions which the more fortunate children in Read's study were allowed to develop.

Nasals

Concerning Read's participants, when a nasal ([m], [n], and [ŋ]) appears before a consonant, it is almost always omitted. This approach applied to words like *bumpy, end,* and *sing*. My children evidenced the same type of omission:

ATE (auntie)	SATCLOS (Santa Claus)
COSRT (concert)	HAD (hand)
FREDS (friends)	DUZT (doesn't)
WIT (went)	WET (went)
WOT (went)	RABO (rainbow)
UBRELU (umbrella)	UDWER (underwear)
UKL (uncle)	

Read emphasized that the omission of preconsonantal nasals was quite common after the age of five, even among first graders, when children begin to notice the nasal but still frequently omit it. He supported this notion by citing an informal spelling dictation given to forty-nine first graders. In that examination, fifteen of twenty-three errors involved the words *went* and *sent* (see previous example for the Kindergartners' varied spellings of *went*). The Kindergartners appear to be in several stages of spelling development. More frequently, they did evidence omission of preconsonantal nasals. Yet they were able to display the more advanced spellings, where the nasals were included:

ANT (and)	NUMBRZ (numbers)
FREND (friend)	UMPIER (umpire)

Interestingly, the children were able to signify preconsonantal velar nasals, which Read's older subjects frequently omitted:

BADENSOOT (bathing suit) AGRING (angry)

In the spelling of *bathing suit,* the child was able to discern the nasal and indicate it with the N instead of the more usual G. In this case, the child did not choose the point of articulation (see below), but instead distilled the [n] sound from the [ng]. In the spelling of *angry,* the child noted the nasal but recorded it as ING. In other words, the child was able to inscribe a velar nasal but confused and reversed it using a more familiar pattern.

The -*ing* ending in Read's study was usually represented with the use of EG and IG, the former used by those children who wrote E for [i]. The explanation given for these children's use of G at the end is that they could not be designating the sound of [g] without a nasal because the nasal is the final sound. In the English language, there is no letter for the sound [ŋ] so the G (as in *give*) most closely corresponds with [ŋ] because it is at the same point of articulation. The reason we find the nasal absent is that the articulatory location is chosen over the nasal (but we should recognize that when a child represents G in a spelling like FIGR [finger], he or she is actually representing the [g]). When it came to velar nasals, my Kindergartners were in contrast to Read's participants in that they preferred the nasal over the articulation point or they spelled the -*ing* with standard spelling. In this area, the -*ing* was pronounced in the conventional manner, so there was no question of the child pronouncing it as *goin'* (although in the first two instances of *going,* one might think that was the case). The Kindergarten children depicted the -*ing* in the following manner:

TACING (with backward G, taking)   RENG (ring)

GOWN (going)   GAWN (going)

GAOING (going)   SWIMING (swimming)

SWIMIING (swimming)

In Read's examples, the children used the ending G to indicate the point of articulation of the nasal as well as the last consonant. This is because when a nasal comes before a consonant, it must be articulated in the same place as a consonant. In consideration that the Kindergartners were not signaling this combination and were simply using the N, they had no way of indicating that the usual [n] ending (as in *man*) was different from the -*ing*. This was the reason for the vowel shift in the second and third examples of *going*. As Read points out, there is no question that the children perceive [ŋ] and [ŋg]. Because all the children knew how to spell *go,* the W was most likely used to express what we can hear as *wing* in *going*. In the first example, the child thought W was sufficient to express the end sound. In the second example, the W was not adequate for the child, thus, the vowel change discussed above. In the last example of *going,* the child did not use a W, so he required a double-vowel substitution because GON would have spelled *gone* and GAN would have spelled those separate letters. There was a possibility of using GAO in order to express this [ŋg] sound that a letter could not represent. In these instances, the Kindergartners relied more on standard phonetic sounds than places of articulation (Paul 1976). It is evident that the children perceived the word as a whole when they were formulating it.

This is because all the children knew how to spell *go*; yet in the second and third examples, they began the word with alterations in order to compensate for the ending. I have found the same results with reading. When a child reads a sentence and there is an unknown word toward the end, the child generally falters with beginning words that he knows well. Thus, it may be that the eye perceives an unknown word toward the end when a child is beginning a sentence. In the same respect, the child's mind may perceive the end before he or she reaches it; thus, the words may be viewed holistically. More research is needed to investigate this phenomenon.

Read called his participants experienced spellers because they frequently wrote at home. The Kindergartners were older and less experienced spellers than the preschoolers, but they gained expertise when they worked on projects in the word centers where they isolated specific sounds from words. Although we did not do particular word work on *-ing,* we talked about it when it arose in shared reading, modeled writing, and at any other time that the children's curiosity presented itself. These things do not automatically transfer to children's writing. The children must, through their own explorations and manipulations, come to decisions concerning their marks on paper. These decisions were based on many factors. Their emerging phonological awareness, learned in school, certainly had a strong impact on their decisions. Of course, it was not only phonics lessons but the fact that the children were allowed to choose the direction of their own learning that made them proficient.

Syllabic Segments

When [r], [l], [m], or [n] occur in English words between the middle two consonants or at the conclusion of a word following a consonant, the segment establishes a loudness maximum (sonority peak) and becomes syllabic; that is, it is distinguished as a separate syllable (Read 1971). Read's preschoolers and first graders never perceived that the peak of syllables was represented by a vowel. A sample of his participants' spellings appears below:

End Sounds	**Medials**
TIGR (tiger)	GRL (Girl)
SOGR (sugar)	BRD (bird)
AFTR (after)	SRKIS (circus)
LITL (little)	SESTR (sister)
WAGN (wagon)	BRATHR (brother)

My Kindergartners sometimes represented the syllable in the same manner. (Note that the children are writing the digraph "th," which they had worked on in the word center.)

FOTHRS (father's)	DOTR (daughter)	BRUTHR (brother)
BRUDR (brother)	OTHR (other)	ESTR (Easter)
BETR (better)	PLUMR (plumber)	

Yet my students' spellings were often in sharp contrast to those of the preschoolers and the first graders. My Kindergartners frequently spelled these syllables with indications of vowels:

KULER (color)	SUMER (summer)	FLAUR (flower)
TABOL (table)	TETHER (teacher)	FAMULE (family)

BRUHARE (brother)

KALLER or KULLER (color—first syllable, A or U, was unclear)

TURTEL (turtle, originally spelled TURTL; the E squeezed moments later)

Avoidance of vowels was practiced with the medials in Read's study as well. Once again, the Kindergartners sometimes duplicated the results of Read's subjects:

CHOLET (chocolate)	TRSRTP (Triceratops)	ASID (outside)
ROBRT (Robert)	HLWEN (Halloween)	FAVRIT (favorite)

Unlike the preschoolers, the Kindergartners frequently wrote the vowel:

LIZURD (lizard)	BURD (bird)	BERD (bird)
FAMULE (family)	SUMTI (sometimes)	SERCIRSIS (circus)
BRUTHER (brother)	CULERS (colors)	

EDAFOSORIS (Edaphosaurus)

BRUHAER (brother, see above for end vowels)

Once again, the Kindergarten group differed from Read's participants in that they displayed more conventional spellings. The first graders that Read reviewed also demonstrated the absence of vowels (1971). Thus, this study's Kindergarten group exhibited more advanced (conventional) levels than the first graders with regard to standard spelling. A dramatic difference between my subjects and those in former studies is that the Kindergarten subjects did not settle on an earlier stage, add a new component, and then move onto a higher level. Often, they seemed to jump into an advanced position. Take, for example, Paul's interpretation of Read's stages (1976). She claims that children initially write with the first phoneme, but follow it with random letters. Next, the children use beginning and ending phonemes, with random letters in between. Third, children gradually move to spelling vowel sounds, and last, to conventional spelling. This is consistent with Gentry's (1979) formulation and has been an accepted model for emergent writing by many teachers of young children. Although my Kindergartners evinced the above qualities, they did so simultaneously. They didn't explore writing until they had a general command of phonetic relationships. After they gained that knowledge, they began writing. This is consistent with their cultural values and the cultural values of other Indian groups. Learning visually, with little discussion, has been found to be the cultural norm for many Indian groups (Romero 1994; Borman 1998; Phillips 1972). These children are reluctant to perform until they feel confident that they can do so. They gain this faith by observing and privately practicing. Frequently, they will not perform until they know they will be successful.

In many instances, the Kindergartners exhibited features of spelling that were similar to those of Read's preschool and first-grade children. More often, they relied on the knowledge of sound/letter correspondences that they learned from their lessons in decontextualized phonics. This is an important discovery because the general image of Indian children is that, chiefly, they learn *holistically*. Two Native American scholars concurred: "Indigenous people around the world are severely disadvantaged because they do not naturally articulate abstraction, because they do not communicate with decontextualized thought, because they do not fare well in school situations of the dominant culture" (Cleary and Peacock 1998, 196). That the children used phonics lessons as their primary method of spelling indicated that they were not only capable of learning through decontextualized information but that they readily adapted themselves to applying that knowledge. This is not to say that we must abandon contextualized learning—if we did, we would be moving backward in time. It is important not only to preserve whole language but also to bolster it with other supportive methods. We owe it to the children to give *all* of them techniques shown to be advantageous to learning. That includes devising new techniques as well as reexamining and readapting old but effective measures. Most importantly, we must combine culturally relevant methods (as well as other methods) that have proved successful with mainstream children while guarding against the pervasive need to assimilate. This is done in great part by offering children literacy that has real purposes and gives children a voice and a choice.

Curriculum: Two Kinds of Literacy

Basic Skills versus Critical Thinking

The student body of Cedarbrook Middle School in a Philadelphia suburb is one-third black, two-thirds white. The town has a very low poverty rate, good schools and a long established black middle class. But an eighth-grade advanced algebra class that a reporter visited in June 2000 contained not a single black student. The class in which the teacher was explaining that the 2 in 21 stands for 20, however was 100 percent black. A few black students were taking accelerated English, but no whites were sitting in the English class that was learning to identify verbs. (Thernstrom and Thernstrom 2003, 1)

*A*s this chapter develops, it is important for the reader to understand that documentation of what is reported as the school climates and curricula given to minorities and the benefits of the same characteristics in mainstream schools are presented as depicting typical, but not universal, circumstances. All along, it has been stated that there are some exemplary teachers and programs in my district, as well as all minority schools, just as there are some poor teachers and agendas in suburban middle-class schools. It was necessary to cite the typical courses of study and methods of teaching common to minority schools in an effort to determine why Indian and minority education has failed. It is only through understanding the causes of this deterioration that the situation might be remedied.

The particular mode in which schools define literacy drives the curriculum (Au and Raphael 2000) and the choice of literacy programs is dependent upon the socioeconomic status of the children (Brown, Palinscar, and Purcell 1986). The more affluent middle-class children have a richer curriculum where there is an abundance of student research resources, lavishly illustrated current texts, and a wide range of courses of study. Here, what counts as knowledge is a highly evolved method of functioning that concentrates on social, scientific, economic, and liberal arts. This can provide the type of encouragement and intellectual challenge that offers students occasions to excel academically. These opportunities for learning are not attendant in a curriculum that concentrates on basic skills, the educational agenda most commonly given to minority children. Bartlett studied two reading programs, one designed for middle-class children and the other intended for those who were said to be disadvantaged (1979). The program focusing on lower-SES children exposed them to a heavy emphasis on decoding, whereas goals for middle-class children centered on a program that emphasized comprehension. The plan for the "deprived" children entailed simpler work locating and remembering items in antecedent text, whereas the middle-class instruction required synthesizing and deliberation in reference to the entire text. Concentration on simplistic awareness leads to disallowance of admittance to the literary inheritance that middle-class children receive. This is because the so-called disadvantaged children's understanding of text is limited to piecemeal scraps of information while they are denied the mental stimulation and pleasure that comes with making meaning from an entire work of literature. Middle-class children have the opportunity to learn how to make meaning from text through provocative programs. This is done with many comprehension-fostering activities. When children were asked the purpose of reading, poor readers (i.e., minority children) were left with the understanding that reading was decoding and vocalizing the words correctly for the teacher. In contrast, middle-class children learned that reading was garnering information (Canney and Winograd 1979 in Brown, Palinscar, and Purcell 1986). This is because children whose curriculum is ruled by basic skills know no other world. Most of their time is spent decoding in order to please the teacher. Thus, they not only are presented with a restricted program but also become extrinsically motivated (Stipek, Feiler, Daniels, and Milburn 1995). On the other hand, middle-class children who learn to comprehend need less direction from the teacher, therefore less approval from an outside source, and accordingly become intrinsically motivated. A diminished motivation to learn leads one down a slippery slope from where there is rarely a return. When children's minds are not provoked and stimulated, their thoughts wander away from learning and move toward other nonproductive activities. This is why minority children are often accused of having behavioral problems. Other disadvantages of fundamental proficiency programs are that children rate their abilities lower, have less expectations of success in school-like tasks, and evidence less pride in accomplishments than the children who experience a more child-centered approach (Canney and Winograd 1979 in Brown, Palinscar, and Purcell 1986). Being in possession of higher-level reasoning entails qualities such as command over skills, ability to comprehend, drawing inferences from reading, applying what was read to other areas, synthesizing and deliberating on printed matter, and acquiring information from text. This type of course brings confidence and pride to schoolwork. Because basic-skills programs dictate an elemental curriculum, underrepresented groups rarely are exposed to these conceptual and critical understandings.

In this rapidly changing world, it is necessary to devise a concept of literacy that will equip underrepresented children for the future. It is not enough that children read fluently. The conception of critical thinking is no longer an extravagance: As we move toward a more global, communicative workforce, judicious reasoning needs to be included in any definition of literacy. Eventually, most Indian children (and those of minorities) do learn to decode. Yet they do not learn to understand or make meaning of texts. This is because they receive little experience in comprehension-fostering activities (Brown, Palinscar, and Purcell 1986), which are taken for granted in teaching middle-class children. For example, it has been learned through the study of the Kindergartners that teaching decontextualized phonics was a necessary *part* of educating young children. Yet schools of underrepresented groups seem to be stuck at this point of instruction. After minority children learn the necessary basic phonetic training, they are continually instructed in the same uses throughout their elementary career. In my district, fourth graders who can already read long and short vowel sounds within the context of their readings are required to spend time with worksheets categorizing these sounds. Teaching phonics to the exclusion of higher-order thinking indicates a mistrust of the intelligence of diverse children. It also speaks to the teacher's low expectations of the students. Finally, it demonstrates that many teachers of minorities actually equate the teaching of reading with the teaching of phonics and other simple fundamental skills. Making sure that children have command over standard competence skills is necessary. But essential to the basic-skills curriculum prevalent in so many minority schools is the constant teaching of simple proficiencies as though they were the only ingredients in the teaching of reading. This is because what is considered knowledge in minority schools is the mechanics of reading, writing, spelling, and math. In stark contrast is the fact that suburban, middle-class schools count knowledge as skills like critiquing, analyzing, theorizing, and thinking about content in general (Anyon 2001). Back-to-basics curriculum is damaging because it impedes students' progress by restricting the children to an abridged course of study. One stunning difference between minority and mainstream education is that it takes almost the entire elementary years for an underrepresented child to learn to read fluently, whereas in mainstream education, basic reading is completed at a much earlier time. In mainstream education, third grade is a crossroads where learning to read transitions to reading to learn. Obviously, this presupposes fluency in reading. American Indians and Alaska Natives meet with difficulty at this juncture (Reyhner 2001). This is because their progress is stifled by their limiting curriculum. Literacy, in schools that serve minorities, is defined in provisos of fundamentals rather than interpretational thinking (Darling-Hammond 1995). This leads to poor readers.

> Where "good readers" are often asked comprehension questions and helped to find meanings, "poor readers" usually get drilled in phonics. As a result, the poor readers, often minority children—improve in phonics but not in understanding what they read. The net effect is to widen the initial gap between good and poor readers, accustoming one group to success and the other to failure. (Neisser 1986, 8)

This country has a tradition of differentiating schooling experiences according to the conviction that some children can more readily or more rightfully achieve excellence. Indian and minority children have generally been denied high-quality schooling. Oakes has pointed out the differences in kinds of knowledge that students in various tracks had entry into: Students in high-track classes were exposed to high-status content such as literature, expository writing, library research, and mathematical ideas (1986). The students in the low-track classes were not expected to learn these subjects but were, predictably, exposed to low-level experiences such as workbooks, kits, practiced language mechanics, and mathematical computation. These students had less time to complete assignments and had more punitive teachers. The more the schools made decisions about the appropriateness of topics and skills, the more limits were imposed upon the children. "The lower the track, the greater the limits" (Oakes 1986, 63). These reports detail the unequal apportioning of learning opportunities between high and low tracks, generally the difference between opportunities for mainstream and minority children (Goodlad 1984). Thus, prospects for learning favor those who are already advantaged. Reform efforts don't usually concentrate on these aspects of inequality but, rather, expend effort in pointing out the deficiencies of the poor. In today's arena, this translates into how underrepresented children fail to do well on tests. This prevailing attitude reveals how deficit theory is punctuated today. Thernstrom and Thernstrom documented the racial gap between blacks and Hispanics with whites, yet blamed black culture (and, to a lesser extent, Hispanic) for their low test scores. Their supposition was that when it comes down to academic success, members of Asian and white cultures were "luckier" than blacks and Hispanics because their cultures supported and promulgated scholarship whereas the minority (other than Asian) cultures were in opposition to it and were, therefore, inundated with cultural deficits. With regard to African Americans, little has changed over the course of the years. Heredity and culture are still blamed for their lack of school success. African Americans still are accused of poor parenting, nutritional ignorance, lack of reading in the home, not preparing their children for school, and having impulse problems. They are regarded as having inherited defects (evidenced in low birth weight), being culturally deprived, disadvantaged, and socially lacking. The schools are still regarded as exculpatory in the face of their black students' failures because these defects are so powerful that literally nothing could be done to overcome them. Thus, are they imprisoned by deficit thinkers:

> [S]omething about the lives of these children is limiting their intellectual development. Some risk factors have been identified by scholars: low birth weight, single parent households, and birth to a very young mother. There seem to be racial and ethnic differences in parenting as well, and the relatively small number of books in black households and the extraordinary amount of time spent watching TV appears related to those parenting practices. . . . African-American children tend to be less academically prepared when they first start school and are less ready . . . to conform to behavioral demands. As a consequence, black students have disciplinary problems throughout their school careers. (Thernstrom and Thernstrom 2003, 147)

Exemplary Practices

Although skills policies have had damaging effects on the reading competency of diverse children, there have been several programs designed to ameliorate this situation. Au devised an intervention in the Hawaiian Kamehamela Early Education Program (KEEP) designed to increase the comprehension strategies of low-SES Native Hawaiian and Polynesian children. This was known as the E-T-R sequence. Here, the children used their own experience (E) to relate to the topic of a story. The teacher then asked the children to silently read the text (T) and then asked the children questions in order to assess their understanding. The final sequence consisted of the teacher and students drawing relationships (R) between the text and the children's experiences. The children and the teacher worked together to form these alliances, and they did so through questioning that encouraged active thought. This study contrasted the children who received the comprehension treatment along with decoding with those who were instructed solely in a phonics program. It was found that the comprehension intervention improved both comprehension and decoding skills of the children in the former program. KEEP demonstrated that when decoding was subservient to comprehension, reading for meaning became the prime consideration for the children. This remedy is especially suitable for minority children because they are the least likely to receive it. Brown, Palinscar, and Purcell devised a similar program, one that had its roots in the E-T-R sequence (1986). Their subjects were black and white low-SES children. The children and the teacher developed a reciprocal relationship where sometimes the teacher taught the lesson and sometimes the child delivered it. After the child's initial reading of the text, the teacher (or student) gave feedback, which included facilitation of the text; that is, summarizing, asking questions, and working through difficulties the child might have encountered. When the children learned the procedure, they were instructed to go through this process when reading text silently. Thus, they were able to learn strategies for comprehension that they later incorporated into their own repertoires. Improvements were found with the E-T-R operation as well as with Brown, Palinscar, and Purcell's interactive method (1986). In both of these programs, Vygotsky's Zoped was supported. The very nature of the teacher-child interactions invited a social place for sharing and deliberating. In both situations, the teacher worked with the children mutually, not as one who knew the answers but as one who knew that the answers resided within the students. The dynamic nature of such a milieu invites students to use actions and dialogue usually reserved solely for the teacher. New social behaviors and dialogues (Wertsch, Tulviste, and Hagstrom 1993) were introduced to pupils and they were required to appropriate them as their own. They were then able to carry them over to the intramental plane. This reciprocity between teacher and students allows the child to move through the Zone. In contrast, in the typical teacher-directed, "teacher-knows-all" curriculum prevalent in minority education, the diverse child's movement toward higher intellectual planes is hampered by the controlling nature of the teacher. This is because the teacher in minority schools genuinely believes that she transfers knowledge from herself to a child's blank slate. This transplantation of knowledge sets the course for the teacher as the dominator and the child as subjugated in a no-nonsense program. Here, active learning is strangled to the point of annihilation.

No Frills

Often, in an effort to help students gain rudimentary reading proficiency, reading for diverse children is assigned to long blocks of time. When the entire school participates in a two-hour reading period, as in my school and others that serve Indian students, characteristic attributes of children are abandoned because young children are forced into learning to read for an inappropriate time period. Furthermore, even the most basic needs are ignored, such as the need for movement and the need for variation in activity to accommodate the students' attention spans. Children who are involved in these reading blocks are again denied stimulating activities which lead to higher-level thinking and which are taken for granted in schools of mainstream children. Problem-solving thematic activities, which incorporate reading, are neglected as teachers of minorities concentrate on skills found on tests. School administrators discount the fact that this constitutes unethical practice (Haladyna and Haas 1991).

This school year, the teachers in my school were actually instructed to teach only those skills found on tests and to abandon those that were not. At a staff meeting, the teachers were presented with a printout of the frequency of each skill on the test and directed to teach only those skills which were recurrently on the tests. There is a troubling urgency in this type of program as schools race, to no avail, to have their children's test scores increase. For example, in traditional reading programs such as Four Blocks or Success for All, "no frills" is the key word. Silence in the classroom is preserved and other interesting activities are often postponed or abandoned until after the specified (and unbending) time period is completed. Some studies of the skills program Success for All have been shown to have significant positive effects on the reading achievement of urban *disadvantaged* (their word) African Americans (Slavin et al. 1990; Madden et al. 1991) and Asian students (Slavin and Yampolsky 1991).

Test results with this program delivered to the Pueblo Indian students in my area appear to be dismal. The low scores on standardized achievement tests after treatment with Success for All prompted the State Department of Education to keep the user school on probation. Poor numbers were demonstrated by children who began reading instruction with Success for All as well as by those who began instruction in other programs and were moved to Success for All upon its implementation several years ago. Therefore, the successful progression of students who were initiated into the program (e.g., Cambodian students in Slavin and Yampolsky [1991]) does not appear, at first glance, to hold true for the Pueblo Indian children who were involved in this course of study. There is now evidence that this program does not provide the achievement that its developers claimed (Pogrow 2000).

My district implemented the Success for All program in a school which has a population of 100 percent Pueblo students, all of whom speak Keres as their first language. It was completely ignored that Keres-speaking children grow up with a dramatically different sound system than do English-speaking children. Thus, phonics programs presupposing that children know and speak the sound system of English (Reyhner 2001) can set these children up for failure. A skills program such as Four Blocks allows teachers to chose their own materials, yet basals are the preferred choice of administrators. While basals are touted as being multicultural, in the early grades at least, they fail to provide provocative illustrations or topics. Many are still in the business of depicting homogenized versions of life, a life that few minorities can relate to. This is because "emphasis on textbook instruction . . . produces passive students who uncritically accept the 'canned' knowledge of the dominant social group" (Reyhner 1992, 103). The enforcement of basal readers to the subordination of authentic literature is simply a continuation of reductionist reasoning: Each lesson comes with specific directions for the teacher, and many of these lessons suggest "correct" responses from the children, thus smothering the children's personal reactions to text, especially as it may deviate from a certain expected type of response. This creates an appetite for mistake-proof learning. When that occurs, there is a decline in explorative thinking.

Another major problem with scripted answers is that the responses are based on the experiences of the textbook's writer rather than on the children's experience. Reyhner and Cockrum (2001) cite an example of Navajo students in Cameron, Arizona, responding to the question of where they would expect to see boats by stating *on a highway*, rather than the expected reply *in the water*. This was because these students often saw boats on passing trailers on the interstate. Most of these children had never taken the trip to nearby Page where they would have seen the boats launched into the waters of Lake Powell.

One way teachers can combat these deleterious effects is to supplement basals with a variety of reading matter, including books written by the children themselves as well as by other children from classes in the school. Language-experience stories written by the children should be utilized. In these ways, children's exposure to more legitimate forms of knowledge can be buttressed and stereotypical images of people from the children's culture can be minimized. Teachers can allow for children's voices through writing and, for very young children, through dictation of drawings. Therefore, teachers of underrepresented groups can overcome programs that they may not have faith in but are compelled to deliver.

In all fairness, publishers of basals are trying hard to overcome their shortcomings. For example, stories in the 2003 version of the Houghton Mifflin basals tend to be longer and more authentic, addressed to a variety of cultures, and many of them are written by well-known authors. However, in their rush to include many heritages, they failed to provide anything socially thought provoking. For example, a beautifully illustrated Indian tale by Bruchac is followed by a fine section on Indian art, and then moves to the next subdivision of the theme "One Land, Many Trails," the pioneers claiming the land, an introduction to a pioneer story. It benignly describes the Homestead Act as a law that provided families with parcels of land, but the Homestead Act was responsible for the theft of Indian land and the relocation of many Indian tribes to lands deemed undesirable for growing crops. No links were made between the two cultures whose stories were featured and also intertwined. In these basals, each story seems to exist in its own vacuum, unconnected to the common history and humanity of the many groups within the American or global culture. It seems that publishers of basals are content to label their work multicultural if the content of their stories contains a variety of cultures and a variety of people of color.

Teachers and those who are in charge of textbook adoption also fall into the guise of this superficiality: They often look at the illustrations and accompanying stories and cite them as being multicultural simply because various cultures and children of color are represented.

Creativity is also suppressed when teachers are mandated to teach in timed intervals. For example, in my school, the teachers of grades one through five are mandated to teach the components of Four Blocks: guided reading, writing, word work, and self-selected reading, in specific time periods, which are strictly adhered to. The purpose of these strict periods is that the whole school is working in the same manner at the same time. This method is thought by administration to be one way of holding teachers and students answerable to the practice of the drill, so to speak. This creates a militaristic environment for everyone involved. In another segment of this program, all of the children are required to read the words from the Word Wall, en masse, with no consideration of the fact that many of these children are "reading" on the coattails of others whom they hear.

There is an unsettling accentuation on standardization as though this could produce higher test scores. "Thus, while traditional reading instruction may have focused on reading the word on the printed page, in today's society—with its plethora of media and technologies—such an approach is limiting at best and detrimental at worst" (Au and Raphael 2000, 150). Schools of diverse students are now including the use of computers in their definitions of literacy but are, again, inundating the curriculum with the basic-skills approach. For example, my school as well as many others in the state (here students of diverse populations are the norm) use technological workbooks and basal programs, and follow skill accomplishment through timed multiple-choice computer testing, such as Star. The option of using computers for advancing critical-thinking skills such as acquiring knowledge through the Internet, upholding the writing process, and communicating with children in other countries would be a preferable use for diverse populations (Au and Raphael 2000), as would investigation of sources of knowledge.

Many questioned two middle-class second graders who attended a small school (2000). Study at this institution was thematic and schoolwide—all grades were exploring the Caribbean—and the two children under investigation were in the process of researching the Bahamas. These children were well versed in exploring sources on and off the Internet. Many's contention was that to be literate, the children also needed to develop strategies for adopting a stance of interrogating the author (of the source), the author's background, and the author's perspectives and expertise. She must have imagined this to be an acceptable task for these young researchers who presumably needed only modeling and extensive instruction, over a period of time, to eventually accomplish this aim. After all, the children easily named books, magazines, encyclopedias, and CD-ROMs as references. Contrast this to Indian children's daily abecedarian reading periods and computer experience with high-tech workbooks and timed multiple-choice tests. Attaining literacy, according to Many, would be a formidable task for them. This is because Indian children do not receive training that demands intellectual scrutiny. In fact, Indian children are denied similar possibilities for an intellectual life because they are not exposed to curricula that provokes high-level thinking, such as making inferences, analyzing and synthesizing information, logical reasoning, and creative expression (Gay 1993).

As technology and literacy instruction converge, the use of networked information and communication technologies will accelerate (Leu and Kinzer 2000) and computerized basic-skills lessons will become as meaningless as current basic-skills curriculum. It is of little value to recognize that these children may have opportunities to learn higher-thinking skills in middle and high school. Many educators and psychologists (i.e., Erickson 1992; Montessori 1995) believe that children have a "window of opportunity" to learn ways of thinking during early years and once this occasion is missed there is no making up for it. Many's conception of literacy is an important one because as knowledge continues to be technologically transformed, the ability to search out, appraise, and utilize information will become essential to all learners (Gaskins 2000). In part, this is the reason why Indian and other minority children need to be involved with critical thinking and problem solving. As the world becomes smaller, they too will be faced with challenging problems.

It is especially important to foster distinguishing thinkers in all parts of the globe, *including* in Indian villages and minority communities. Because of First Amendment rights, the Internet transmits negative as well as positive information. For example, hate rhetoric, haphazard advertising, and alternative political and religious discourse will increase the need for discriminating thinking (Cunningham 2000). Therefore, teachers are obliged to help children not only to read the words but also to examine them and make judgments upon the material. The conception of literacy must also include critical responses to reading the words, reading the world, and moving with distinction from one to the other.

Maintaining the Status Quo

In minority communities, problems of preserving ethnicity will be increasingly combined with those of communicating with others. Maintaining *old ways* is a dominant force in the pueblos, but as civilization progresses this becomes a more difficult task for the people. For example, only one generation ago, storytellers were active in Pueblo life. Today, they are all but gone. This is, in great part, due to the influence of television (Suina 1992). We can only imagine the impress of the Internet. This emphasizes the importance of involving the children in problem-solving, thinking skills so that they will be able to make informed decisions about their life and community rather than allow circumstances to dictate their future. This can come about only through involved education and *not* the continued reiteration of elementary skills. If attaining higher test scores is a priority, the way to attain this is to provide minorities with the same educational opportunities as those who do well on the tests, that is, by integrating real problems into interesting subject matter. "Drill and kill" will never provide informative educational advantages.

Children involved in this type of rote learning are not able to apply knowledge to new problems; they can merely repeat or parrot back what they have been "taught." This is often acceptable to teachers of minority children. In contrast, children involved with hands-on learning, experiments, and developing understanding through projects, are more self-reliant, creative, and better able to resolve problems. Therefore, an essential task of schools that serve minorities is to allow adept teachers to abandon the skills curriculum so they might foster absorbing activities that promulgate discriminating thinking. Administrators in minority districts rail at this type of proposal, arguing that the children will not be able to do well on tests with what the administrators consider a capricious type of learning (not everyone is on the same page). Like broken records, they point out the central skills minority children failed to accomplish during the heyday of whole-language learning. This becomes their *raison d'être* for following the fundamental-skills model.

The decline in California's test scores due to the influence of whole-language curriculum is commonly pointed out. Yet there are impressive arguments that prove this a myth (see, e.g., McQuillan 1998). Moustafa brought to light data from the National Assessment of Educational Progress, the reading "report card" which measured fourth-grade standardized reading tests nationwide. She discussed the contortion by conservative back-to-basics advocates which blamed the whole-language movement for the failure of test takers to meet minimal standards in reading, accounting for California's poor test results. These adherents ignored the inordinate number of students with limited English proficiency who took the test, the fact that California had the largest class size in the nation, the poorest library system, and that only 2 percent of its teachers had actually been exposed to whole-language methodology.

Similarly, I knew of only two teachers in my system who knew about, and practiced, whole language. As a result of the low scores, the conservative planners bolstered the need for the back-to-basics curriculum for the "illiterate" population, which, of course, turned out to be minority groups. Basic-skills learning is commensurate with what is known as reductionist education, or what I have referred to as traditional education, the most common form of knowledge that children of color are exposed to. Here, learning is *reduced* to isolated subskills. Those that follow this philosophy assume that children must be taught skills and information rather than engaging in reasoning activities first; that they learn the skills allied with reading, writing, mathematics, science, and so on, rather than learn the concepts behind these subjects. Teachers expect students to know sound/letter correspondences before engaging in reading a simple text. This attests to the fact that a memorized set of subskills must be learned before engaging in the actual discipline. Learning then becomes reduced to having gained knowledge about the rules of reading as opposed to actually engaging the students in reading. Before (or while) children learn the sounds of letters, they can be involved in shared reading, modeled writing, and language-experience stories. These activities will entrench the children in the love of reading, which will in turn motivate children to read. Reductionist learning, whether in science, writing, reading, or mathematics, involves children in learning a set of skills divorced from thinking. It is reductionist in that it curtails learning to preordained linear stages rather than seeing it as holistic and connected to other subject matter in a multidimensional context.

Society considers schooling as preparing children for life and, as part of that mission, the kind of work they might be involved with in the future (Leu and Kinzer 2000). Aside from the important need to communicate from a community, such as an Indian pueblo, to the world and vice versa, minority children deserve to be educated in the currency understood by those that hold power. Not conversing in the language of the dominant group alienates the poor from civic life even at the local level because affluence undermines efforts to involve the estranged (Shannon 2000).

If mainstream children learn through problem-solving curricula, the obvious conclusion is that mere fundamental competence cannot give children the rich experience that others experience in school. The incessant emphasis on basic skills suggests that this is a form of subjugation because the end result can only be competence in elementary abilities. Variations of skills curricula are more frequently delivered to the poor than to the more prosperous (Anyon 2001; Brown, Palinscar, and Purcell 1986). Thus, schools and their respective curricula have been used primarily to represent and foster the social status quo in the United States:

> When we consider the intersection of the history of reading and politics in the U.S., we look to the paradoxical nature of their coexistence. As has been pointed out, literacy and politics have worked hand in hand as barriers for many people of color, the poor, and females throughout the 20th century. From the onset, reading has been politicized to support the status quo and to deny access to nonmainstream groups. A review of the history of reading suggests several common themes: (a) legal and customary battles over whose notions of knowledge, truth and values are considered legitimate; (b) denial of access to literacy as a means of controlling certain groups; and (c) the creation of a means of assessing literacy that supports philosophically narrow and biased (race, class and gender) viewpoints. (Willis and Harris 2000, 58)

Herrnstein and Murray, neohereditarian contemporary deficit thinkers, argued that those who *have* profit because they are smarter and those who *don't have* are lacking as a result of their inferior intelligence (1994). Inherent in this theory is that middle- and upper-class whites possess this preferred intelligence whereas minorities are without it. These authors represent current educational conservative thought that views the basic-skills curriculum as necessary for those who *have not*. Functional literacy, composed of phonics, grammar, and conventional spelling, is viewed by present-day deficit thinkers as education that is to be projected toward those who are lower on the hierarchical scale of intelligence. In almost antithetical contrast, at the upper end is a curriculum characterized by the sophisticated application of scholarly criticism (Shannon 2000). I am arguing that minorities must share in the more elevated program.

How do we move from agendas that reflect distrust of children's aptitudes to those that incorporate confidence in their ability to progress? First and foremost is the necessity of changing the values of administrators and teachers. A good start might be effectuated through antiracism/diversity/multiculturalism training. Pewewardy, a Native who is the principal of the American Indian Magnet School in Saint Paul, Minnesota, advocates restructuring teacher-training programs in order to promote the concept of a culturally responsible pedagogy (1992). This includes developing "craft wisdom," which incorporates an understanding of Indian students' language, code switching, style of presentation, and communal values. Learning about Indian students' home lives can be accomplished by visiting public events in the villages and inviting community members to speak to teachers during inservice days. It would be wise to hold these meetings in the local neighborhood so community spokespersons can host teachers on their own "turf" rather than the usual school tradition of teachers receiving family members on school property. This would eliminate the constraints a Native person might feel when in a white man's school. In a typical school setting, the Indian speaker is at somewhat of a disadvantage because the principal is the one who has the vested authority. At home, the speaker can communicate from his own dominion. This was exemplified in the following true story:

> A Pueblo Indian woman who works as a secretary at the University quietly and efficiently performed her job over the years. She had an amiable relation to the Dean but not overly so. For example, she did not impart personal information nor discuss family situations with him. In short, her conduct was appropriate to her job, especially befitting the mainstream world. When the Dean and other professors visited her village on its annual Feast Day, they found not the staid worker they had come to know but an exuberant hostess, one who readily made known her home life and family. She was quite jovial and especially gregarious as the Dean and other professors joined her and her family for a meal in her home, a dinner which she supervised. (Suina 1985)

We can describe her behavior as emanating from her comfort zone. This account can be extended to diverse children in school. To the Pueblo Indian Kindergartners, school may appear to be an alien place: Their culture is remarkably different from that of the traditional school. Those that teach diverse children must learn to appreciate their worth, culture, language, and ways of knowing. As teachers learn to accept diversity in children, they will learn to explore diversity in responses. Embracing differences will help us move from the uniform, timed reading and writing programs to the honoring of varied ways of teaching and learning, which include appreciation of spontaneous comments and reactions of children. Instead of "right" and "wrong" answers, it is beneficial to investigate how children reach their answers, guiding them to arrive at accurate responses through their own discoveries. For this to come to fruition, teachers must have the permission of administrators to explore a varied course of study. "Mandated assessments, legislated curriculum, and shackling policies can place teachers in a state of educational gridlock, denying them the opportunity to exercise professional judgment and pedagogical prerogative" (Baumann 2000).

The Traditional Model

The traditional pedagogical orientation is one that has been discussed as the temper and curriculum given to minorities. It goes largely unquestioned because, historically, it has been the accepted model of education. It operates out of the transmission mold. This orientation views the teacher as one who dispenses her knowledge and skills to children who are "empty" in that they do not yet possess knowledge themselves. This conveyance of knowledge necessitates that the teacher maintain control over every aspect of the classroom so she can transfer the information to the children. She directs all interactions, continually aligning them toward the accomplishment of instructional objectives (Cummins 1992). She expects quiet in the classroom and strict conformance to inactive behavior. In order to receive this knowledge, children are placed in passive roles where they are obligated to respond to "display" questions (questions for which the teacher already knows the answer) and filling out worksheets that concentrate on rote memorization.

When Boykin described the mainstream character of traditional schooling, he pointed out that, inherent in school cultures, there are certain tacit understandings that are thoroughly written into what makes a school a school. They are so putative as to be seen as universal factors that belong in all schools. Indeed, they reflect what is thought to be "correct" in education and, pertaining to actions of students, what is "civilized" behavior. These properties orchestrate most happenings at school: They conduct what is to be taught and how it should be taught, what attributes students should possess and how they should comport themselves. They represent the ideal model of Anglo-European rules for schooling and the narrowness of this view extends to a disallowance of any deviations from it. Let us examine these traits: Embedded in the values of conventional schools are competitiveness, rigid time periods with time viewed as a commodity (Katz 1985 in Boykin 1994), minimal noise, staying "on task" to the point of averting talking, sitting still for extended time periods, and emotional suppression. I have already explicated many of the factors that drive the curriculum at the school where I work—competition with rewards for the winners, inflexible timed periods for each component of reading, limited noise in order to stay on task, and sitting still for inappropriate time periods.

These attitudes can have troublesome effects on schools. Competitiveness occludes working well in group situations, rigid time periods prevent teachers and students from engaging in expansive deliberation and conveys the message (to both teachers and students) that one cannot augment or append the curriculum. Minimal noise inhibits exchanging ideas with others and, in general, aggrandizes low physical stimulation. Imposing sitting still for long periods is inappropriate for young children and encourages movement repression over movement expression. These characteristics emanate from the Eurocentric mold of the strong, acontextual individual and, thus, belongs to those who come to school with cultural capital of the mainstream, namely, children who belong to the middle and upper classes (Boykin 1994). These children are better prepared to follow conventional regulations because they have had years of conditioning in learning this code.

For diverse others, these regimens only serve to alienate and disempower. This is because children who grow up in a culture different from that of the mainstream are chastised for not knowing the rules of the establishment. Consequently, two conditions need to change: The school environment needs to be reformed so that it can accommodate diverse learners and, in explicit ways, minority children must be taught the currency of the culture of power so that they, too, can succeed in conventional places (Delpit 1988). Minorities need to become "fluent" in the mores of mainstream culture but not inculcated with them. This means that, with proper training, minorities can have the Euro-American pandect available to them so that they can be on a commensurate intellectual level with their middle-class counterparts. Schools can begin to change their environment through abrading the more pernicious characteristics of traditional schools. This must begin with administrators and teachers of minorities becoming aware that they can modify the standards of firmly incorporated practices by replacing them with more thoughtful ones that better suit all children. This can come about only through dialogue and education.

For example, in teacher training or on inservice days, teachers can be involved in a type of forum setting where they are asked to discuss the benefits and pitfalls of the attributes (e.g., a quiet class versus one in which children are free to speak and learn in cooperative settings; keeping to a rigid time schedule versus having a flexible, creative, yet productive one; allowing one or two children to win a competition and "shine" versus having all the children succeed, and so on). Nor does this examination need to end with all of the traditional attributes appearing as completely undesirable. The characteristics should be brought to light because they go largely unexamined. "They are often taken for granted as appropriate to such an extent that educators may not even realize that they are promoting, advocating and imposing their centrality and indispensability on the students" (Boykin 1994, 247). Seeking alternatives to these modes challenges the traditional ethos and sanctions entrance to cultural acceptance of minority groups. By acknowledging other cultural currencies, we ratify the integrity of diverse children. In this way, we can view them as being capable in their own right. This becomes the most important aspect of minority education.

Homogenization and Oppression

Through the never-ending meetings, administration and staff try to figure out why our students fail. Time after time, the content of these meetings is met with a predictable monotony. Literacy speakers, often those with little education of the knowledge-construction process, are hired because they give presentations that support our present reading program. The schools won't give up advocating particular agendas, even when our students have been shown not to excel in them.

One might suggest that they persist in the same program because of monetary considerations, but this is not so. When the schools are provided with the resources to purchase new materials, they persist in ordering variations on the same agendas. The curriculum is always one in which the most important value is that skills are spelled out and built upon from grade to grade. Everyone must use the same basals so that these competencies can be followed, taught, and tested through the grades. As far as programs, there must not be any that disallow this progression, nor any that are not equivalent in form from grade to grade, and none that permit deviation (often innovation is perceived as deviation).

In recent years, frequently, there is a reading specialist whose main job is to ensure that these programs are followed through exactly as prescribed. Sometimes, his or her knowledge of the reading process is limited, but as long as he or she polices these procedures, the reading specialist is regarded as a valuable tool. He or she is a major instrument in maintaining the reading customs of the traditional school culture. This constant surveillance creates a feeling of subjugation in the teachers, who, if at first do not agree with the "new" program (invariably a variation of an older one), finally relent in order to keep their jobs. At first, names (among teachers) like "gestapo" have actually been given to these supervisors. As the programs become embedded within the culture of the school, these labels disappear because the teachers know the school's agenda is more important than their own.

For several years, a Montessori Kindergarten was effectuated in our school. The children excelled beyond all expectations. For no "logical" reason, the principal wanted a traditional Kindergarten, so she removed the teacher from her position and placed her in one where she would be forced to amalgamate into the school's curriculum. No matter that the teacher had spent years learning and effectively carrying out this potent form of education. The Montessori program seemed to be a threat to the school not only because the curriculum did not homogenize with the Other's curriculum but also because if one teacher demonstrated that the children weren't lacking, the blame could logically be shifted from the students to the school. Therefore, excellence and innovation are avoided. They scare, challenge, and ask the question: Who, really, is to blame? The minority-school culture is so inculcated with charging the students and their families with the school's shortcomings that it robs the children of good programs rather than reproaching itself.

There are many instances where the misuse of administrative power against good teachers goes unchecked. This happens most often between the school's principal and teachers simply by virtue of the fact that they have daily contact with one another. When authority is used to control, teachers cannot speak out against abuse because their jobs are endangered. They have very little recourse and, consequently, shrink under the rule of domination. This mistreatment occurs in minority schools more often than in those where white middle-class children are situated because parents exert more of an influence in more affluent schools than those where children are underrepresented. After all, underrepresented means that there is little or no genuine advocacy for the children. Where this type of environment exists, there is often no support for teachers either. Prosperous families care about the well-being of teachers, realizing that their state of mind and degree of expertise influence the way that they approach their students. Because of the generally poor participation of parents in minority schools, the principal is frequently the sole decision maker, often answerable to a committee made up of families who rarely disagree with him or her. In minority schools such as the ones I have described, colonization is exerted through curriculum, values, and student comportment (the administration can be of any race, yet they buy into the white model). Also, authority is wielded over teachers because dominance becomes a way of being. In other words, one cannot act without equity to one group and justly to another. Either integrity is the standard or it is not. It is difficult to separate where the sword of authority that rules over children ends and that which subjugates teachers begins. Once the blade is raised, whether it is in curricular command or control over a teacher's freedom, the stab can be devastatingly injurious. When higher administration stays quiet about teacher mistreatment, permission is given to principals to continue their intimidation. When there is no fear of reprisal, those who abuse power will continue to do so.

Teachers lose their voice when curriculum and decisions about teaching are dictated from above. I have already discussed how the Word Walls in the Four Blocks program was a requirement in my school. One day, at a meeting, a teacher who (rightly) didn't see the value in using them meekly asked if she could dispense with them. Without asking why the teacher didn't see the use, the principal, blindly following the program, said she must keep the Word Walls.

The teacher's initiative was quickly stamped upon. This sent a dire message to all teachers who were present in the meeting.

The principal who trampled upon the Montessori program undermined most of the teachers by announcing that she planned to change everyone's grade assignment for the next school year. It was thought by parents and much of the staff that she used this as an excuse to oust the Montessori instructor and end that successful course of study. Those teachers who had devoted their professional lives to learning how to effectively teach a certain grade would not be able to continue to do so. Most teachers have grade preferences and situate themselves in that place. Over the course of teaching for a number of years, they accumulate materials and educate themselves, often by trial and error, in what works best for that particular grade. Changing teachers' grades while ignoring their choice is very much like pulling the proverbial rug from under their feet. Moreover, it vitiates their will to perform with excellence because discharging one's duties with quality means putting a great deal of time and effort into it, effort which may seem worthless if one's job is changed on a whim. If that weren't enough, the principal told everyone that the assignments must be kept secret until she publicly announced the changes some nine weeks later. In short, she imposed a gag order on the teachers under an express threat that if an individual told another she would find out and there would be a price to pay. Many of the teachers were frozen into silence. Others spoke in quiet whispers with their eyes always on the door, in case the principal should enter the room in which they were speaking. If she did happen to come in, the subject was immediately changed and one of the parties, in a loud voice, would utter something innocuous, like "And so I will pick up the book from you." The question of who would be assigned to teach what grade was rampant among school gossip. There were many tears and many complaints, but no one dared to question the principal's authority. At that time, it struck me how similar the school's atmosphere was to a dictatorship—everyone was afraid to speak their minds because of the tyrannous use of power and the resulting punishment if that power were questioned. The school's environment was one under a totalitarian regime. In this climate, the teachers were expected to do their best in the classroom. Who could do so? Teachers who were preparing materials and learning centers ceased doing so with the justification that it was useless to make ready materials that would not be put to use for long. The atmosphere was stifling for those who loved their jobs. Enthusiasm dropped to an all-time low as the teachers realized they, in fact, had not an iota of a voice. So in minority schools, the misuse of power can cripple the school, as it did mine. Energy that could have been used to teach children was diverted into emotional turmoil for many of the teachers. Yet there were those who were so inured to not having power that they readily agreed to whatever the principal's decision would be. This became the more dangerous camp because they were the followers who would obey any order that was imposed. They completely disregarded any preferences or special interests they had in favor of what authority dictated. This acclimatization is what makes minority schools so comparable, so expendable, so bland, and so dispensable. Ethics and school happenings are woven together in a fabric that can either withstand inspection or unravel in the face of spurious exploitation. The most important aspect of education is to nurture children's character, to keep them from corruption or becoming corrupters themselves. This can be accomplished only by providing an environment that adheres to principles of probity.

An Example of the Oppression of Families

I have already discussed the Pueblo's practice of religion; that is, that numerous families believe in both the Catholic and their Native faiths, many exercise only their Native beliefs, and a very few devote themselves only to Christianity. When the conquistadors entered the scene in the 1500s, they were represented by the Catholic clergy who, in the end, vanquished the Pueblo and severely punished the people for what was deemed "idolatry." Thus, the Pueblo were forced to conceal their Native religious practices.

Today, even with those who exercise the two systems simultaneously, there remains a very distinct dichotomy between the two faiths. The Catholic doctrine is adhered to mostly as a subordinate religion with the Native gods and spirit world taking precedence in village life. For example, it is known by those who work with the Pueblo that prayers before eating concern feeding spirits who are hungry. Devotions are demonstrated by throwing cornmeal to Mother Earth, protection is afforded by wearing an arrowhead blessed by a medicine man, attendance at religious events takes place in the *kivas,* and a potent source of petition is actualized through dance.

Daily village life is permeated with Native holy practices. In the beginning, the Catholic faith was followed as a way of surrendering to the clergy for the sole purpose of staying alive and avoiding harsh penalties. Later, its practice was actualized through fulfilling secret Native obligations on the Church's calendar, thus deceiving Catholic priests into thinking that Catholicism was adhered to. This too was a necessity for survival. As the Church became a regular fixture on the pueblo (all pueblos have a Catholic church with attending priests), it meshed with the Native faith. But the people have never forgotten their subjugation and subsequent punishment for practicing their Native religion. This is the reason that their religion is kept hidden today. Children are warned by their families and officials of the village not to reveal any facet of religion and new teachers are admonished not to ask questions about it. Because Native faith is so important to the people, it must be respected by the schools.

The principal and many teachers in a minority school in my district resisted this regard in favor of their own. The teachers formed a committee in order to decide the theme for the school's Christmas program. The committee chose the

Nativity. Where religion is thought to be threatened (if its celebration is out-lawed by the state), it often becomes the mission of followers to transcend the law and interpret it according to their will. Thus, when the celebration of a public display of worship at Christmas was legally banned, most of the school's population ignored the legal decision and decided to celebrate it anyway. The school sent an announcement informing the families that they intended to use the theme of the Nativity for their winter program. It asked parents, if they had any concerns or objections to the theme, to fill out a form and have their child bring it to school. It stated that if the form was not returned, the school would take it as acceptance. The form had two parts: The first was *I do not object to the Winter program theme "The Nativity"* followed by a space provided for the signature; the second part read *I object to the winter program theme "The Nativity"* followed by a place for the signature and comments. Because our school is largely a Christian setting, most of the parents signed the notice, agreeing with the school decision. There was one holdout—an Indian family who practiced only their Native faith. For several days, it was announced on the intercom that there was only one family blocking the attainment of the Nativity theme and that it was hoped that the family could be convinced to relent. The two children of that family were forced to listen to these announcements. By the end of the week, the family finally succumbed to the pressure. A declaration was made on the intercom that everyone had agreed to the theme.

At the time of the decision, and before the notice was sent out to parents, I asked an Indian colleague about those families who might not believe in Christianity and wondered if she thought having a Nativity theme was fair to them. I also mentioned that the law favored non-Christian families on the matter. Her answer was vague and spoke to the usual muteness of underrepresented people. Especially for Indian people, who underwent the theft of their children, lost first to slavery by the Spanish and, later, to the white man and his boarding schools, secrecy is the last weapon against encroachment by the dominant society. It is better to relent to the dominators because a battle against them, especially concerning Christianity, could never be won. If mouths were kept silent, the Native religion could prevail in its concealment and, in that way, the Indians would be able to keep a semblance of self-determination. It was interesting that the Kindergarten class that performed a Native dance and did not allude to the Christian holiday received a standing ovation by the Indians who witnessed the unmistakable honoring of their culture.

If we are ever to experience Indian and other minority people's participation in schools, we must communicate a genuine milieu of respect and equity. Most of all, psychological subjugation must cease to take place. Authorities must relinquish their own agendas and listen to the voice of the people, however small that voice may be. When small voices are heard, others will inevitably join in. The climate of some minority schools that "you must listen to me because I am the authority" must end. A coalition of families and communities can be formed.

It is often said that only the same parents come to Parent-Teacher-Student Organization (PTSO) meetings and other school functions. A continual defense by both administration and school staff consists of presenting a litany of attempts to increase parent participation. After these recitations, in which the school is always presented as guiltless, the blame is inevitably placed on families and cultures for not having the participatory qualities of the white middle class.

When blame is erased, when deficits are not attached to people, it will be possible to change the paradigm and, thus, truly welcome diverse families into the school arena. This will be hard work, but once the autocratic hold is released, families will feel as though their opinions are sought after and valued.

Pseudo-Multiculturalism

According to administrative thought, authorization to deviate from basic-skills curriculum can be given only if the test scores increase. The irony is that minority children must, literally, pass the test in order to receive an equitable education. I argue for true multicultural education. Before examining it, it is necessary to examine what multicultural education is not.

In its most basic design, multicultural education is interpreted (in my school as well as many others) as the observance of holidays in order to represent culture. In the district where I work, it is common to observe Cinco de Mayo and also Indian Day, an arbitrary day set aside for the celebration of Indian culture. On Indian Day, the children and staff are invited to wear Indian garb, Indian bread is baked, and often, nonceremonial Indian dances are performed. Other cultural holidays are observed, the most common one being Martin Luther King Day, when the concentration is invariably on the "I Have a Dream" speech. The incessant focus on this famous speech demonstrates a reluctance of schools to confront the real nature of King, who was, in fact, a social revolutionary who criticized unrestrained capitalism and formed associations among capitalism, racism, and war (Nieto 1992).

Instead, educators prefer to tailor or sanitize their heroes (Laughlin, Martin, Jr., and Sleeter 2001), hiding them behind a facade of values that fit the mode of what is commonly thought to be the best of American traditions, such as heroism. When a hero is of European descent, such as Thomas Jefferson, his misdeeds are ignored (i.e., his slaveholding) while his contributions to mainstream American culture are extolled. Minority heroes are rare, and even when they appear they are whitewashed so that they come to represent the best of Eurocentrism. In other words, minorities can be included in history only when European ethnocentric paternalism is preserved.

One might conclude that there is a certain amount of benevolence in the glorification of "great men," that the intention is to teach young children basic values of courage, bravery, and valor. Yet masquerading historical heroes as something they are not can be devastating to minorities. I am reminded of a recent Columbus Day bulletin board exhibited in my school. Here, the children were simply told the myth of Columbus: He *discovered* America and he did so by sailing three famous ships. The children were asked to draw the three vessels that they had learned the names of, and this composed the entire display; that is, the three ships drawn by each child were featured on the bulletin board. True to American mainstream folklore, the caption read: *In 1492, Columbus Sailed the Ocean Blue.* The teacher was completely unaware that she had committed a transgression against the Indian children and their families, most of whom consider the appearance of Columbus their darkest moment in history. Other holidays are sometimes commemorated: A teacher will occasionally celebrate Kwaanza, or the Chinese New Year. Usually, a teacher and his or her students will make or order a Chinese meal from a restaurant. Although thought of as multicultural education, this is what Spring (1995) quips as the "pizza and chop suey approach," conveying that educators often limit ethnic heritages to food, clothing, and housing. Banks refers to this as multicultural education's lowest level, the contributions approach (1999). This is not genuine multiculturalism. Celebrating holidays and foods will do little to teach the children about respecting diversity, yet these isolated cultural days are the accepted, and even desired, curricula. This disjointed course of study is aptly named *pseudo-multiculturalism* (Boutte and McCormick 1992) because of its inauthenticity; *tourist multicultural curriculum* because classes "visit" other cultures and then return to their European-American curriculum (Perez 1994); and the *play-kit approach* (Clark, DeWolf, and Clark 1992), where certain "props" are taken out to represent a particular culture.

Signs of this ersatz multiculturalism are: (1) Disconnection, in which the activity is supplemented into the curriculum at a special time rather than integrated into all aspects of the general program; (2) Patronization, in which the culture studied is depicted as "quaint" or "exotic"; (3) Trivialization, in which cultural happenings separated from the daily life of the people trivialize that culture; and (4) Distortion, in which too few reflections on a group oversimplify the variety within the group (Hohensee and Derman-Sparks 1992). Authentic multicultural activities should be ongoing and connected daily to both conventional and informal activities: "Multicultural ideas are 'caught' not 'taught' and are developed through everyday experiences rather than formal lessons. They should be thoroughly integrated throughout all activities every day—not only in fragmented units" (Boutte and McCormick 1992, 140). I have pointed out many of the flaws in the educational system I work for only to accentuate how many Indian and minority students are taught. Curriculum and attitudes must change if we are to effect education for the ever-growing numbers of diverse children. Members of the dominant society need to participate in multicultural education so that they may effectively function in a pluralistic society.

True Multiculturalism

Let us now examine true multiculturalism. I have elaborated upon Banks's (1999) characteristics of multicultural education but have made modifications as will be explicated below. Because of the importance of an equitable pedagogy, I have included the issue in chapter 7.

Content Integration

This deals with the level of content that is derived from a variety of cultures in order to represent concepts and theories. Contrary to the popular notion that with content integration comes multicultural education, this particular facet comprises only a part of nondiscriminatory schooling. For example, science and math teachers who feel no relevance between multiculturalism and their subject matter would concentrate on other features of multiculturalism, although they could follow this aspect by calling attention to minority individuals who contributed to their field (Banks 1999). By making diverse cultural knowledge part of the curriculum, we are able to publicly recognize it and endorse those groups who have heretofore been excluded. In order for the dominant culture to preserve its hegemony, minority groups have been ignored or have been purposely excluded (Cazden 2000). Hegemony is a pestiferous construct because it inundates the culture with dominant meanings, values, beliefs, and actions (Apple 1979 in Boykin 1986). Hegemony and its accomplice, lack of content integration, cause alienation among minority groups because their own culture is rendered mute while the dominant culture is tacitly accepted as the only way of life. Continual exposure to Eurocentric ideals makes Anglo culture appear normative. Therefore, cultural elements that deviate from this criterion can readily be seen as deficient because departures from the cultural ideal appear as imperfections (Boykin 1986; Laughlin, Martin, Jr., and Sleeter 2001). Suina, a Pueblo Indian, passionately described his childhood feelings of inferiority for his culture, his grandmother, himself, and even his dog due to the daily exposure to the "perfect" American family portrayed in the Dick-and-Jane readers of the 1950s. We must be cautious as we look at the new books that claim to portray minorities but who may actually subjugate them:

> The multicultural curricula many educators and textbook publishers end up creating are too frequently colonizing, Eurocentric, patriarchal curricula in disguise, still structured around a worldview rooted in the European immigrant experience. . . . Such curricula implicitly stress individualism, upward mobility, broad social consensus, and the legitimacy of the status quo. (Sleeter 1996, 92)

An authentic example of content integration is given in Lipka and Yanez, where Yanez presents a lesson on smelting to a group of first graders from her village (1998). She attempted to bring the native language and culture into the classroom by modeling and having the children prepare smelts for drying, a common activity in the homes of that locale. The lesson actually conveyed the essence of the culture to her students. This was because she wove the Yup'ik values of helping, sharing, and respecting both animals and the land with Yup'ik ways of being, such as working together in a group (consistent with Yup'ik hunting rituals, a survival technique): learning by observation ("Go watch her so you could learn. Go by her. Galik, you should go watch April" [126]); withholding overt praise ("I tell the students 'good' but I try not to make a big thing out of it" [126]); being careful not to waste ("I teach my students not to waste any part of the fish because being wasteful in our culture is not allowed; Good, Deanna, you're not wasting your string" [124]); and teaching only when one is ready ("Who's ready to string?" [125]). At the same time, the children were engaged in science concepts such as learning smelt physiology, migration patterns, and animal behavior. The students were able to bring in knowledge and experience (Student: "When we were far away we net them, we net them, my dad caught ten sea lions" [118–19]). Activating prior knowledge has been shown to be an effective strategy for teaching Native American students as well as those who are mainstream. This is because when prior experiences are called upon, there is a validation of one's encounters and the framework within which they occurred. Thus, culture and home life are validated in the school setting and corroborated as meaningful.

When Kawakami and Au wanted to improve the school performance of K–3 Polynesian-Hawaiian children, they found that instructional issues should build upon the strengths of the students. These strategies included drawing on home and community speech events. The lessons were organized in a talk-story style of interchange with overlapping speech that was reminiscent of talking taking place at home. This style of interaction helped the children to find relationships between text and their own background experiences.

Prejudice Reduction

Bigotry begins at an early age because children learn intolerance from their families and cultures. In the area where these children lived, there was an undercurrent of racism between the Hispanics and the Indians, although they worked well together in school and were outwardly cordial to each other at home. For the Pueblo, this intolerance is derived from their subjugation by the Spanish that began in the 1540s with the arrival of the Spanish. By 1598, not only were the Pueblo forced to give up their stores of food, but when they refused, they received brutal reprisals. At Acoma Pueblo, women and children were burned alive and all males over the age of twenty-five endured having one of their feet cut off before being placed in servitude. Women over twelve years of age were forced into slavery for twenty years, while the children under twelve years of age were stolen and brought up as Christians and slaves (Sando 1992).

The Indians are also keenly aware of the hazards they endured from Caucasian domination. When the boarding schools were established in the late 1800s, the Pueblos had their children taken from them again, this time by the white man. History tells us the subsequent reservation day schools gave the Indians voice in their education, but this is not true. As late as two generations ago, Anglo teachers in the day schools of Santa Ana tortured their students in their own villages. The children were lined up and forced to consume castor oil daily. They were then subjected to scalding hot baths under the guise of keeping the children clean (Santa Ana Pueblo, personal communication, 2001). There is much reason for the Pueblo people to have feelings of injustice. Yet it does not serve them to retain these ties.

Prejudice abatement can be especially helpful in a region such as this, where perceptions of the Other are tainted by many years of grievousness. Actively pursuing its demise promises to help the children uncover and explore their racial attitudes with the expectation that these attitudes can be improved after intelligent reckoning. Negative racial dispositions of children have been responsive to change with the advent of various strategies implemented by the teacher. Some of these include authentic representations of ethnic groups on a consistent basis, role playing, and involvement in cooperative activities (Banks 1999). Accurate accounting and understanding of actual past events from multiple perspectives must exist in the classroom. Understanding how knowledge is assembled, particularly as it is formulated through cultural assumptions, frames of reference, and biases, can elucidate why certain groups are looked upon more approvingly than others. It explains that knowledge construction can be subjective and can be influenced by partiality, whether through ethnicity, gender, or the like. The inclination to favor groups, such as those who hold power, directs prejudice toward groups outside the standard, which in turn leads to feelings of resentment by diverse groups toward the preferred one. This is why prejudice becomes a vicious cycle from which it is difficult to remove one's culture, family, and self. The only exit is an education of how the knowledge was actually conceived, by whom, and for what reason. American schools select knowledge carefully, and the proclivities are unidirectional, in the direction of the dominant group. For example, the firmly rooted construct that literacy is developmental stems from the controlling group:

> When that assumption is taken for granted and seen as real (as it is today), those students who do not grow naturally along appropriate lines are seen as having a deficit of some sort. The linear progression through a series of developmental levels is considered normal and those students who do not progress in this way need to be "caught up" or given what they missed . . . whatever the

cure, it is a deficit model, as if literacy skills are given to those who don't have it. The learner who is not learning according to the plan is assumed to have a developmental deficit, and a series of interventions (if you're young) or remediations (if you're older) are created to give the gift, to fill the holes . . . it follows from this that if the student still doesn't get it, there must be something wrong with the student, the parent, or poverty in general, but certainly not the system. (Hammerberg and Grant 2001, 77)

Programs such as Limerick's The Legacy of Conquest, in which multiple perspectives are presented in regard to "How the West Was Won," could be used. For example, in the Indian view, the European settler is seen as an intruder. Programs such as this would help clear up misinformation and help children understand worldviews of different cultures (Laughlin, Martin, and Sleeter 2001). When Peacock and Albert interviewed American Indian high-school students, they found that racism was inextricably woven with content (2000). One of the students in their study put it this way:

> I haven't heard nothing about Native Americans. It's completely based on Caucasians. In English, I have never heard nothing about a Native American author, nothing about Native American language. There's one culture class. I'd like it to tell us more about the background and the culture of Native Americans on the positive side of it and not just on the negative. Racism, I get tired of it. Sometimes I feel like the teachers treat the Caucasians different than the minorities. Schools need more minority teachers to teach the Caucasians about what the minority has gone through. I want to learn the minority side! (Rachel in Peacock and Albert 2000, 4)

Wherever possible, underrepresented children should be given the historical background of their group. Schlessinger decries that minority groups cannot gain self-esteem by learning about their history but must gain this quality only through personal achievement (1994). Yet, American Indians place little emphasis on solitary accomplishment. Whereas Anglo concepts focus on the individual, the Pueblo concentrate on the community. The Pueblos focus on group practices and avoidance of self-promotion, while Anglo-led schools focus on competition and self-promotion. Therefore, the suggestion that minorities can gain self-esteem only through individual accomplishment ignores how nonmainstream groups actually form their sense of worth. For the Pueblo, this is derived from working harmoniously within a group and solving group predicaments. Therefore, we may say that learning about one's ancestors, for example, how they survived by living in cooperation, would feasibly raise feelings of self-esteem. There are several important history books written by Pueblos that would most likely spur interest in that field while also generating pride (see, e.g., Ortiz 1994; Sando 1992).

Every ethnic group is important in history and many have made indelible contributions. It would be of considerable advantage to learn about one's past, especially as it may deviate from the Eurocentric model. It could be of significant value to compare various versions of the same time period, for example, the Pueblo and the Hispanic accountings of New Mexico in the latter half of the six-teenth century, allowing voice for both heritages. It would also be of merit to study the bondage of other people such as the Jews in the Holocaust and African Americans during slavery and learn it from their own accounts and the accounts of the dominators while critiquing and comparing them. This could raise the important issues of racism, subjugation, and dominance, and could apply motives for colonization, rebellion, and wars. By studying history through multiple perspectives, the children learn from a social-empowerment approach. However, it should be noted that critique alone could lead to cynicism, alienation (Cazden 2000), and more racism, so critique should move in the direction of transformed practice, "Where the students operate in the genuine world, with the possibilities of social action in which they live and have to communicate in the contact zone of cultural differences" (Cope and Kalantzis 2000, 237). By learning within their own cultural history, minority children will begin to overcome feelings of cultural domination and become empowered while also gaining *amour-propre* (Spring 1995).

Of course, when studying history, the question arises: *Whose history?* Chronicled accounts are always subjective. These biases should be examined so that lessons can be organized around powerful concepts (Banks 1999). Once again, I argue for programs that impel thinking. In the school where I teach, the book *The Courage of Sarah Noble* (Dalgliesh 1954) was banned by the fifth-grade teacher because of a misguided view of protecting the children from prejudice in the use of offensive words such as *squaw* and *brave*. It would have served the children more if they were allowed to explore the historical *milieu* in which these words came about. Some words, although racially motivated, have simply become part of American jargon. Rather than barring the children from reading this particular work, it would have been more advantageous for them to examine the pernicious words (and thoughts) in the book along with studying their historical and political reality. This can have the beneficial outcome of helping the children understand the effects of bigotry.

Studying words and their historical and political significance has the more advantageous effect of teaching their strength. How racism can be dismantled by diffusing a word's power rather than shielding Indian students from words that have derogatory origins could have provided a better lesson. In my district, many other books have been censored by well-meaning teachers—sometimes printed material was actually ripped out of books. The motive behind these actions was that these materials could cause further feelings of bitterness. It is important to allow the children to see how they were portrayed in history, whether it was shown in a positive or negative light. When we censor books "for the benefit of the children," we steal their ability to reason. The forthright acknowledgment of differences, whether they reflect a group advantageously, disapprovingly, or neutrally (Glock 1975 in Reyhner 1992), will bring prejudices to the light of day, where they can be explored so that children won't feel deceived about history. Research on story content leads to the conclusion that censorship should be avoided and that stories should realistically mirror the world in which they are set (Reyhner 1992). Even folktales should not be watered down as they contain symbolic truths (Reyhner 1992).

In the ways described above, Indian children can become informed about history and learn to intelligently discuss important issues while investigating their own feelings without the taint of prejudice blinding them. The ultimate aim is Freire's (1974) critical pedagogy, in which the students will have an increased awareness of their political, economic, and social circumstances and, thus, will ultimately effect social change (O'Cadiz and Torres 1994).

Indian governments are political by virtue of their continual negotiation of land, and water rights, restitution of land, and sovereignty of their nation. Knowledge of racism helps the people understand the political system that they must deal with as they moderate their place in the white world. The children that attend our schools are, literally, tomorrow's leaders of their tribes and they need to be instructed in the role of racism, especially as it pertains to social and political movements.

An Empowering School Culture and Social Structure

Here, the school is rearranged so that balanced achievement and participation occurs for all races. There must be a total reevaluation of the school culture that enables all students to succeed. This includes analysis of testing without bias, de-tracking, and reconceptualizing the school environment so that students of any race or cultural group can achieve as well as any others. Because this is a rural area, where Hispanics and Indians are predominant, there is a numerical balance of both races. Over the years, I have witnessed that most of the teachers view both races as equally able to succeed (or equally unable). I have been told repeatedly by Pueblo teachers and other Pueblo staff members that their voices are the ones least heard. As an example of this claim, the large number of Hispanic employees in the district's central office compared to the small number of Indians sends a message of the undesirability of Indians in the workplace. Another issue, closely related to this, is the politicization of job opportunities in my district. When employment prospects arise, teachers, aides, and other staff often converse about the importance of "who you know" in obtaining a position. Although this may be a common occurrence in many places, it remains problematic and unethical. I have seen very qualified individuals emotionally defeated before they have even applied for a position.

Thus, we can see that authentic multicultural education can move schools to a curriculum where students engage in thoughtful scrutiny of issues concerning heritage, race, prejudice, and learn that generally accepted definitions of knowledge can be opinionated and faulty. These characteristics empower students, staff and schools to reorganize thoughts and policies so that they are in accordance with fair and equitable procedures, providing all students with a comprehensive education and all staff with equitable practices.

7

Multiculturalism Enacted:

An Equity Pedagogy

The Myth of the Indian Language Deficit

This study demonstrates the abundance of the Kindergartner's use of language. Not only was their language use prolific but it also revealed the children's ability to discriminate between various forms and functions of speech, choosing, creating, and adapting those aspects that would serve many purposes. As the children worked and communicated with their peers, they displayed an adept usage of language that made the very notion of language deficits appear to be a preposterous presumption on the part of schools. It raises questions about why teachers and administrators continue to promote the theory that

141

Indian and minority children have language deficits. These conclusions about shortcomings often are based on culturally biased tests, Anglo notions of book knowledge, and the ability to label things according to how a teacher (who is typically Anglo or Anglo influenced) does so. Expecting exact answers rather than accepting the variety of rich ways that children speak about their world is limiting at best and racially biased at worst. Accusing Indian children of having extreme language deficits permits schools to create themselves as having preferred status and thereby gives rationale to subordinate Indians to a lower rank, those who cannot speak as intelligently or with as much embellishment as the dominant class. This supposed differentiation of language use leads to differentiation of schooling experience. The most extensive and the loftiest type of education is available to those who are expected to do the best; those who *know* how to speak, how to act, and how to learn (all according to mainstream values) while the "minimum competency" education causes curriculum for Indian and other minority children to remain at the level of basic literacy and computational skills (Oakes 1986). With few exceptions, these children are the ones assigned to carry on the serviceable jobs in our economy. Differentiation in their education disallows a giant leap toward the higher end. In meeting after meeting I attend at school, the most pervasive pleas from teachers and administrators are the constant call for learning phonics, decoding words off of "word walls" (the latest addition to rote learning, thought to be a progressive innovation), and learning arithmetic. Concern for increasing vocabulary through reading good literature or understanding mathematical concepts is rarely (if ever) expressed. These educational goals are reserved for those who already *know* how to speak, how to elucidate their phonetic sounds, and how to add and subtract. The conspiracy that Indian children suffer from language deficits may be unintentional. Most teachers of young Indian children are thoroughly inculcated into the belief and surety that their charges lack an extensive language base that is inferior to that of white children. This is the consistent explanation given for the children's failure to progress. Thus the reasoning behind the language-deficit theory was originally, and still is, the preservation of the ascendancy of the governing class. The hegemonic assault on Indians continues today through the retention of language-deficit theory, cultural deficits and their direct result, and differentiation of schools, which, in turn, leads to differentiation of privileges. The only means to break through this barrier is to bring equality of curriculum to minority children so that the playing field might be counterweighted.

Learning Styles

The standard of an equity pedagogy was created so that teachers could examine their programs and methods to determine to what extent their practices reflect multicultural approaches (Banks 1999). Here, teachers modify their instruction in order to promote academic accomplishment among the population they serve. This includes addressing the varied learning styles of their students. Learning styles have been defined as habitual patterns or favored ways of doing things that are steady over long periods of time and across an assortment of activities (Sternberg 2000 in Hilberg and Tharp 2002). These styles should be regarded as strengths because they are the preferred, therefore the most often chosen, mode of perceiving, incorporating information, and taking action. Learning styles are "influenced by the values, norms and socialization practices of the culture in which that individual has been enculturated" (Swisher and Deyhle 1992, 82). Various cultural settings cause their cultures to exhibit different orientations, demeanors, and comportments; different responses, adaptations, and perform-ances. Many researchers have called for teachers to adjust their instructional methods to the learning styles of minority students so that these children can meet with achievement in school (Au and Kawakami 1994; Swisher and Deyhle 1992; Reyhner 1992). The cultural-differences theory ascribes that aligning ways of learning at home with ways of learning in school creates continuity be-tween home and school culture that can help underrepresented children to suc-ceed.

American Indian children may have similar learning styles. This may be the result of similar ways that Indian children learn to construct knowledge at home. Life on most reservations is communal. Existing in a collective lifestyle in these places means sharing a common history that binds people together in social, political, and religious ways. Swisher and Deyhle have noted that the research has suggested that Indian students come to know the world in ways that differ from non-Indian students (1992). Many of these manners of learning have been remarked upon in this book and will now be reviewed and expanded upon so that implications for teachers can be affixed to a particular style. It must be cau-tioned that the consensus on Indian learning styles has been based upon small studies performed on one or another Indian tribe—the temptation to apply what is learned from one study to all Indians can be dangerous and verges on stereo-typing. There are more than five hundred tribal groups, two hundred languages, and a variety of Indian cultures (Cleary and Peacock 1998). Yet, because culture has a strong effect upon ways of learning, and because Indians share many common characteristics of culture, the general consensus of Indian learning styles will be presented in this chapter. I have chosen to focus on the three most cited styles: observation and practicing in private; collaborative versus competi-tive; and holistic thinking. Other styles, which have already been discussed in earlier chapters, include modeling, reflection, and visual thinking.

Observation and Practicing in Private

Pueblo children learn by observing a modeled situation, listening, and practicing in private (Romero 1994). Other tribes acquire information similarly: Warm Springs Indians achieve proficiency through observation, mindful listening, guided participation, and self-examination to determine if a skill has been acquired (Swisher 1991; Phillips 1972). The mores of the Ogala Sioux of the Dakotas dictate that a person should not undertake an action unless he or she knows how to do it. If this knowledge is not known, one should watch until one understands how it is done (Wax, Wax, and Dumont 1964). This is confirmed by Brewer, an Ogala Sioux, who informs us that the children of this particular tribe learn from family and community socialization in a very informal manner (1977). The children observe the adult models and if they so desire, can ask questions. They are given some guided participation, then left alone. When the children are ready to perform an activity, they first do so in private with no external help. The tasks are self-initiated and self-tested before publicly demonstrated. Navajo children have also been reported to continually observe an activity before undertaking its performance. They do so in a solitary manner and only after reviewing it will they perform it in front of an audience. There are no adult figures nearby prodding them (Longstreet 1978 in Swisher and Deyhle 1992). The antithesis of practicing in private and trying in public is representative of the larger American conventional society. Here, one is given credit for trying, as the adage goes: *If, at first, you don't succeed, try, try again.* Because most schools follow the mainstream ethos, they also promote the dictum of trying out tasks, which is done most often in front of a classroom. Indeed, students who do not attempt tasks on command are labeled as noncompliant and lazy. For Indian children, making mistakes in public was never (and is not presently) an acknowledged way of learning at home (Brewer 1977; Swisher 1991). In class, Indian children who are not yet ready to perform are faced with the arduous responsibility of doing so in front of peers while they are uncertain of their own aptitudes and have reason to anticipate a negative attitude from the teacher (Wax, Wax, and Dumont 1964), especially if they get it "wrong." However well intentioned, most traditional teachers feel that it is their duty to let the students know when they perform "incorrectly" and to announce that publicly. *How else can they learn?* Therefore, students whose cultural background encourages them to rehearse tasks while sequestered may feel unprepared, unprotected, and exposed when asked to execute a task in the open.

Teachers should be careful when calling on Indian students to perform unless they know that the child will feel comfortable with the assignment (Cleary and Peacock 1998). Not every cultural characteristic needs to be aligned with school practices as long as the teacher demonstrates sensitivity to that practice and helps the child comfortably shift routines from home to school while avoiding a cultural clash. The teacher must be culturally sympathetic but may also help the child attain expertise in mainstream mores, especially when those are characteristics that the child is likely to encounter in school settings. In order to help students perform a public act in school, they may have to be taught. This can be accomplished by allowing children "getting-ready" time when they can practice. This can be done in small groups. The process of trial performance can be taught and explained in the larger context of rehearsals. For example, children presenting scientific projects can prepare their recitations in small groups (with peers first, then with teacher guidance and support). Later, when they are ready, they can perform in front of the class and eventually be prepared to present to the school and larger audiences. This example demonstrates how learning styles can be modified to fit school settings. The key to this adaptation is initially preserving cultural congruence and then slowly moving away from it while keeping the integrity of the value intact, so that accommodations could be made for the school setting (e.g., those times when practicing in private may not be feasible). In all events, the teacher should shy away from putting students on the spot. Teachers should prepare for the success of their students and avoid situations that may engender discomfort or failure. Errors could be celebrated. One of my strategies is to let students know when I make a mistake. I announce it publicly with a comment such as, "Oh, I made a mistake." Then, I state what the oversight was, appending it with, "It's OK to make mistakes; everyone does." Then we go through a litany of who makes mistakes, such as moms and dads, sisters and brothers, principals, and so on. This is a constant message in the room so that when the children make mistakes, they often announce "I made a mistake" and the class again goes through the familiar litany of who else makes mistakes. In these ways, we can make the transition from home to school an untroubled event.

Collaborative versus Competitive Environments

Pueblo Indians live together in small villages. Although each family, often extended, has its own home, most of the activities in village life are carried out communally. Collaboration is the main vehicle that Pueblo Indians use to realize common activities. Most aspects of their lives require the participation and cooperation of each other. The culture does not endorse the singling out of specific people, even if they accomplish a task more easily than others. This is because the concept of achievement is different from that of our Eurocentric one. In Pueblo society, individual achievement outside the realm of community service is a foreign concept:

> A lot of it, I feel, is based on the fact that within our traditional lives one is not . . . noted for being, I guess in a sense, being recognized for something, being blessed or more perceptive of or receptive of the activities we have. Basically, [the way] we look at it when we do our activities is that everyone is on an equal basis. . . . Mainstream Anglo society really deals with how much better you can do this than the next guy. (Laguna man in Romero 1994, 42)

When the Pueblo dance, their concept of beauty is found in group movement. The motion of the whole group is considered more important than the performance of any individual. There are no stars who yearn to stand out. Conformity in carrying out steps is the standard—a single dancer should not destroy the mirage of the group moving as one. Unity in performance not only bolsters aesthetic interests but, more importantly, fortifies the Pueblo concern for the needs of the community over those of the individual (Sweet 1985).

Wax, Wax, and Dumont found no evidence of Dakota children viewing any aspect of classroom learning as rivalry (1964). In contrast, if one learned easily, the proper action was to help those who did not. This is commensurable to the ways Pueblo children are instructed: They are taught to learn from one another and to help those who have difficulty (Romero 1994). Miller and Thomas researched Blackfoot Indian and urban middle-class white children when playing games (1972). The first involved a group reward condition, where each child in the group received a piece of candy. Here, both Indian and white children cooperated effectively. However, when the reward system was changed from group to individual effort, Blackfoot children continued to cooperate to the extent of developing a strategy whereby each player took a turn at winning, while the non-Indian children showed competitive behavior that impaired their performance. Thus, the Indian children demonstrated preference for communal efforts and were able to gain points by developing cooperative strategies whereas the white children competed even when it was counterproductive to do so. During these games, if competitive behavior was evinced by an Indian child, it was quickly suppressed by the group. "Standing out" is a trait that many Indian groups regard as a quality to be avoided. Swisher reported that Indian children may hide academic proficiency to escape seeming superior to others (1991). She cites Brown's evidence that Cherokee children, who preferred cooperation over competition, wanted to maintain their norms of harmonious relations, and did so by repressing knowledge when that knowledge exceeded that of the group, even though it meant that they, as a group, would produce lower achievement (1980 in Swisher 1991). Deflecting kudos in school for excellent performance was also found among the Ogala Sioux because attaining prominence was interpreted as collaborating with "the enemy" [the teacher] (Wax, Wax, and Dumont 1964). For whatever reason,

> in many Native societies, the humility of the individual is a position to be respected and preserved. Advancing oneself above others or taking oneself too seriously violates this key value. If Native children learn best cooperatively, they will experience discomfort and conflicts in classrooms that are too competitive or in which the competition is unfair. (Swisher 1991, 4)

Thus, the teacher can plan for cooperative, rather than competitive, learning environments. He or she can establish cooperative groups for solving problems and building projects. Rather than having children work individually, cooperative learning centers can be made available. Activities such as working within a small group should be included in Indian education, and for all children of color (Davidson 1990 in Banks 1999). In this way, not only would Indian children's learning be consistent with home but also they would become more adept in working with others toward common goals, such as solving problems, a trait necessary for the socialization of all people. The use of cooperative learning is compatible with minority group values (Banks 1993) and, in particular, with those of American Indians (Bray 1999). As the children in the study taught each other through cooperative peer teaching/learning, so can other groups. Vogt, Jordan, and Tharp demonstrated how lessons could be congruent with home settings that advocate cooperative peer learning (1987 in Au and Kawakami 1994). Hawaiian students were seated in small groups at learning centers, where the children were encouraged to help one another. At the same time, the teacher was engaged in a small-group reading lesson. The children were indirectly supervised by the teacher, so they became dependent upon each other for assistance. The peer situation was similar to the home setting of the Hawaiians in that the children had informal access to other children where they are accustomed to cooperative peer interactions. Yet, when independent small-group learning centers were attempted in Navajo culture at Red Rock (Vogt et al. in Au and Kawakami 1994) the same procedures were unsuccessful. This was because there is more separation of the sexes in Navajo culture. Preliminary results showed that when the Navajo children worked in small groups according to sex, the children engaged in peer cooperation. This difference between the Hawaiian and Navajo children makes it clear that although there may be a general likeness in Indian learning styles, there can also be subtle differences between Native groups. When teachers admirably institute culturally compatible practices in the classroom, they must monitor and adjust them to fit the needs of their particular populations. This must also be applied to individual students, each of whom may have their own personal preferences for learning. Competition and reward for the victor is so ingrained in traditional schools, children will undoubtedly encounter it in its most virulent form: being excluded from the limelight. All schoolwork cannot be cooperative, nor should it be. There are many times when it is appropriate to develop individual potential. The teacher should encourage the children to always do their best, whether working individually or with others, not to gain a prize but for self-satisfaction. Therefore, intrinsic motivations should be encouraged.

Holistic Learners

Almost exclusively, Native children have been depicted as having a holistic learning style. The holistic learner is one who construes meaning by first understanding the entire context. This is in contrast to the analytic or linear thinker (Hilberg and Tharp 2002), who first interprets the parts and then joins them together in order to make meaning of the whole. Several studies grounded in this conceptual contraposition examined the intellectual organization of American Indian students. Davidson used the Kaufman Assessment Battery for Children to determine the distinctions in learning styles of American Indian and white children (1992 cited in Hilberg and Tharp 2002). It was discovered that the American Indian subjects scored higher on simultaneous processing (comparable with holistic thinking) and the white children scored higher in sequential processing (associated with analytic, or linear, cognition). In another study, Browne described learning styles in terms of brain hemispheric propensities (1986). She argued that hemispheric preference is influenced by cultural background because cultures emphasize particular beliefs and activities and, thus, pursue action in one or another hemisphere. She explored the test results of 197 American Indian children on the Wechsler Intelligence Scale for Children-Revised (WISC-R) (Browne 1984 cited in Browne 1986). Her research disclosed a characteristic pattern unlike the normed children of that test, who generally favored left brain operations. This new pattern revealed a definite preference for right brain hemispheric functioning. This was consistent with Ross's (1982 cited in Browne 1986) and Cattey's (1980 cited in Browne 1986) work that demonstrated that Native American culture encourages the development of the right brain processing style. Cajete, a Pueblo Indian, agrees: "Traditional Native American approaches to teaching/learning tend to emphasize right brain modes of information processing because Native American cultural sciences include metaphoric and symbolic approaches to perceiving and understanding the natural world" (1999, 170). Right hemisphere cognitive processes specialize in relational, simultaneous processing and holistic thinking. In contrast, left hemisphere operations concentrate on linear, sequential information processing and abstract reasoning. Browne relayed that, although any task requires the use of both hemispheres, some tasks require more of the specialized functioning of one or the other sides of the brain. Musical and artistic endeavors use more of the right hemisphere, whereas language, especially English language (Browne 1986), utilizes the left hemisphere processes. Backes used the Gregoric Style Delineator to establish learning-style processing and organization of information in American Indian (Chippewa) and non-Indian children (1993 cited in Hilberg and Tharp 2002). The American Indian students principally fell in the abstract-random range and the non-Indian students chiefly fell into the concrete-sequential range. The characteristics of these styles are as follows: Abstract-random learners evaluate learning experiences as a whole. They prefer activities that include multisensory experiences and a busy atmosphere. They favor learning in unstructured settings, where they have freedom from rules. This gives them the liberty to organize material through reflection (Browne 1986). The children who place in this category enjoy being part of a social group where a holistic approach is taken. Here, discussion, reflection upon feelings, flexibility, and adaptability are emphasized (Butler 1984). Concrete-sequential learners value distinctly arranged presentations that follow in logical sequence. They strive for and comply with directions and seek a quiet environment. They favor straightforward experiences with concrete materials (Browne 1986). They are orderly, step-by-step, structured, practical, accurate, factual, standardized, directions oriented, organized, hands-on, reliable, detailed, particular, and exact (Gregorc and Butler 1983). Concentrating on right brain activities would be a departure from the traditional left brain analytical curriculum so that art, music, and dance could be incorporated as essential ingredients in *all* school programs. Teachers should concentrate on giving children opportunities to learn holistically, as in whole-language programs. Here, children learn to make meaning from text while they learn to appreciate authentic literature. Functional exercises, like learning to write through a school post office or doing a science project while observing real events, would be helpful to left brain learners (as well as enjoyable for all children).

Many other researchers report on the Native propensity for holistic thinking. Swisher, a Standing Rock Sioux, and Tippeconnic, a Comanche, both speak of a Native holistic worldview (1999). So does Cajete, a Pueblo, when he contends that indigenous people historically have used the thought processes of creative science within contexts of culture, deeming this a holistic approach. Numerous other Native and non-Native researchers have supported the holistic learning style of American Indians, often teaming them with Alaskan Natives (see Hilberg and Tharp 2002; Swisher and Tippeconnic 1999; Swisher 1991; Tunley-Daymude and Begay-Campbell 2000). While indigenous people of the Americas and Alaska are often clumped together when results are discussed, there have been relatively few studies that have remarked on the real differences within individual tribes. For example, while Hawaiian children speak in overlapping structures (Au and Jordan 1981b), the Pueblo at Santo Domingo become offended if speaking is interrupted by another party. Although much of the research demonstrates that there are many similarities and values shared between indigenous people, differences should also be investigated.

It remains significant that children of the Inuit culture created art from whole to part, while children of the Pueblo culture in this study created from part to whole (see above, chapter 4). I have remarked on Cox's contention that Inuit children created their art in like manner as the elders in their culture: specifically, that the Inuit children created art from whole to part as did their families when they created pottery (1993). From that assumption, I stated that Pueblo children, who created their art from part to whole, also followed in like manner from their tradition of creating pottery. I gave several examples of how Pueblo and other Southwestern art was created from part to whole. The Kindergarten subjects gained literacy, to some extent, from decontextualized phonics. They were totally involved in their word work, although the words had no intrinsic meaning in themselves. They showed no signs of boredom or of feeling uncomfortable in an atmosphere that was vastly different from their home experiences. The children were then able to compose words and invent spellings—similar to, and in many aspects in a more advanced manner than, their white middle-class peers (see above, chapter 5). The only conclusion that can be reached is that these children did not always think holistically, but they were very much sequential thinkers. Especially with respect to brain functions, Sternberg (2001 cited in Hilberg and Tharp 2002) makes clear that research on learning styles has not generally been replicated, while Hilberg and Tharp (2002) report that most studies on learning styles have been anchored to a particular instrument where there is inadequate evidence of construct validity or internal consistency. In addition, the Gregorc (the test mentioned previously) is a self-reporting instrument, so the accuracy of the categorizing of learning styles depends upon how objective a person is able to be, concerning himself. Consequently, although the preponderance of documentation informs us that American Indians do both think and learn holistically, we should remain open to other avenues of learning that can take place by concentrating on differences between groups, within groups, and individually. The reader is warned to beware of applying the learning styles to all Indian children because

> the common pattern that emerged from existing research and the voices of teachers that we interviewed was that there is no single American Indian learning style, nor any combination of learning style preferences that fit all American Indian groups or individuals. Good teachers use multiple teaching methods to meet the unique learning style preferences of all learners, regardless of their cultural or racial backgrounds. (Cleary and Peacock 1998, 172)

While teachers should use these styles as general guidelines to address Indian students' needs, they should not limit their students to the general prescribed styles but should always be open to children being able to learn in unanticipated ways. When interpreting research on Native people, important questions must be asked: When do we generalize from one group of Indians to another, and when does that generalizing become stereotyping? For example: Navajo learning styles are frequently portrayed as nonanalytical, nonverbal, and visual, and the learners are portrayed as "doers" rather than "talkers" (McCarty, Lynch, and Bennally 1991 in Marlowe and Page 1998) who may consider it rude to disagree in public or not worth the risk of hurting someone's feelings by stating an opinion in class. They may also be slow to respond verbally (Marlowe and Page 1998). The traditional implications for teaching are that the teacher should employ "right hemisphere" approaches such as art, dance, and music. Other prevalent suggestions are that instruction should employ a lot of "wait time" after questions and the teacher should try to avoid asking direct questions that highlight a particular student. Yet, Marlowe and Page found that these characteristics develop when the children are in traditional classrooms, where teachers operate from the model in which knowledge is dispensed (1998). In that situation, it was found that teachers of minorities took more time talking "to" the children compared to teachers of white children, proving that minority children spend more time inactively listening to the teacher rather than being heard. Thus, it is the classroom culture that produces passive, nonverbal, nonanalytical students. McCarty and others found that Navajo students enthusiastically and verbally responded to questions when they were in an environment where dialogue occurred among teachers and students, where the children's thoughts were sought and valued, where the curriculum meaningfully incorporated the students' social background, and where students were allowed to use their cultural and linguistic backgrounds. Thus, Indian children may not be confined by reported learning styles but by the traditional environment that causes them to shy away from active participation. We should not allow ourselves to be constrained by teaching children only according to a particular style. We must make sure the classroom environment is one where children's ideas, actions, and responses are encouraged and looked upon as being valuable and where the curriculum is challenging, meaningful, and draws upon the children's background. These interactions are characteristics of a social constructivist environment. In these settings, all children can learn.

Social Constructivist Learning and Environments

My Kindergarteners learned by constructing their knowledge in the social plane. They constructed their learning by being thoroughly occupied in their work through playing, talking, and cooperating with others, by investigating and discovering, and by constructing and reconstructing conceptions of dialogue, art, drawing, writing, and being. Social constructivist learning is active learning where children acquire knowledge in collaborative settings, where they have the opportunity to think critically, solve problems, and cooperate with each other. It involves learning through personal and group initiative and responsibility. It is a way of having children use higher-order thinking as a means to creatively investigate and discover real life issues. Social constructivism is not a *new method* of teaching; it is an explanation of how children come to know and make sense of the world around them. A social constructivist view maintains that children construct knowledge from a social atmosphere by building onto their own knowledge base. This becomes internalized and develops into the child's inner sphere. A sociocultural setting is important because it is the foundation from which the children build new knowledge. This theory of learning is especially useful for diverse children due to the importance placed on valuing where children come from and how they have learned to learn.

Rather than emphasizing the schisms between Indian children and non-Indian or minority children and middle-class children by catering strictly to diverse learning styles or cultures, it is preferable to acknowledge that constructivist learning is the way that all children learn. This way, Indian children don't have to be constrained in an isolated quarter and we can address their needs in a more universal way. This does not vitiate the important research on learning styles of Indian children but links Indian learning styles with the constructivist expectation that children can perform and persist when they are encouraged to generate their own ideas, granted the authority to think critically, and allowed to make informed decisions about their own learning. Social constructivist environments naturally take into account the teacher's necessary sensitivity toward children. Cooperative learning, peer teaching, and holistic learning are essential elements of the constructivist setting. By being finely attuned to the children, the constructivist teacher is able to see that a child who does not willingly offer knowledge is one who is not ready to do so. He or she investigates what is going on with the child: Does the student need more experience in a particular subject matter? Is the student unsure of the concepts? Does a feeling of modesty dictate the child's actions? After exploring the child's reluctance, the teacher acts upon the knowledge available to him or her. Similarly, a teacher who wants to help diverse children feel represented in the class also wants to bring culture into the school setting. This is because learning for meaning is at the forefront of constructivist education. We know that all children enjoy authentic, hands-on activities that stimulate their minds and their sense of enjoyment. The traditionalist views of school are outdated and ineffective for all children. Seats and desks are no longer bolted to the floor. This is a metaphor for ending the reigning-in of the students' voices, where prior experiences in life count for very little and, in fact, interfere with the teacher's constant flow of information that he or she feels necessary to complete curriculum requirements. In traditional education, the atmosphere is competitive rather than cooperative; correct answers are valued over inventiveness; and rote learning takes precedence over risk taking, deeper awareness of concepts (Reyes 1998), and active thinking. Social constructivism reverses these processes.

The principles of social constructivist learning are presented below. They are followed by a brief comparison of what appears to be the traditionalist diametric correlate (for a detailed explanation of traditionalist education, see chapter 6). The constructivist standard is succeeded by linking the prescript to the strengths of Indian children.

Principles of Social Constructivist Learning

Learning Is Contextual

Cognition (learning) is the outcome of mental construction. Social constructivism is a philosophy of how we come to know. When applied in school settings, it furnishes children with expansive opportunities to construct knowledge in context. In this way, learning can "connect" to the children's existing knowledge, which is grounded in prior experience. Knowledge occurs by experiencing, by piecing new information together with what is already known. The children construct their knowledge by testing ideas and approaches, often *with others,* based on their prior knowledge and experience, applying these to a new situation, and integrating the new knowledge gained, with preexisting intellectual constructs (Botela 2003).

Traditionalism reasons that knowledge comes from the teacher, through the banking model (Freire 1974) in which the teacher (the banker) deposits knowledge into the bank (the student), where it is passively received and "saved" until needed to answer a question or for a test. Here, the emphasis is on knowledge reproduction rather than knowledge construction.

Like all children, Pueblo Indian children live in the context of their culture. Imagine the excitement of gathering with many other villagers at a friend's house to participate in a throw, a statement of community sharing. Here, an assortment of household goods, candy, toys, and other interesting things are thrown from the rooftop. Standing with friends and relatives, you vie for the goods by lifting your arms, trying to catch everything you can. You join in the squeals of excitement when something is caught. Everyone enjoys the process because there is a lot of laughter and many thrills when someone catches an item. Because an abundance of effects are thrown, everyone goes away with something. If one person did not catch anything, he or she is given something by someone who did. Everyone participates in a joint construction of cooperation. This is an example of contextual learning. It takes place in an engaging atmosphere, with others, in the context of an activity. From a young child's viewpoint, he or she learns how to catch things, how to amicably participate with others, and how to share. With each additional attendance at a throw, the significance of the event becomes deeper. Whereas preliminary participation meant receiving toys, candy, and other household goods, later participation comes to instill its more abstract import—giving to others in the society becomes receiving a host of intangible gifts such as community, togetherness, and the promotion of tribal values. The Indian children have participated in a plethora of activities with people of all ages, spoke at will, listened to many voices, and shared input with others. Then, they go to school, where they are often forced to listen passively to a dominant figure telling them about unrelated facts, very little of which relates to their lives.

There is little opportunity in the traditional environment to make meaning out of monotonous drills. When knowledge comes from a result of experiences in context, children can construct meaning by internalizing those new experiences and knowledge into their existing schema. Much of the research has informed us that Indian people are holistic learners who construe meaning by first understanding the entire context (Cleary and Peacock 1998). Whether a child is "holistic" or "linear," learning is a search for significance. Meaning requires understanding of wholes as well as parts—and parts must be explained in the context of wholes. Therefore, in contrast to the traditionalist teacher's isolated facts, the learning must ultimately focus on whole concepts. The drill, the isolation of unrelated facts, must be brought to a meaningful conclusion. In order to capitalize on the strengths of Indian children, instruction should be designed to simulate, facilitate, and re-create real life experiences in context (Cey 2001). This is how social constructivism can vitalize education for Indians and other minorities.

Grounded in Social Interactions

Imagine this scenario from a traditional classroom: Students are sitting in an orderly arrangement, raptly attentive to what the teacher is saying. The classroom is quiet and orderly. When the directions for a learning activity are given, every student gets quickly down to business, working on the same assignment.

Or take this scenario from a constructivist classroom: Students are working on a problem that is relevant to their lives and experiences. They work individually, in pairs, and in small groups. They share their ideas, ask probing questions, challenge concepts, and collaborate with one another in constructing their own knowledge. Because of all the activity, the classroom is a buzz of student voices. (Koki, van Broekhuizen, and Uehara 2000, 3)

Learning is a social operation. It is intimately tied to our interdependence on others—families, peers, teachers, and friends. Social constructivism emphasizes the influences of cultural and social relationships in learning. Knowing is not based on a straight interaction with a separate reality. The course of learning involves transactions and negotiations with other people. Consequently, culture and society mediate and modulate thought (Quinn 2003). Thus, social constructivism emphasizes the social outlook on learning and employs conversation, socialization with others, and the application of knowledge as integral aspects of learning (Hein 2003). In this context, cooperative learning is the norm.

Baking bread is a prime example of how Pueblo Indians work together in a social setting to carry out a task. Women gather together and mix the dough. They apportion the loaves on tin pie plates. They beat down the loaves when they rise. Young girls help with the apportioning and pressing down of the loaves, so they learn by participating in the process. When the bread is deemed ready for baking, they summon a male family member to carry the wood to the outdoor ovens (hornos). Here, they warm the wood to a perfect temperature until it is ready to receive the portions of bread. Next, they put the loaves in the oven until they are baked and when those loaves are done, they are replaced with others. Usually, fifty or eighty loaves are baked at a time. All the while, the women engage in a social atmosphere where they entertain themselves with jokes and conversation because the process takes many hours. The young learners also share in the conversation and camaraderie and, therefore, are integral partners in the entire social event. Over time, and as they grow, the young girls take more active roles until they become full participants in the process. In this very social event, the child gradually takes more responsibility from experienced allies until the time she is grown and is able to take full responsibility. The more experienced associates trust and *expect* the learner to learn. This is not unlike the manner in which the children learned to write words, where they worked in a duet, gradually taking on more responsibility from an experienced confidant.

In the traditional model, the learner is isolated from all social interaction and is viewed as having a one-on-one relationship between himself or herself (the learner) and the objective material to be learned. The desired environment is minimal noise so the learner can stay on task. Indeed, many teachers complain about children who "cannot focus" on their work because they are not able to sit quietly (refrain from talking) and silently attend to their work. I have witnessed many children who were accused of this incapacity and who were later placed on medication to become more placid and close mouthed. Of course, there are times when children need to learn the skill of quietly concentrating on a task. This is best accomplished not by forcing the child into being stationary and immobile ("Sit down and listen!") but by engaging the child in activities that he or she will want to concentrate all his or her efforts upon. In the case of my Kindergartners, when they were occupied in various activities, they often silenced themselves in order to concentrate on solving an intellectual problem.

Indian children are inclined to join in social gatherings, as was shown with the Cherokee who were "predisposed to participate more readily in groups or team situations" (Miller and Thomas 1972 in Cleary and Peacock 1998, 157). Collaboration is a strength of Indian children (Tunley-Daymude and Begay-Campbell 2000) as well as their typical way of relating to others. Thus, it is an appropriate method to have them learn within social settings such as cooperative groups and peer situations.

Learning Is an Active and Authentic Process

The learner receives sensory input and constructs meaning out of it. Learning is active in the sense that the learner needs to do something when he or she engages in activities. Thinking is active engagement. Constructivist learning is grounded in children's active partaking in problem solving and higher-order thinking concerning a learning activity that they regard as interesting and meaningful. These activities involve participation, self- and group direction, asking questions, using information effectively, and critically examining data. In social constructivist classrooms, there is a multiplicity of projects and activity centers. Experiments that solve real problemss are devised. While teachers plan general learning tasks, students assume a great deal of responsibility for planning what learning activities they will take part in. This was demonstrated by the fact that although I set up particular activities for the children to do they made decisions as to what work they chose, who they wanted to work with and how long they took to complete a task. These plans originated from goals the students set for themselves. Once they had chosen a task, they assumed responsibility for the work. This is because they were encouraged to be dependable and efficient. In order to think critically, teachers must not only provide the opportunities but also the permission of children to do so. Children feel empowered when they are responsible for their own actions. They must be trusted to set objectives, plan projects and proposals, and figure what approaches to take in order to accomplish their goals. This will give them the confidence in their own ability to take control over their lives later on (Barrell 1991 in Davis-Seaver, Smith, and Leflore 2003).

Giving authority to think and decide strategies to problem solving is in contrast to passive learning of traditionalist education, in which the learner only needs to listen, receive, acquire, and accept information that the teacher dispenses. Learning is minimal through this model because knowledge is not formed during the transmission of it (Cey 2001). Learning materials in traditional classrooms are often unrelated to the learning. Workbooks are employed for the learning of skills. Traditionalists believe that knowledge can be taught directly, that the accumulation of facts must come before thinking critically about them.

We have discussed the learning style of Indian children practicing in private in order to perfect their accomplishment of a task. It must be realized that, here, they have received the trust and authority of their families to take on responsibility for their own learning. Constructivist classrooms can utilize this self-taught competence by continuing their practice of entrusting children to independently accomplish their work. The teacher can accomplish this by opening centers where the children take responsibility for completing their work. When constructivist classrooms treat children as though they are dependable and reliable, they take advantage of the home models of trustworthiness. This empowers children to be responsible for their school activities (as they are for home activities) by making informed decisions, solving conceptual problems, and reflecting, through discussion with others, various vantage points, thereby coming to a deeper understanding of ideas.

Authentic learning opens the door to culture in the classroom. Resources for activities can be cultural artifacts from home. For example, in the Southwest, where chilies are eaten daily, there could be a numeration activity of counting miniature chilies. Village potters can help the children create a vessel. Planting and learning about native plants can be accomplished on the school grounds; complete with community instruction; the children can help pick the harvest corn if the planter of the crop is elderly or incapacitated.

Students who learn holistically derive meaning globally, by first seeing the finished product and then breaking it down into constituent parts. Therefore, holistic learners benefit from seeing a "blueprint" or plan of the entire concept before an explanation of its parts, with discussion focusing on the total picture and the use of visual presentations (Hilberg and Tharp 2002). As meaning takes precedence in constructivist classrooms, the children could see an assortment of clay pots before selecting which one to emulate. They could discuss reasons why it would be helpful to go to the fields to pick the corn for someone who was incapacitated. Current research on American Indian dropouts make evident that high-school students reject school because they do not see the connection between what they are learning and its pertinence to their lives (Reyhner and Davidson 1992). When learning is relevant to their lives, children want to solve problems and find solutions that arise during projects.

Learning Involves Language

Through the interchange of language and social interactions, children learn the rich body of knowledge that exists in their culture. Because thoughts and words are inextricably combined, culture becomes intertwined in a child's thought system. In the Pueblo culture, the linguistic domain is concerned with competence in Native language use, composing and singing songs, and giving good advice and counsel. Thus, excellence is not reflected solely in the rendition of speech acts (speaking, composing, singing) but also in sharing that knowledge with others by delivering wisdom to another, by putting linguistic abilities to use for the benefit of others in the community. Because social constructivism encourages manifold interpretations, Native language has the potential of being galvanized. We have only to examine KEEP, which has adjusted itself to Native Hawaiian language structures by vitalizing the original "talk story" once so prevalent in Hawaiian life. Talk story involves open turns and overlapping speech, thereby creating a comfortable environment of learning for Hawaiian children.

KEEP has already turned Hawaiian schools into success stories (see Au and Kawakami 1994). It is not only the language itself that influences learning but also the thoughts, attitudes, and values that originally emanated from the language. Thus, in those areas where Native language use has become endangered, schools that align themselves with the Native outlook will be more successful. The Pueblo value system of delivering knowledge to others is an important one in that the temper of sharing is essentially transmitted as an intrinsic part of language learning. This eliminates the coveting of knowledge and invites all sorts of in-class cooperative endeavors. These types of activities are useful in learning higher-order critical thinking and, subsequently, in future employment. In nearly all careers, committees and groups are expected to communicate effectively in discovering and solving problems. Leu and Kinzer describe how the effective use of information and communication in schools will later become an essential ingredient in the global workplace of the near future:

> The change to a high performance workplace requires organizations to value people with problem-solving skills. As collaborative teams seek more effective ways of working, they are expected to identify problems important to their unit and seek appropriate solutions. This has consequences for schools that will need to provide students with greater preparation in critical thinking, analysis, and problem solving. Students, when they leave school, will need to be able to identify central problems, find appropriate information quickly, and use this information to solve the problems they identify. (2000, 91)

Traditionalist education views "English only" as an important aspect of everyone carrying on the American heritage. This straight and narrow path limits diverse ways of thinking because it abridges ideas that may be found in other languages and cultures. Even if a traditional school, such as mine, declares to accept and even celebrate the children's first languages, there are numerous staff discussions on why this first language is responsible for holding the child back or why the child can't quite readily adapt to the *intricacies* of English. In this example of contemporary deficit thinking, English is again held up to be the more complex and elaborate language (for a historical discussion on this fallacy, see Nott and Gliddon's ideas of language in chapter 1). Statements such as "Well, there is no *-ed* ending in Indian and that is why Maria can't grasp the *-ed* concept in English" are often announced. In short, the deficit view is contemporaneously applied to the negative influence of the culture's language upon the child. The language is blamed for holding the child back. The undercurrent of thought is that if the child did not speak this "other" language his or her learning would not be impeded. The argument never takes into account the teaching method, in this example, of teaching the *-ed* concept and how the lack of proper instruction may be the true culprit. Thus, the traditionalist perspective carries traditional thoughts and traditional words that, historically, have been weighted with feelings of superiority. In these instances, superiority of the dominant language prevails, which of course carries with it superiority of the dominant race.

Motivation as a Key Component in Learning

In order for children to feel intrinsic motivation, they need to exercise independence and self-rule. Motivation entails enjoyment, fun, and active engagement. When children are actively occupied in their work, when they have voice and independence, learning becomes meaningful and pleasurable to them and they want more of it. Because human beings are social animals, the prospect of working with others is appealing to most children. When children welcome the opportunity to work with others, they have more of an opportunity to remain focused on the activities. In the social constructivist settings, sharing responsibility with others encourages conversation and interactions and makes for livelier feelings among the participants. Due to the reduced lecturing, the children are able to gain more mobility and make connections to personal meaning. All of these elements contribute to the natural motivation of students.

In traditional classrooms, children may be bored and might not be interested in learning or using the material because they often do not know the purpose for learning particular subject matter. In addition, the traditional attitude presents information in a linear, didactic manner that is divorced from children's previous learning experiences at home. Therefore, school may strike children as rigid, uninteresting, and ultimately alienating (Cey 2001). The motivation in traditional schools is based upon extrinsic factors and is intimately connected to rewards and punishments; therefore, the children become initiated to acknowledge and respond to the control of others. In opposition, Indian students learn experientially (Reyes 1998), without the constant surveillance and correction of traditional teaching. This gives the children a sense of self-governing with which they decide issues for themselves, for example, determining when their private practice is ready for public performance. Social constructivist classes encourage intrinsic motivation by allowing and encouraging this type of autonomy.

Freedom to Choose, Freedom to Move

· Choice ·

When students have choice, they feel ownership of their learning. In the social constructivist classroom, choice is valued and supported. Instead of pursuing ways that demand that children learn what the teacher has ordered, social constructivist teachers concentrate their undertakings on discovering what students are interested in and help them create their own agendas to further their knowledge in those fields (Oldfather, West, White, and Wilmarth 1990). In social constructivist classrooms, there are a variety of ongoing projects and diverse materials and activities. Children choose what they will work on. This does not mean that "anything goes." It is not a room out of control. For example, if the class has decided to study the rain forest, the teacher can help the children assemble books and materials on that subject. He or she would help the children find their passions within the periphery of the topic. The social constructivist teacher may have a reading workshop where the children are free to choose what they want to read, who they want to read with, and where they want to enjoy their books. Toward the last facet of this workshop, group sharing time, the children choose to use their voice in the ways that are meaningful to them. The children may ask questions and participate in their own way with whatever style feels comfortable to them—they may act as teachers, students, or a combination of both. This is because in social constructivist classrooms, student/teacher roles are shared.

In the traditionalist mode, the teacher tells the students what they will be working on. She tells them how to do the work, what pages are to be covered, and how they will enact their projects. We saw the participants of this study learn through decontextualized centers at the behest of the teacher. Yet, an important modification took place—the children were allowed choices in what work they did and, also, they were allowed to work in collaboration with their peers. This transformed the didactic nature of traditional learning into a place where the children were trusted to work and take responsibility for that work.

Movement

In constructivist classrooms, the children are actively engaged in projects. They are free to move about the classroom: to go get materials, look up information, and put together their project. The class is usually abuzz with activity.

> The listless fly on the wall, in the industrious classroom of a constructivist teacher, may require shoes with suction grips to keep from vaulting off the wall and into the swarm of accomplishment and engagement that promises to invigorate its academic senses. . . . This is in stark contrast to the tiny starched straightjacket, and readily available Ritalin the fly will require in the hushed and restrained atmosphere of the "listen-to-me-and-learn" classroom down the hall. (Cey 2001, 1)

Traditionalist classes limit movement. The desired environment is a quiet, immobile class. Teachers are praised and rewarded for having quiet and inactive classrooms because it is thought that children will learn more when they are subdued, placid, and can, therefore, concentrate on their work. Children must obtain permission for the most basic of actions: "Native children are used to being free at home. At school, where they have to ask permission to use the bathroom, they feel constrained and their intelligence and common sense feel questioned" (Tunley-Daymude and Begay-Campbell 2000, 4). They also dislike being confined in one place for long periods of time (Brewer 1977). On reservations, Indian children are given extensive freedom to roam about as desired. This is due, in part, to the fact that families recognize the free will of the person, even if that person is a child. When teachers suggest interventions to families that they believe will benefit the child, they often hear statements like "I will ask Carlos if he would like to do it" or "I will ask Maria what she wants to do" or "I will leave it up to Santiago." White- and mainstream-thinking teachers are often annoyed when parents don't make decisions for the child (particularly the decision that the teacher has suggested). Ultimately, educators blame the culture for allowing the child to determine his or her own fate. At the same time, the Anglo paragon is held up. (The child is not old enough to make his own decisions. They must be made for him.) The minority culture is, once again, demeaned. Additionally, reservations are still relatively safe places. Everyone knows one another. Therefore a stranger or even a known outsider is obvious to all. As the children freely traverse their village, they see friendly faces and greetings wherever they go. Because of their accustomed liberty to move, they feel best when allowed to do so in the classroom.

Collaborative Learning Opportunities

When children deliberate over an uncertainty together, they are able to reach a rich level of understanding, while also learning multiple perspectives. Collaboration invites cooperation, while rejecting rivalry. This is because children in cooperative settings come to see one another as sources of knowledge, rather than competitors. Learners begin to form their own views because they have the opportunity of expounding on opinions while having others comment, interpret, and clarify on their [the learner's] outlook while also learning through the elucidation of other standpoints. Through interdependent dialogues such as these, learners come to form more enlightened visions, conglomerations of their views and others'—ones that they would not have had originally, were it not for the interactive conversations and discussions. Through communication and dialogue, they may begin to master concepts that, once again, they may not have understood alone. The teacher's and children's roles are shared and they form interchangeable relationships. Responsibilities for the school program are negotiated and the power structure of classroom dialogue and interactions are shared. While the teacher has important knowledge about content, skills, and instruction and provides that knowledge to the students, he or she values and builds upon the students' knowledge, personal experiences, language, strategies, and culture

(Tinzmann et al. 1990). In traditional classrooms, the teacher is the giver of information. He or she dispenses the information, without much effort or exertion (to create or construct) for the learner. The teacher is the sole authority who grants rewards and gives punishments, who issues orders and expects the students to follow them with military precision. If they are obeyed, accolades are bestowed. If orders are not followed, the teacher immediately disciplines the offender. The exception is devotion to the teacher's favorites, who can do little wrong. Thus, the classroom atmosphere becomes one of trying to please the teacher rather than engagement in content. In Indian communities, there is rarely a single leader directing activities (Brewer 1977). I have illuminated the fact that Indians work and engage in recreation in collaborative, cooperative structure. Locust explains that the vinculum of collectiveness is due to the survival instinct by which Indians still live (1988 in Cleary and Peacock 1998). For the group to subsist, they depend upon each other and share, knowing that when they need another, others will be there for them. All the members work mutually and assist the group, an inherent part of Indian culture. When children are mature enough, they are also expected to contribute to the group.

The Teacher's Role

Students learn from teachers; teachers learn from students. Both teachers and students come to recognize contributions in the creation of classroom learning. Learning is cooperative, related, and reciprocal. The teacher ensures that the class setting supports learners in making meaning from their experiences and in communicating that meaning to others (McCarty and Schaffer 1992).

The lessons have to be prepared with a great deal of attention. The teacher must set the course and, while the direction of the route is open-ended and arranged with the students, the teacher must be sure that each child learns the concepts and skills to competently complete the passage. He or she must be aware of each student's needs and make sure that they are met. This may involve individual and group instruction, modeling, and scaffolding. Disciplined learning and structure are the norm for all projects.

Classroom structure and behavior should be spelled out. These are rules and standards of behavior that are developed with collaboration of the teacher and students. Because knowledge and control are shared among teacher and students, the teacher's capacity becomes one of mediator. He or she successfully helps students connect their new experiences to prior information, helps the children reach a conclusion when they are uncertain, and adapts the amount and kind of information given to the children so that they may take responsibility for their learning (Tinzmann et al. 1990). The teacher's role is to provide the class setting as invigorating, interactive, immersive, and informative. He or she should guide and facilitate, rather than hand down information. Teachers create learning tasks that aim at promoting high standards of performance for all students. These tasks involve the students in high-level decision making and problem solving that provide the means to make links to real-world objects and experiences, tapping into multiple perspectives. The tasks are challenging and, at the same time, promote confidence. The teacher continually assesses the children's conceptual understandings. This may be done, in part, through miniconferences with the student. In this way, the teacher will gain access to the student's thinking and determine, through questioning and other forms of conversation, to what extent the child understands the concepts and where the gaps are in his or her understanding and knowledge base.

For teachers to transform their practice from traditional view to a social constructivist one, they first have to understand the ways children construct their knowledge. They must "buy into" this learning theory and this would best be done through professional development. In order to avoid isolation, this should be done in collaboration with other teachers. Change is effected best by those who have the will to reform, so the process should be completely voluntary. Often, new programs in minority schools are instituted by administration and forced upon teachers, so inner resentment and resistance to modifications thwart conversion processes. It is beyond the scope of this book to spell out how this transformation can be done, but the book *Learning through Children's Eyes: Social Constructivism and the Desire to Learn,* written by Penny Oldfather and Jane West with Jennifer White and Jill Wilmarth, serves as a guide to prospective social constructivist teachers while offering concrete exercises and a wealth of information for consideration.

I will now turn to one model of social constructivist teaching. Teachers can implement these practices in their classrooms. In this way, they can "try on" social constructivism while seeing the opportunities it offers for transforming their classrooms in ways that will help their students gain a sense of self-determination while learning in meaningful ways.

Framework for a Social Constructivist Classroom

There are many frameworks for a social constructivist classroom. The one I have chosen encompasses many of the elements of a thinking curriculum. This learning model includes anchored instruction, reading and writing workshops, situated learning, games, and balanced language.

Situated Learning

Situated learning occurs when students work on authentic and realistic tasks that relate to the real world. It weds learning with doing, thereby treating knowledge as completely dependent upon the situation in which it is learned and used. Therefore, both the activity and context in which learning takes place are constitutive to learning. Situations coproduce knowledge through activity. Accordingly, activity and situations are central to learning and cognition (Brown, Collins, and Duguid 1989). In traditional schools, knowing and doing are often separated and knowledge is viewed as a distinct piece of the learning process, one that can be transferred because it is independent of the situation in which it is learned and practiced. Brown et al. (1989) point to Miller and Gildea's work on teaching vocabulary to exemplify how knowing and doing can be divorced from each other, thereby ignoring how situations structure cognition (1987). They studied children learning vocabulary from dictionary definitions and a few ensampled sentences and compared the results to how children learn vocabulary in the context of customary human interactions. When children learn words through dictionary definitions, the words are viewed as discrete entities of information and the students are accessing abstract information that is severed from everyday use. Thus, examples of student-learned vocabulary from dictionaries yielded nonsensical meaning in sentences. The participants wrote:

Me and my parents correlate, because without them I wouldn't be here.
I was meticulous about falling off the cliff.
Mrs. Morrow stimulated the soup.

Learning in this fractionate manner disregards the way awareness is advanced through situated use. Words actually derive their meaning from the situation in which they are said, so depending upon the circumstances, one can determine the meaning of a word from the context in which it is spoken (for example, the difference between *a pair* or *a pear*). Children learn words from the environment, gleaning their meaning from the what, where, and how these words are delivered, and also by preceding and succeeding utterances. Under the normal conditions of usual conversation, children learn words with remarkable understanding of their meaning. They are enculturated into these authentic experiences through the use of activity in social climates. Brown et al. term this usage cognitive apprenticeship (1989). It addresses the development of concepts out of, and through, continuing authentic activity. They cite Lampert's teaching of multiplication to fourth graders (1986). Lampert involved her students in mathematical exploration that she tied to their everyday knowledge. This was taught in the setting of coin problems, because the class shared implicit views concerning coins. The lessons began with a problem such as "using only nickels and pennies, make 82 cents." Lampert helped the students explore their tacit knowledge. Next, the students created stories for multiplication problems. They enacted a series of decomposition problems and discovered that there was no one right answer. The last phase introduced students to the conventional algorithm, now that it had meaning to the children. In the end, the children ascertained ways to abridge the operation, usually coming to the standard algorithm. In this way, Lampert bridged the gap between conceptual knowledge and problem solving, between knowing and doing. Teachers can produce cognitive apprenticeship by enacting similar procedures:

1. Begin with a task embedded in a familiar activity. This will demonstrate to the students the justifiability of their implicit knowledge and the practicality of transferring this knowledge to unaccustomed tasks.
2. Emphasize that "a cat can be skinned in different ways" by helping children see the diverse approaches to a problem. Have them work various solutions "hands-on," constructing, deconstructing, and reconstructing.
3. Allow the students to originate their own solutions. Enculturate the children into the vocabulary and ways of the project (i.e., be a mathematician, a scientist). Encourage children to consider, deliberate, and assess the shared vocabulary and procedures of their collaborative environment.
4. Use the process of situated modeling, coaching, and fading (Collins, Brown, and Newman 1989 in Brown et al. 1989). First, model strategies for students in authentic activity. Second, support and guide the students' attempts at the task. Last, empower the students to proceed independently.

Most children enjoy discovery rather than being eventually told the answer. The mathematics curriculum can permit children to discover answers to specific problems, especially when the children are in a common setting. Students are able to formulate answers that may, or may not, be correct. Making mistakes and talking about them can lead to multiple solutions for solving the same problem and to perceptions of why an answer may not be feasible whereas another solution is. This is because dialoguing with others often creates reflection (DuCharme 1991).

Lave argued that social interaction was a vital element of situated learning because learners become immersed in a community of practice which constitutes certain beliefs and behaviors (2003). Lave and Wenger addressed "legitimate peripheral participation" (1991, 29). Here, newcomers and beginners enter the community on the periphery. From their legitimate position, they are able to learn about the community. This position fits well for the Indian student as quiet observer. In their home locale as well as in this place of peripheral participation, their observation is seen as learning, not slow or reticent (Romero 1994). The need to watch and examine before partaking is how learners acquire information about the culture; to "observe how practitioners at various levels behave and talk to get a sense of how expertise is manifested in conversation and other activities" (Brown et al. 2003, 12). As the learners become more active and engaged within the culture (or, at home, as they learn to do things within the culture), they move toward the center, where eventually they become the old-timers. This is an important aspect for teachers to remember—that learning discourse does not have to be commanding and assertive, that teachers can take the lead from the children by giving them credit for knowing when to "jump in."

Reading and Writing Workshop

The reading/writing workshop is a way of teaching reading and writing as literacy processes that promote a student-centered, active-learning approach. Much of the decision-making responsibility is given to the children. They decide what (and why) to read and write. They address the cooperative and collaborative nature of learning (Stevens 1995). The workshops have three components: mini-lessons by the teacher, activity time, and sharing time.

• Mini-lessons •

The teacher gives mini-lessons to an individual or a small group. The teacher and children sit together as the teacher instructs in a reading or writing strategy that he or she has observed is needed by the children. The teacher may use scaffolding, modeling, or direct teaching as needed. This is to ensure that the children are not falling behind and are continually challenged. The teacher keeps careful notes during these lessons so that he or she can analyze the children's movement through the Zoped. This time will be used to provoke and assess the children's learning. Often, the teacher will discuss a particular strategy and provide the means for the children to actively use that strategy. Although not customary, word-work centers could be utilized here. The children would have choice in which work they would pursue, as well as have the social opportunity to work with others. The teacher could later assess their work and review the accomplishments, choices, and needs of the children.

• Activity Time •

In reading workshops, the children read, respond, participate with peers, and attend individual conferences with the teacher. For some teachers, activity time may go on while the teacher is giving mini-lessons. However, it is preferable for the teacher to be available during this segment. That way, he or she can offer coaching and scaffold reading and writing strategies within teacher/student conferences. This is the time that children learn an appreciation for literature because they are "allowed" to read what they want, with whom they want, and where they want (i.e., tables, library corner, or the floor). Children often form small groups in which they read to each other or with each other. In writing workshops, the children write. Students participate in all stages of the writing process. They form small groups and hold discussions on aspects of writing, they share drafts as well as finished products, and they exchange and comment on journals, sharing with peers. They also join in peer and/or teacher conferencing.

• Sharing Time •

The children share what has been read or written. They discuss ideas and, in the case of writing, written products. Children bring up problems so that they can get feedback. For example, if a student is having a problem with the writing process or if a child has noticed something puzzling about a book he is reading, the child would bring these up. Norms are established for group discussions and they emanate from the children, under the teacher's tutelage. These are changed as needed, drawing attention to what works and what doesn't, thereby opening the door to children's deliberating on these matters. Instead of directing actions, the teacher views every opportunity to expose children to learning new ways of problem solving and decision making, remembering that the children can only construct this type of knowledge through actual practice. The teacher may ask provocative questions. He or she may model questioning and help students make connections (PWCS 2003). Students ask questions and act as teachers as well as students. Reciprocity of roles occurs during these workshops. Collaborating in order to make meaning, rather than repeating, retelling, and restating teacher-held opinions and information, is the function of small and large group sharing (Stevens 1995).

The workshops are collaborative and should open possibilities for sharing ideas, reflecting, responding, and deliberating. In reading and writing workshops, children should be trusted to construct and direct their own learning.

Anchored Instruction

Anchored instruction is a major prototype for (primarily) technology-based training. Its focus is on the utilization of interactive videodisc apparatus that encourages students to solve complex, realistic problems. The design of the equipment is not to be confused with equipment typically used in school settings. The purpose of these materials is to create interesting, realistic contexts that encourage the active construction of knowledge (Bransford and the CTGV 2003). The video tools serve as "anchors" for teaching and learning. It is an approach for training and investigation that takes place in a shared environment. All the activities involve a group of students who solve a problem around a realistic situation or anchor. The apparatus provides a motivational focus that affixes students to the learning task. Such problem-solving macrocontexts offer a deeper and more complex experience than text itself. Anchored instruction is used as a learning environment where students pursue and implement relevant knowledge, form new connections between concepts, and therefore construct a more complex conceptual understanding. An example would be students exploring the effects of various weather conditions on plants by growing plants and tracking the weather, simulating different weather conditions, and observing how the plants grow (Ruzic and O'Connell 2003). The curriculum materials are often, but not always, grounded in technology. All of the data needed to resolve the problem are embedded in the situation on the videodisc apparatus. The learners examine aspects of the situation so that they can gather the relevant information to solve the problem. This formula for exploration invites children to view knowledge as tools that can be applied to new situations rather than as facts to be memorized (Ruzic and O'Connell 2003). The paradigm of anchored instruction is grounded in general models of problem solving. Its principal applications are focused on elementary and middle-school reading, language arts, and mathematics learning. The anchors are stories, rather than lectures.

> One example of early anchored instruction activities involved the use of the film "Young Sherlock Holmes" in interactive videodisc form. Students were asked to examine the film in terms of causal connections, motives of the characters, and authenticity of the settings in order to understand the nature of life in Victorian England. The film provided the anchor for an understanding of storytelling and a particular historical era. (Bransford and the CTGV 2003, 1)

A set of interactive videodisc programs called "The Jaspar Woodbury Problem Solving Series" has been devised to teach middle-school mathematics (Bransford and the CTGV, 2003). It is a series of adventures that tell stories upon which mathematical concepts are used to solve problems. A group of students watch video segments to understand the situation and the problem. The materials have "embedded data" to plant the environment with ideas pertinent to problem solving. This sequence goes way beyond the "word problems" ordinarily found in middle-grade math workbooks because, here, children are enjoying themselves while working on higher-order thinking tasks.

Games

Traditional schools operate on the standard of isolating the learner from social interaction while he or she establishes a one-to-one relationship between him- or herself and the material to be learned. Conversely, social constructivism stresses how children construct their knowledge from their experiences in social environments. This would be appealing to Indian students because this is how they learn at home. Games deal with "real" situations, real in the sense that children learn about, play, and/or solve problems in a setting that has rules or patterns. Games have rules that children follow, yet the provocative ones leave room for problem solving where students are involved in thinking through predicaments, uncertainties, and dilemmas. Children learn that there are multiple ways of solving a problem. Games can be technological or not.

Games arouse students' minds. They are pleasurable, and many of them invite and solicit collaboration. All games are not constructivist in nature; many are simply intended as drills or tutorials and give the children little opportunity to make choices. The teacher must evaluate the games to see if they are constructivist. That is, they should give the children flexibility, be open-ended, and have the ability to have students think and make decisions. Teachers' catalogues have plentiful games. The teacher can investigate which ones would fit into a thinking curriculum. Games should not be considered only for "free time," nor should they be implemented as rewards. They should be an integral part of the problem-solving curriculum. They could be used in the mini-lesson segment of reading and writing workshops or during math time. They should not be used as busywork to free the teacher but certainly could be used when the teacher needs to give individual instruction to others. The children should sign off on games they play so that a record can be kept. In that way, the teacher can evaluate if the children are continually challenged. Also, rules should be established as to the games' usage. A games workshop could be instituted where the teacher models games, the children are involved in activity of them, and sharing time could consist of students telling the particular problems that arose during the playing of games. Teachers can find games for almost every occasion and they can be integrated into the curriculum.

Balanced Language: Whole Language and Phonics

Whole language is a holistic view of learning literacy. It is grounded in the recognition that children learn language naturally when it is whole, intact, and complete. Children learn language as they listen and attempt to reproduce and reconstruct the sounds and meanings of the language in which they are immersed. The goal of the whole-language approach is to make language instruction meaningful by allowing the students to take an active position in their learning (Fox 1992). Because children learn whole words in context, breaking down words to component parts can be unnatural, especially because it robs children of essential meaning. When students have a genuine purpose for using language, when it is relevant and meaningful to their lives, they learn fairly easily. In whole-language classrooms, children are involved in authentic literature, not parts of stories but actual whole ones. Whole language is cognitively challenging because when a learner approaches a text, he transacts with it, untangling and resolving uncertainties and manufacturing and expanding psycholinguistic strategies (Goodman and Goodman 1990). In whole language, spoken and written language involves the child, through functional and authentic activities, by learning through doing. For example, through writing letters for the school's post office, the children learned how to write as well as the meaning of writing (communication). Yet, it must be remembered that the Kindergartners also mastered decontextualized phonics, which is a momentous departure from whole-language philosophy. The Kindergartner's learning in this area fits in with social constructivist settings because, in these instances, the children had a choice of what work they wanted to do, choice to decide who they wanted to work with, and choice of where they worked. They had the freedom to move at will. Their work was designed in such a way as to give them the ownership of their work, that is, they were able to perform the work independently. The children had to actively *do something* with the work and this led to the construction of knowledge. We may say that when children have the liberty to interact with their work, the work itself mediates literacy learning. Thus, analytical elements can be added to holistic learning as long as the children have independence, choice, freedom, movement, and active engagement in tasks within a social environment. Much of the argument of literacy learning stems from the question of who has the control of the learning. When the teacher retains the sovereignty, the children become the subjugated; when the teacher allows the control to be passed on to the children, they become self-governing. When children are autonomous, they can use their intuitions to try out the rules of the language around them; they can experiment with language; they can acquire language by using language for its purposes at the moment (McCarty and Schaffer 1992).

Thematic Learning

Language arts is not a separate part of the curriculum to be "done" during a specific time slot. Language should be integrated throughout the day across the curriculum, through thematic learning. During writing time, the Kindergartners created their own themes. Creating topics from assorted information is the way the Kindergartners created meaning. Out of a mass of facts, humans clump information together in order to draw significance from them. Thematic learning involves children in using language to investigate and research a topic from many angles. When the class begins to focus on a topic, the teacher can mediate the weaving of language skills, rich language, and content into a meaningful context. The integration is accomplished by emphasizing a topic, grounding lessons in and activities on the theme, and then branching out into a variety of subject matter as the children's interests evolve (Wright Group 1992). One theme can move to another quite naturally. For example, the children might express interest in the falling leaves in autumn (they usually do!). Later, this topic might merge with the study of trees; later move to the forest, animals in the forest, hunting (common in this area as a way of obtaining food), and camping (how the people hunt). Because thematic teaching is child centered, the children and the teacher reciprocally decide upon themes, using the children's interests as the motivation for the themes.

Let us examine how language can be used in thematic learning:

1. As the theme is decided upon, the teacher charts the ideas and involves the children in a discussion (K-W-L would be appropriate here).
2. A gathering of language resources, where the teacher and students collect poems, stories (fiction and nonfiction), books, magazines, photographs, newspapers, and articles in order to create a thematic class library.
3. Words can be suggested by the children and activities can revolve around them. The words can be placed in word centers (i.e., children have to match pictures of forest animals to their written names).
4. Use a balance of language by engaging the children in reading (shared book), writing (stories of personal experience in the forest), listening (to taped sounds of wind through the trees, animal sounds in the forest, books on tape about animal life, camping), and speaking (from personal experience). Children need opportunities to use cognitive skills such as summarizing, predicting, drawing conclusions, making inferences, classifying, and so on.
5. Activities can be centered on the various subject areas, such as comparing forest animal tracks to pictures of the corresponding animals (a different type of reading), drawing animal tracks and labeling them, making a mural of the forest with its animals, counting and classifying animals, writing and singing songs such as "A-Hunting-We-Will-Go" or "Camping" (Wright Group 1992), and so on. One idea is to write the words of a song on strips of paper, place the strips around the room, and have the children track the words "sing-around-the-room" with their pointing devices.

McCarty and Schaffer agree that interests and themes should be generated by the students (1992). They cite the Tohono O'odham first graders who investigated themes related to their desert environment: native plants and animals, shelter, water, local village life, and the idea of community itself. This way, children can connect their experiences in school with those out of school, while the children investigate new content using their own prior knowledge and experiences. This provides a natural setting for collaboration among the students, teachers, and knowledgeable resources (people) in and out of the school.

Using Culturally Relevant Materials

to Support Literacy

Because whole language capitalizes on the experiences that children bring to school, the culture and prior knowledge of the children become especially important. When children are able to link these features to literacy activities, their learning becomes meaningful. In order to acknowledge and welcome children's encounters both in and out of school, it becomes necessary to connect them to culturally relevant materials and activities. Such materials are indispensable to the success of Indian children (Reyhner 1992).

As textbook companies become more politically correct, they are beginning to include Indian stories. Various Indian cultures present differing lifestyles. For example, the Pueblo traditionally live in adobe homes and hunt deer and elk in a forest environment. This differs dramatically from the Inuit, who still create ice houses from an environment of snow and frost when they hunt for whales and sea lions. The Sioux lead a different lifestyle from the Navajo, as do the Cree from the Seminole, and so on. In order for a text to be culturally relevant to an Indian child, it must portray the lifestyle of that child. To an Indian child, the concept of generic Indians has no meaning (although it certainly does for middle-class white children). If a Pueblo child reads a story about Inuit children, it may be interesting to him or her but would have no particular significance. To be relevant, an Indian story has to be a story about that child's particular culture. Therefore, with the exception of a few stories representing that Indian child's culture, there is little else. Of course, one of the capacities of the talented balanced-language teacher is to draw upon the experiences of the children and help them to relate to many different stories of many different cultures. In that way, the children begin to see a shared human culture. Yet, as the basals of the 1950s taught us, children need to see themselves in literature (Reyhner 1992; see Suina 1985). One solution is to create homemade materials. This can be done covering all aspects of the language arts: reading, writing, listening, and speaking. It has been documented that Indian children need more exposure to these elements in order to meet with more success (Fox 1992; McCarty et al. 1992; McEachern 1990). McEachern and Luther studied the effects of culturally relevant materials on the listening comprehension of seven- and eight-year-old Indian children in Alberta (1989 in McEachern 1990). They used one commercially prepared and one homemade "Indian" text. The text that depicted Indian children yielded higher listening comprehension than did the nonspecific text.

Experienced balanced-language teachers are accustomed to making homemade books and other texts. When children make books, they write through their perspective, often writing about their lives. For younger children, class books are often created. Here, the children create a story together while the teacher writes it down on chart paper. The children illustrate it, often drawing pictures of things familiar to them. Storytellers can be invited to school. The younger children will see their cultural values honored while they become more adept at learning to listen. Older children can transcribe the stories so that they are preserved. These can be placed in the school library. The children can imitate the model of the storyteller and create their own oral stories. A reservoir of culturally relevant, locally produced materials could be accumulated.

> Language arts programs must incorporate the linguistic background, prior knowledge, and experiences of Indian students to support the key function of comprehension. . . . These principles can help teachers validate their student's lived experiences to bring about learning and empower young Indian students' . . . literacy. (McEachern 1990, 3)

An Outstanding School: No Excuses

As exemplary schools emerge and demonstrate the effectiveness of social constructivist settings on children of color, schools that are truly interested in change can become aware that they should no longer concentrate on their students' purported deficits in order to rationalize their students' failure. One such school is Central Park East in New York City. Its students have met with inordinate success, yet critics can never be satisfied that the usual crop of minority students can accomplish elevated incidences of success because this contradicts their view of the country's minority populations and it raises troubling questions as to why so many other schools are failing minority children (Bensman 2000).

Central Park East

Central Park East is a school that serves African American children. In Central Park East, classroom activity is centered not around textbooks or skills programs but around an integrated and thematic curriculum. Each theme emerged from the children's or group's interests or teachers' notions based on challenging, engaging, exciting ideas. All themes were ultimately designed so children could develop multiple skills through a variety of activities, many of them project-based. The students were encouraged to choose among the various activities and these choices were honored as being essential to developing good habits of mind. The courses of study were organized to challenge students to think for themselves, and they learned to do so through questioning, searching and evaluating evidence, and developing and expressing their own opinions. Students were encouraged to assume responsibility and this was accomplished, in great part, through collaborative activity. Far from being a "free-for-all" curriculum, the teachers designed themes that covered a wide variety of disciplines. Teachers provided support and assistance by observing their students and making suggestions so their charges would build on their knowledge and be on a path of constant development. Competition was deemphasized and, therefore, sharing and cooperation became a preeminent feature of the program. Rather than the usual grading evaluation, teachers furnished in-depth progress reports in which they were able to build on the strengths of the students by encouraging them to follow their interests in order to create areas of academic potency.

Central Park East's success has been distinguished by the fact that ordinary students of color have been able to meet with extraordinary accomplishment. These achievements include academic as well as social and emotional growth. Graduates have attributed this development to the following lessons:

1. Learning is enjoyable.
2. They can trust their own judgment, experience, and artistic impulses.
3. They possess valuable strengths on which to build.
4. Asking others for help in solving problems and overcoming weaknesses brings support and yields successful solutions.
5. Working with, helping, and being helped by others yield power and satisfaction beyond what an individual can produce alone.
6. The world outside their homes and neighborhoods contains resources they can access and utilize. (Bensman 2000, 120)

Smell the Roses

How can a system such as the one in which I work accomplish these goals? However admirably teachers try, they cannot fulfill momentous tasks by working alone. Even when administrations make decisions based on staff committees, the parties' knowledge of school reform and best practices is limited to what they have read. In order to successfully continue, the school system must collaborate with others who have successfully met with school reform. It would be wiser to combine forces with those who have specifically formed a successful plan to raise the educational levels of poor children than to try to reinvent the wheel, so to speak. Two such organizations are Accelerated Schools and the Coalition of Essential Schools.

I will briefly outline the Accelerated Schools program because of its similarities with programs I have recommended and because it has concentrated its efforts on actively pursuing the achievement of minority children (for more detailed accounts, see www.acceleratedschools.net).

Accelerated Schools

The underperforming students are exposed not to the usual remedial efforts that ultimately slow down their learning but to an accelerated program usually reserved for the gifted. As with other enriched curricula, the children are involved in problem solving through higher-order reasoning, the production of authentic ideas, and the making of decisions in the context of developing ingenuity while working in cooperation with others (Levin 2001). The process enjoins the school to make significant changes in its belief system, attitudes, and practices. This is effected through a series of steps designed to, ultimately, move the culture and practices of the school to a place where dynamic learning becomes an everyday experience. The framework for this procedure is engulfed in its three living principles (below).

• Unity of purpose •

This involves the operative collaboration of families, administrators, teachers, support staff, and community to decide on a set of goals for the school. These collective aims and values become the focal point for everyone's undertaking.

• Empowerment coupled with responsibility •

This pertains to the capacity of the partakers of the school community to make significant educational decisions, be accountable for implementing these decisions, and be answerable to the outcomes of these decisions. This is vitally important. When Levin asked hundreds of teachers, administrators, school-board members, and parents, "Why are the educational results so poor for at-risk students?" and "Who is responsible?" (1991, 3), not one of these participants took responsibility for the insufficient educational outcomes, but each blamed everyone except him- or herself: Teachers blamed the students and their families for not having the preparation and support from home (see chapter 1). They blamed the students for not being able to sit still and listen, for lacking motivation, for their lack of respect for authority. They blamed poverty with its attendant alcohol and drug abuse, violence, child abuse, and a noncaring home life. Furthermore, they blamed administration for being more concerned with requirements and mandates than student outcomes. They blamed the principal for pleasing the central administrative office instead of looking into valid concerns of parents, students, or teachers. Administrators blamed students and parents in much the same way teachers did. In addition, they blamed taxpayers for the lack of funding and state and federal regulators for hampering their ability to make significant improvements. Additionally, they blamed teachers' unions for limiting flexibility in decision making and for impeding meaningful educational reform. Board members were perplexed about the inability of minority students to succeed. They blamed funding and innumerable regulations that limited their role. They also blamed administrative bureaucracies and teachers' unions for the lack of ability to improve learning outcomes. The parents held the schools responsible for educating their children and accused the educators of incompetence or laziness. In short, everyone pointed his or her finger at someone else.

Therefore, the solution to the paralysis of shirking responsibility is to increase the capacity of school staff, families, and communities at the local school to be answerable for the educational outcomes of the students by furnishing the resources, expectations, and empowerment to make educational decisions in the interest of the students. It is in this area that the deficit concept has the most potential to be dismantled. When blame shifts from students and their families and culture to the school which then takes accountability for educational outcomes, the on-site school supporters can take the lead in changing the situation.

• *Building on strengths* •

This involves employing all the assets that students, parents, communities, and school staff bring to the educational setting. The aim of Accelerated Schools is to build on the strengths of these people by bringing their various talents into the learning community, thereby creating a more democratic atmosphere.

Schools who look for reform need to join forces with others who have already done so. Accelerated Schools has demonstrated that minority children can do well. However, it has made clear that curriculum must change from reductionism to constructivism. It has demolished the notion that poor children need to be spoon-fed the curriculum in small doses because they are culturally starved. Rather, minority children are finally allowed to satisfy their hunger for intellectual pursuits by actively feasting on an enriched curriculum.

Multicultural Education for Young Children

How does multicultural education translate into the teaching of young children? The classroom environment should reflect the society in which the children live; although the teacher highlights differences, he or she must always stress similarities so that the children understand and are empathetic to their connections with a common humanity. *The Anti-Bias Curriculum* guides teachers in implementing such a multiculturally sensitive approach in the classroom (Derman-Sparks and the ABC Task Force 1989). The essential quality of this program is that the children learn not only how to combat inequality when it is directed toward them but how they themselves can become "peacemakers" and transmitters of fair practices.

Teachers should provide supportive environments by helping children feel their culture is fully represented in the classroom. What do the children see when they enter the room? Can they find themselves represented there? This is important because "children from dominated cultures often failed in school because they considered the school to be representative of the dominant white culture" (Spring 1994, 101). Images of many different ethnic groups should be displayed in the room in the form of photographs, posters, paintings, magazine illustrations, and the like. While I do not limit visuals to the children's culture, I give it priority because I want them to feel present in the class. Articles from regional magazines feature the Indian and Hispanic cultures and I often cut them out and place them in the room. For example, last month a local Indian magazine featured photographs from the children's pueblo. When I hung the photographs, the Kindergartners had fun identifying the people they knew (in this area both the Hispanic and Indian communities are well acquainted with each other). Enlarging photographs of community events and class activities brings the children's milieu into the school environment and affords the children opportunities to engage in authentic conversations about each other *with* each other. Educators can draw on their students' culture by locating photographs and other likenesses in books, magazines, and on the Internet. The children especially enjoy seeing blown-up photos of themselves, especially when engaged in cooperative class activities. Paintings, such as those of Mexican and Indian artists, afford aesthetic understandings of one's own culture and that of others. It also conveys the message that the children's cultural artifacts are valued. All of these portrayals convey a sense of who the children and their families are. In fact, the aforementioned pleas for problem solving and critical thinking would be reduced to immaterial tactics unless the children were provided with numerous opportunities to learn and reflect upon their own culture and other cultures. In other words, discriminating thinking needs to be embedded in authentic situations that are meaningful to the children. Acceptance of themselves and others means teaching not only the differences and sameness in cultures but also in issues of gender, class, race, and differing abilities (Robinson 1993). Educators are obligated to teach their students to embrace differences with equanimity. This includes attitudinal obstacles that keep people from forming connections with each (Hardaway 1993). Because at a young age learning takes place through manipulation of objects, materials take on special importance when instructing or remediating racial issues. Let us take a closer look at how particular items can contribute to an equitable early-childhood classroom: The housekeeping area should represent many cultures in that cooking utensils and play foods can be indicative of many regions. Special accessories should be added, such as chopsticks, tortilla makers, and other cultural devices. Each item should be presented when that culture is taught so that the children have an understanding of how these accoutrements are used and how they fit into the particular culture studied. The items should be kept within context of instruction.

Dolls should be used to teach sensitivity about races: Asian, Latino, Native American, African American, Anglo dolls. The area needs equipment adaptive to disabilities such as doll- and child-sized wheelchairs, walkers, a stuffed Seeing Eye dog and a cane, glasses for the dolls, hearing aids, crutches, leg and arm braces, and prostheses. Many early-childhood catalogs carry these items. The dolls are sometimes given a persona, where each has its own life story. This allows children to solve problems of the doll's tales because the wise teacher will construct lifelike stories based on antibias themes.

Art and writing centers need to contain multicultural crayons, markers, paper, clay, various color and texture of hair yarns, and a variety of materials to make differing eye and hair colors. A successful theme that can run as a strand throughout the year is "All Colors Are Beautiful." This is outlined in *The Antibias Curriculum* (Derman-Sparks and the ABC Task Force 1989). It depicts ways we can help children appreciate different colors of skin, eyes, and hair while they learn to celebrate the varied colors in our colorful world (Schmidt 1995). The children look at themselves with mirrors and place their hands together, observing the varying colors of skin, while they discuss the uniqueness and beauty of each tone. Other activities follow—they make clay figures out of multicultural clay, which represents differing color skins; draw people with varying skin tones using multitoned crayons and markers; use buttons to represent contrasting eye colors; make use of different color yarns for the hair; create people figures from multicultural colored paper; and paint their portraits with skin-toned tempera paint. Respect for differing skin, hair, and eye colors should be elaborated through discussions of variations and sameness within the class and school. If school is a homogeneous place, the use of books, posters, photographs, and so on should be used to introduce the students to other cultures. This must occur with the general everyday demeanor of fairness and equity that should take precedence in the classroom. The teachers of all populations ought to help their students know that one culture should not be preferred over another. In order to appreciate who they are, children can be taught to look within themselves and their communities for their power. The reading area should reflect a plethora of books that tell stories of children from many backgrounds and of differing physical abilities, and those that represent children in real-life situations such as divorce, unemployment, homelessness, strife within the household, and so on. Contemporary and historical images of different ethnicities should be presented. The makeup of Block and Duplo (large Legos) areas should reflect multicultural and environmental issues by containing figures representing people of many ethnicities and gender-neutral occupations. Animals should be representative of many areas such as deserts, mountains, rain forests, and plains, with emphasis on endangered species. Because we are striving to have the children view life through a morally responsible lens, it behooves us to teach them accountability, with regard to issues of not only the human race, but also of animals and the environment of which they will eventually be the keepers. Teachers should enlist the help of community members in order to form school-home partnerships and learn how to acquire culturally relevant items for the children to play with. Because my Kindergartners are approximately 30 percent Hispanic and 70 percent Native American (depending on the year), I have brought these cultures into my classroom. Instead of ordering from catalogs with my yearly allotment of money, I commissioned a community member to make doll-sized versions of the Pueblo Indian cradleboards and swings that have been traditionally used in the children's culture. The dress-up clothes consist of American Indian, Hispanic, and Euro-American clothing, many of which are dramatic, such as Indian mantas (dresses), ceremonial men's shirts, traditional Hispanic clothes, as well as everyday wear.

However, the crux of the antibias curriculum lies not in the physical features of the environment but in the messages and activities that are given about diversity and equity. The central feature of the antibias curriculum is the delivery of these topics. The children's self-identity is cultivated as they learn to interact with others, think critically about bias, and gain the ability to stand up to it (Hohensee and Derman-Sparks 1992).

Involving the Community

The teacher must also be cognizant of events in the community, thus giving him or her more of an understanding into the children's lives. Classroom activities can involve the community. Because tortillas are a staple in the Hispanic and Native American populations where I teach, and because we were involved in a unit on "Breads Around the World," I invited the families to come up to school and help the children make tortillas. Native-language speaking was encouraged, as usual. The parents became the teachers—they were in charge of the lesson because they were the experts. This elevated them to a place of importance and responsibility within the school setting. On the surface this may appear as a pseudomulticultural activity itself, but the basic premise here is the celebration of the children, their families, and activities in which they take part on a regular basis. It honored me to relegate the role of teacher to a newly arrived mother from Mexico. I saw her transformed from a shy woman to one who became very animated and talkative as she became involved in helping the children learn how to make tortillas.

Other activities can be planned within the community. Again, when we were studying our thematic unit, my Kindergarten class visited the Indian pueblo to bake bread "the old way." This way of baking bread has persisted throughout generations and is a common activity on the pueblo before their ceremonial feast days and on many other occasions. Most of the families have an outdoor oven, a *horno*, adjacent to their homes, and bread baking in this way is familiar to all the children. We involved parents, friends, and relations. In fact, as the people of the village saw us involved in the activity, they volunteered their services—soon we had many helpers. Our baking coincided with the seniors' lunch, so we also had many of the seniors helping us. When families are involved in school activities, whether on school premises, as was the tortilla activity, or based in the community, as was the bread baking, trust for the school and its teachers grows. In these types of home-school endeavors, dialogue between teachers and community members become more informal and amiable because teachers relinquish their authoritative role in order to learn about the home culture. Both the tortilla and oven bread activities are "alive" within the community. That is, the people partake of them naturally and on a frequent basis. We must be careful, when studying other cultures that we ourselves have not grown up with, that we not present former customs as happening today. If we did that, we would be studying a culture frozen in time. When we utilize activities such as the ones I have described, those that are currently "in use," we can help bridge the gap between school and home.

Because the children live in a specific environment, and since environments exert influences on culture, it is also wise to celebrate and convey an ethical responsibility for our surrounding environment. Sunflowers flourish in our area every September, and because they will shortly die, we pick them and place them in vases and put them on our tables. We take them outside and produce paintings of them. The results are masterpieces in their own right. We count the petals and make graphs; we count and eat the seeds. Mesas (flat-topped mountain tables) are a native landform, and we spend time outdoors examining them. Watercolor paper is placed on clipboards and as the children observe the scenery, they paint their own versions. We take walks in our area as we draw specimens of flora, fauna, and insect and animal life around us. Because Pueblo Indians are averse to taking anything out of its environment, we continue this tradition and are careful not to do so. In these early years, the children learn to enjoy and respect the land as precursors to being stewards of it. Becoming keepers of the earth has always been part of indigenous culture. When we honor autochthonous values, we begin to appreciate that Native literacies can have impacts on European ones. In fact, the history of European use of the environment has been a dismal one, fraught with disregard for moral issues concerning the land. It is now necessary to encourage the exemplar of the historic Native Indian view, one of being environmentally conscientious. Ethical issues concerning the land should also be included in efforts to include multiculturalism.

Whose Cultural Literacy?

Multicultural education has often been portrayed as an either/or learning experience. That is, it has been said that the experience of concentrating on other cultures robs children of learning about the Euro/American store of knowledge, thus producing children who are in a sense culturally illiterate (see, e.g., Hirsch 1988; Schlessinger 1994). This need not be the case. In the above activities, opportunities arise where the teacher could and should introduce that common repository of European "core" knowledge. After all, it is not only the inheritance of middle- and upper-class children, but of all children in our society. For example, Van Gogh could be introduced when investigating sunflowers, the meaning of *purple mountain majesty* when observing the mesas, and the introduction of nursery rhymes such as *Pat-a-Cake* when studying *Breads Around the World,* and so on. I agree that minority children should learn the pool of knowledge that makes up what Schlessinger terms is essential to "the American creed" (1994) because it affords ethnic groups an education equal to that of white America. Both facets of wisdom should be imparted but ethnicity should never be diminished to a place where white America supersedes it. For example, Hirsch's *Cultural Literacy* (1988) underrepresents groups such as Chicanos, Native Americans, African Americans, Asian Americans, women, and others as does his new version (see Hirsch, Kett, and Trefill 2002), although in the latter publication there is at least an attempt to reconcile the earlier absences. Students might even be invited to write their own "cultural literacy" books; that is, they can research what they, their families, and communities deem essential to their cultural literacy. The primary damage of books like Hirsch's is that they add to the assumption that traditional ideas are normal and other nonmainstream ideas and values are somehow peculiar (abnormal), "exotic, strange, unnecessary, or possibly immoral or evil" (Laughlin, Martin Jr., and Sleeter 2001, 92). Although "American" core knowledge bases should be utilized, it is equally important to include those of minority cultures. It is clearly necessary that materials and curricula portray underrepresented cultures. In doing so, minority students will be better able to match their experiences with those in books (Reyhner and Cockrum 2001), and other aspects of school culture. The match must not only be between the child's culture and appropriate school subject matter but also must be one that creates investigation, appreciation, and styles of all cultures. After all, most minority urban schools have their own pluralistic societies. We must be fair and just while also being kind, considerate, and empathetic to feelings of alienation that minority children may suffer when they come into contact with a dominant culture that often has little sympathy for their plight. There must be a balance of the *pluribus* with the *unum*. This can never be accomplished by insisting on only the *unum* (e.g., the English-only movement). Just as the insistence on dominant values can produce a state of hegemony, so too can exclusive attention to ignoring mainstream culture cause negligence. For example, when the American flag procession was carried out in the local high school at graduation time, the audience had to be told to rise because they lacked the essential knowledge of the formalities of the flag. Next, because the audience sat as the national anthem was played, they again had to be asked to stand because they didn't know to do so. Likewise, when patriotic songs were heard in the media in memory of September 11, 2001, I realized that most of our students had no knowledge of songs such as "Our Country 'tis of Thee," "God Bless America," "America the Beautiful," and so on. As I watched on TV the sailors aboard a battleship smiling and waving as "Anchors Aweigh" was played, I thought that few of our students could relate to such a song because most had never heard it. We cannot deny that there exists an American experience because in doing so we rob our minority children of an essential common adventure. Although this book begs for the plight of minorities to gain voice and cultural recognition, we must be careful not to throw the proverbial baby out with the bath water. Ogbu rightly points out that the problems with conventional pleas for cultural education are that they are noncomparative; that is, they don't account for successful minority students who are not trained in their language and culture; there may exist some cultural values that are not compatible with scholarly pursuit; and future work in the global workplace will not depend on minority cultural way of life (1995). Minority children should be afforded equity. We must be able to combine multicultural with middle-class core education (explicitly instructing, of course, what and whose core). The key is that middle-class standard values should not be transmitted as the preferred way of living. Children should be involved in a critical and transformational education where histories of minorities are examined. Here, children should be allowed to investigate their voices. For many, this would be a new experience. Students could be educated to intelligently express beliefs and opinions. This includes, but is not limited to, learning how to give speeches and partake in debates. Minority children deserve an equitable education where they become as equipped as any other child in America. With regard to teaching with cultural sensitivity, this is best achieved with community input because teachers need to be instructed by the community concerning their mores.

Alternatives in Native and

Minority Education

There are many successful Indian programs as well as other minority education programs that could be adapted to fit particular districts: For example, the Sky City Buddy Works program (Office of Educational Research and Improvement 1995) has achieved the 1993 Outstanding Schools Program award from the Bureau of Indian Affairs. In this program, Kindergarten students were tutored by sixth-, seventh-, and eighth-grade students. The older mentors prepared forty-five-minute lesson plans under the aegis of certified teachers. Each lesson contained a double component: An academic activity as well as a physical one, so a lesson such as teaching the alphabet would also have a motor component. In this case, the community became an integral part of both students' education: The older students communicated with family members in order to discover strengths and weaknesses in the younger student. The plan included Keresan-language instruction and was driven by the Pueblo value system in which each child "wins" in a noncompetitive environment. The Kindergartners advanced more rapidly than usual and the older students gained a sense of responsibility. The families of the Kindergartners were pleased with their children's one-on-one attention, the community's language and values were preserved, and the goals of the school's curriculum were met. There was cultural congruity when one child from "home" taught another. When the lessons were completed, the duos were met with recognition in the village.

Another exemplary program—Santa Clara School, a Pueblo day school, has devoted itself to restructuring (Office of Educational Research and Improvement 1995). The students in grades one through six met in small groups several times a week. They participated in reading stories aloud and later acted out the parts they enjoyed most. The curriculum was literature based, and the emphasis was on drawing from cultural backgrounds while reading for pleasure. This school received the 1989 and 1990 Blue Ribbon Schools Award from the Department of Education.

The program, the Circle of Life, is a Choctaw innovation (Office of Educational Research and Improvement 1995). The program has developed a culturally based American Indian curriculum for early-childhood education. This serves as a model for teachers who are well intentioned and are able but not "ready" to teach Indian children because they don't have the know-how. Although each Indian tribe has its own particular culture and language, many American Indians have similar values and world attitudes. Samples of units in the Choctaw program include: The Child: A Member of a Community; The

Child: A Cultural Being; and The Child: A Member of the Wide, Wide World. Information from this curriculum could be transferred to other Indian and minority communities.

Schools need to approach their problems with creativity and input from staff, community, parents, and students. Administrators must see themselves as being only part of the solution. Teachers need the desire and the motivation to honor children. A good deal of learning takes place by trial and error, and the results are worth it. If the children experience true multiculturalism in the microcosm of the classroom, they will be better prepared to practice it throughout their lives. There is no doubt that the ability to conduct one's actions with minimal prejudice is an important factor in leading a fulfilling life, but along with prejudice reduction is the ability to freely choose one's occupation, lifestyle, and personal opportunities. Until educators of minorities provide an education that will enable these students to be as equally equipped as their middle-class counterparts and as empowered to enact social change, minorities will continue to be victims of the elite social class that keeps them in a position of oppression. The end to racial intolerance and class division is essential to the future of personal fulfillment, community recognition, and global peace.

Providing the Best

Radical educational ideas were established when Central Park East Elementary was designed. The founders made a decision to model a minority-populated public school after the best private schools by instituting progressive practices. They immersed their students in supportive learning communities where they were able to thrive in the academic environment, form lasting relationships, learn lifelong lessons, and achieve personal growth (Bensman 2000). These are expected outcomes of America's foremost private schools. The success of Central Park East defied the assumption that children of color cannot overcome what was typically thought to be insurmountable deficits of their background. It demonstrated that those children, who were ordinarily expected to be low achievers, could accomplish much. Looking back to the beginning of this book, I paraphrased Pearl's belief that the differences theory was an extension of deficit thinking because it failed to credit minority students with the capacity to adapt to new situations if given the encouragement that middle-class students receive (1997). By substantiating the crushing effects of the basic-skills curriculum typically given to minority children, it was made clear that children of color rarely are given the opportunity through curriculum, attitudes, or expectations that middle- or upper-class students receive. What if they did? What if they received an exemplary education as outlined in the social constructivist principles described in this book? What if, instead of imposing a rudimentary curriculum, we involved Indian and other underrepresented children in a dynamic thinking one? What if administrators and teachers looked upon Indian children and their families (and all minorities) as having an abundantly rich knowledge base, something so tangible that it could easily be built upon? "Why not the best for the country's most needy children?" (Bensman 2000, 1). This can be accomplished by building upon the strengths of these students, fostering their fascinations and interests, and establishing a problem-solving curriculum. Most of all, each voice must have the opportunity to speak and be heard.

Traditional public schools were never meant to shape the lives of leaders of nations; that was always reserved for the elite private schools. Public schools were intended to impart fundamental skills to its recipients, such as basic math facts, spelling, names of capitals and rivers (Meier 2001) and pacifistic knowledge. Thus, the existence of the basic-skills curriculum so common in schools of poor children today. Indian and minority children are entitled to a more universal kind of elite—that of being architects of their own lives, constructors of consequential knowledge, thinkers, and movers and shakers in their own (and in the larger) society. They are entitled to an education that will bring them to that place.

References

Allen, J., and E. Carr. 1989. Collaborative learning among Kindergarten writers: James learns how to learn at school. In *Risk makers, risk takers, risk breakers: Reducing the risks for young literacy learners,* eds. J. Allen and J. M. Mason, 30–48. Portsmouth, N. H.: Heinemann.

Anderson, G. L., K. Herr, and A. S. Nihlen. 1994. *Studying your own school: An educator's guide to qualitative practitioner research.* Thousand Oakes, Calif.: Corwin.

Anyon, J. 2001. Inner cities, affluent suburbs, and unequal educational opportunity. In *Multicultural education: Issues and perspectives.* 4th ed., eds. J. Banks and C. A. Banks, 85–102. New York: John Wiley & Sons.

Au, K. 1979. Using the experience-text-relationship method with minority children. *The Reading Teacher* 32: 677–79.

Au, K. H., and J. M. Mason. 1981a. Social organizational factors in learning to read: The balance of rights hypothesis. *Reading Research Quarterly* 17:115–52.

Au, K. H., and C. Jordan. 1981b. Teaching reading to Hawaiian children: Finding a culturally appropriate solution. In *Culture and the bilingual classroom: Studies in classroom ethnography,* eds. H. T. Treuba, G. P. Guthrie, and K. H-P. Au. Rowley, Mass.: Newbury House.

Au, K. H., and A. J. Kawakami. 1994. Cultural congruence in education. In *Teaching diverse populations: Formulating a knowledge base,* eds. E. R. Holins, J. E. King, and W. C. Hayman, 5–23. New York: State University of New York Press.

Au, K., and T. Raphael. 2000. Equity and literacy in the next millennium. In *Envisioning the future of literacy,* eds. J. Readence and D. M. Barone, 143–59. Delaware, N.J.: International Reading Association.

Aubrey, M. J. 1987. A teacher's action research study of writing in the kindergarten: Accepting the natural expression of children. *Peabody Journal of Education* 64 (2): 33–64.

Backes, J. S. 2003. The American Indian high school drop out rate: A matter of style. In *Journal of American Indian Education* 32 (3): http://jaie.asu.edu/v32/V32S3AME .htm (accessed July 17, 2003).

Baghban, M. 1992. *What happens to children's drawing?* ERIC Document No. 350 609.

Bakhtin, M. 1981. *The dialogic imagination.* Translated by C. Emerson and M. Holquist. Austin: University of Texas Press.

Ballenger, C. 1993. *Children's voices, teachers' stories: Papers from the Brookline teacher researcher seminar.* Technical Report #11. Newton, Mass.: The Literacy's Institute.

Banks, J. A. 1993. Multicultural education as an academic discipline. *Multicultural Education* 39: 8–11.

———. 1999. *An introduction to multicultural education.* Boston: Allyn & Bacon.

Barnes, D. and Todd F. 1977. *Communication and learning in small groups.* London: Routledge and Keegan Paul.

Barnhardt, C. 1982. "Tuning in": Athabaskan teachers and Athabaskan students. In *Cross-cultural issues in Alaskan education* 2, ed. R. Barnhardt, 40–49. Fairbanks: University of Alaska, Center for Cross-Cultural Studies.

Barry, J. W. 1984. *American Indian pottery.* Florence, Ala.: Books Americana.

Bartlett, E. J. 1979. Curriculum, concepts of literacy, and social class. In *Theory and practice of early reading* 2, eds. L. B. Resnick and P. A. Weaver, 229–42. Hillsdale, N.J.: Lawrence Erlbaum Associates.

Baumann, J. F. 2000. What will classrooms and schools look like in the new millennium? In *Envisioning the future of literacy,* eds. J. E. Readence and D. M. Barone, 109–10. Newark, Del.: International Reading Association.

Benjamin, R., R. Pecos, and M. E. Romero. 1997. Language revitalization efforts in the Pueblo de Cochiti: Becoming "literate" in an oral society. In *Indigenous literacies in the Americas,* ed. N. H. Hornberger,115–36. New York: Mouton de Gruyter.

Bensman, D. 2000. *Central Park East and its graduates: "Learning by heart."* New York: Teachers College Press.

Bernstein, B. B. 1972. A critique of the concepts of compensatory education. In *Functions of language in the classroom,* eds. C. B. Cazden, V. P. John, and D. Hymes, 135–51. New York: Teachers College Press.

———. 1975. *Class, codes, and control.* London: Routledge.

Bijiao. 2003. *Social constructivism.* www.bijiao.com/tel700/book/Games.html (accessed July 16, 2003).

Bissex, G. 1980. *Gnys at wrk: A child learns to read and write.* Cambridge, Mass.: Harvard University Press.

Bleiker, C. 1995. *Teaching young children art: An analysis of the studio method of instruction.* Paper submitted for the 1995 European Education Research Association (EERA) Conference.

Borman, K. 1998. *Ethnic diversity in communities and schools.* Stamford, Conn.: Ablex.

Botela, L. 2003. *Links: Constructionism / Contructivism.* www.members.shaw.ca/ncpg/links_constructivism.html (accessed June 17, 2003).

Boutte, G. S., and C. B. McCormick. 1992. Avoiding pseudomulticulturalism: Authentic multicultural activities. *Childhood Education* (Spring): 140–44.

Bowman, B. T. 1994. The challenge of diversity. *Phi Delta Kappan* 83: 218–24.

Boykin, A. W. 1986. The triple quandary and the schooling of Afro-American children. In *The school achievement of minority children: New perspectives,* ed. U. Neisser, 57–92. Hillsdale, N.J.: Lawrence Erlbaum.

———. 1994. Afrocultural expression. In *Teaching diverse populations: Formulating a knowledge base,* eds. E. R. Holins, J. E. King, and W. C. Hayman, 243–56. New York: State University of New York Press.

Bransford, J., and the Cognition and Technology Group at Vanderbilt (CTGV). 2003. *Anchored instruction.* http://tip.psychology.org/anchor.html (accessed July 16, 2003).

Bray, S. 1999. *The Emancipation Proclamation for Indian education: A passion for excellence and justice.* ERIC Document No. 432 421.

Brewer, A. 1977. On Indian education. *Integrated Education* 15: 21–23.

Brittain, W. L. 1979. *Creativity, art, and the young child.* New York: MacMillan.

Britton, J. 1983. A quiet form of research. In *Reclaiming the classroom: Teacher research as an agency for change,* eds. D. Goswami and P. Stillman, Upper Monclair, N.J.: Boynton/Cook.

Brock, D. R., and V. P. Green. 1992. The influences of social context on kindergarten journal writing. *Journal of Research in Childhood Education* 7: 5–18.

Brown, A. L., A. S. Palinscar, and L. Purcell. 1986. Poor readers: Teach, don't label. In *The school achievement of minority children: New perspectives,* ed. U. Neisser, 105–43. Hillsdale, N.J.: Lawrence Erlbaum Associates.

Brown, J. S., A. Collins, and P. Duguid. 2003. Situated cognition and the culture of learning. *Educational Researcher* 18: 32–42. Available at www.ilt.colombia.edu/ilt/papers/johnbrown.html.

Browne, D. 1986. *Learning styles and Native Americans.* ERIC Document. No. 297 906.

Bunzel, R. [1929] 1972. *The Pueblo potter: A study of creative imagination in primitive art.* New York: Dover.

Butler, K. A. 1984. Quoted in The American Indian high school drop out rate: A matter of style by J. S. Backes. In *American Indian Education* 32 (3): http://jaie.asu.edu/v32/V32S3AME.html (accessed July 17, 2003).

Cajete, G. A. 1999. *Igniting the sparkle: An indigenous science education model.* Skyland, N.C.: Kivaki Press.

Canella, G. 1991. The sociocognitive growth and the young child: Comparisons with special and literacy content. *Child* 25 (3): 213–31.

Cazden, C. B. 1986. Classroom discourse. In *Handbook of Research on Teaching,* ed. M. Wittrock, 432–63. New York: Macmillan.

————. 2000. Taking cultural differences into account. In *Multiliteracies: Literacy, learning, and the design of social futures,* eds. B. Cope and M. Kazlantzis for the New London Group, 249–66. London: Routledge.

Center, Y., L. Freeman, and G. Robertson. 1998. An evaluation of schoolwide early language and literacy (SWELL) in six disadvantaged schools. *International Journal of Disability, Development and Education* 45: 143–72.

Cey, T. 2001. *Moving towards constructivist classrooms.* www.usask.ca/education/coursework/802papers/ceyt/ceyt.htm (accessed June 14, 2003).

Chang-Wells, G. L., and G. Wells. 1993. Dynamics of discourse: Literacy and the construction of knowledge. In *Contexts for learning: Sociocultural dynamics in children's development,* eds. E. A. Forman, N. Minick, and C. Addison Stone, 58–90. New York: Oxford University Press.

Chomsky, C. 1971. Write first, read later. *Childhood education* 47: 296–99.

Clark, L., S. DeWolf, and C. Clark. 1992. Teaching teachers to avoid having culturally assaultive classrooms. *Young Children* 47: 4–10.

Clay, M. 1985. *The early detection of reading difficulties.* Portsmouth: Heineman.

Cleary, L. M., and T. D. Peacock. 1998. *Collected wisdom: American Indian education.* Boston: Allyn & Bacon.

Commins, N. L. 1986. *A descriptive study of the linguistic abilities of four Hispanic bilingual students.* Unpublished doctoral dissertation. Boulder: University of Colorado.

Cook-Gumpertz, J. 1986. Caught in a web of words: Some considerations on language socialization and language acquisition. In *The Social Construction of Literacy 1986,* by J. Cook-Gumpertz, W. A. Cambridge [Cambridgeshire], N.Y.: Cambridge University Press.

Cope, B., and M. Kalantzis. 2000. Pedagogy: The *"how"* of multiliteracies. In *Multiliteracies: Literacy learning and the design of social futures,* eds. B. Cope and M. Kalantzis with the New London Group, 237–38. London: Routledge.

Copple, C. 1981. *Children's interactions as they draw: Hypotheses about peer influence on representational awareness* ED# 202 591. Annual Symposium of the Jean Piaget Society.

Cox, M. 1993. *Children's drawings of the human figure.* East Sussex, U.K.: Lawrence Erlbaum Associates.

Cummins, J. 1992. The empowerment of Indian students. In *Teaching American Indian students,* ed. J. Reyhner, 3–12. Norman: University of Oklahoma Press.

Cunningham, J. 2000. What will literacy look like in the new millennium? In *Envisioning the future of literacy,* eds. J. E. Readence and D. M. Barone, 49–50. Newark, Del.: International Reading Association.

Dalgliesh, A. 1954. *The courage of Sarah Noble.* New York: Scribner & Sons.

Darling-Hammond, L. 1995. Inequality and access to knowledge. In *Handbook on research in multicultural education,* eds. J. A. Banks and C. A. M. Banks, 465–83. New York: Macmillan.

————. 1997. *The right to learn.* San Francisco: Jossey Bass.

Davis, B. D. 1995. *Promising programs in native education.* ERIC Document No. ED 385 420.

Davis-Seaver, J., T. Smith, and D. Leflore. 2003. *Constructivism: A path to critical thinking in early childhood.* www.natonalforum.com/07seaver.htm (accessed July 18, 2003).

Delpit, L. D. 1988. *The silenced dialogue: Power and pedagogy in educating other people's children.* Harvard Educational Review 58 (3).

Derman-Sparks, L. [1993]1994. Empowering children to create a caring culture in a world of differences. *Childhood Education* (Winter): 66–71.

Derman-Sparks, L., and the ABC Task Force. 1989. *The Anti-bias curriculum: Tools for empowering young children.* Washington, D.C.: NAEYC.

Deutsch, M. 1967a. The disadvantaged child and the learning process. In *The disadvantaged child: Selected papers of Martin Deutsch and associates,* ed. M. Deutsch, 39–59. New York: Basic Books.

———. 1967b. Some psychosocial aspects of learning in the disadvantaged. In *The disadvantaged child: Selected papers of Martin Deutsch and associates,* ed. M.Deutsch, 31–38. New York: Basic Books.

DuCharme, C. C. 1991. *The role of drawing in the writing processes of primary grade children.* National Conference of Teachers of English. Indianapolis, Ind.: ERIC Document No. 363 878.

Dyson, A. H. 1982. The emergence of visible language: Interrelationships between drawing and early writing. *Visible Language* 16: 360–81.

———. 1983. The role of oral language in early writing processes. *Research in the Teaching of English* 17: 1–29.

———. 1985. Three emergent writers and the school curriculum: Copying and other myths. *Elementary School Journal* 85: 497–512.

———. 1986. Transitions and tensions: Interrelationships between the drawing, talking, and dictating of young children. *Research in the Teaching of English* 20: 379–409.

———. 1988. Appreciate the drawing and dictating of young children. *Young Children* 43 (3): 25–32.

———. 1989. *Multiple worlds of child writers.* New York: Teachers College Press.

———. 1991. Viewpoint: The word and the world—reconceptualizing written language development or do rainbows mean a lot to little girls? *Research in the Teaching of English* 25: 97–123.

———. 1993. *Social worlds of children learning to write in an urban primary school.* New York: Teachers College Press.

Eisner, E. W. 1982. *Cognition and curriculum: A basis for deciding what to teach.* New York: Longman.

Erickson, E. H. 1992. *Childhood and society.* New York: Norton.

Erickson, F. 1986. Qualitative methods in research on teaching. In *Handbook of research on teaching,* ed. M. Wittrock, 119–61. New York: MacMillan.

Fassler, R. 1998. "Let's do it again": Peer collaboration in an ESL Kindergarten. *Language Arts* 75: 201–9.

Fayden, T. 1997a. *Writing time for a group of Pueblo Indian Kindergartners.* Unpublished doctoral dissertation. University of New Mexico.

———. 1997b. Children's choice: Planting the seeds for creating a thematic sociodramatic center. *Young Children* 52 (3): 15–20.

Ferreiro, E., and A. Teberosky. 1982. *Literacy before schooling.* Portsmouth, N.H.: Heinemann.

Flores, B. M. 1982. *Language Interference or Influence: Towards a Theory of Hispanic Bilingualism.* Unpublished doctoral dissertation. Tucson: University of Arizona.

Foley, D. E. 1997. Deficit thinking models based on culture: The anthropological protest. In *The evolution of deficit thinking: Educational thought and practice,* ed. R. Valencia, 113–31. London: The Falmer Press.

Forman, E. A., and J. McPhail. 1993. Vygotskian perspectives on children's collaborative problem solving activities. In *Contexts for learning: Sociocultural dynamics in children's development,* eds. E. A. Forman, N. Minick, and C. A. Stone, 213–29. New York: Oxford University Press.

Fox, S. 1992. The whole language approach. In *Teaching American Indian students,* ed. J. Reyhner, 88–177. Norman: University of Oklahoma Press.

Freire, P. 1974. *Pedagogy of the oppressed.* New York: Seabury.

Funderstanding. 2003. *Constructivism.* http://www.funderstanding.com/constructivism .cfm (accessed June 20, 2003).

Gallas, K. 1992. *The languages of learning: How children talk, write, dance, draw, and sing their understanding of the world.* New York: Teachers College Press.

Gardner, H. 1980. *Artful scribbles: The significance of children's drawings.* New York: Basic Books.

———. 1983. *Frames of mind: The theory of multiple intelligences.* New York: Basic Books.

Gardner, H., D. Wolf, and A. Smith. 1982. Max and Molly: Individual differences in early artistic symbolization. In *Art, mind, and brain,* ed. H. Gardner, 110–37. New York: Basic Books.

Gaskins, I. W. 2000. What will classrooms and schools look like in the new millennium? In *Envisioning the future of literacy,* ed. J. E. Readence and D. M. Barone, 110–12. Newark, Del.: International Reading Association.

Gay, G. G. 1993. Ethnic minorities and educational equality. In *Multicultural education: Issues and perspectives.* 2nd ed., eds. J. A. Banks and C. M. Banks, 171–94. Boston: Allyn & Bacon.

Gearing, F., and P. Epstein. 1982. Learning to wait: An ethnographic probe into the operations of an item of hidden curriculum. In *Doing the ethnography of schooling: Educational anthropology in action,* ed. G. Spindler, 240–67. New York: Holt, Rinehart & Winston.

Gentry, J. R. 1979. An analysis of developmental spelling. *The Reading Teacher* (October): 255–64.

Ginsburg, H. 1972. *The myth of the deprived child: Poor children's intellect and education.* Upper Saddle River, N.J.: Prentice Hall.

———. 1986. The myth of the deprived child: New thoughts on poor children. In *The school achievement of minority children: New perspectives,* ed. U. Neisser, 169–89. Hillsdale, N.J.: Lawrence Erlbaum Associates.

Giroux, H. 1987. Introduction. In *Literacy: Reading the Word and the World,* eds. P. Freire and D. Macedo, xxi. South Hadley, Mass.: Bergin & Garvey.

Golomb, C. 1981. Representation and reality: The origins and determinants of young children's drawings. *Review of Research in Visual Arts Education* 14: 36–48.

———. 2002. *Child art in context: A cultural and comparative perspective.* Washington, D.C.: American Psychological Association.

Goodenough, F. L. 1926. Racial differences in the intelligence of school children. *Journal of Experimental Psychology* 9: 388–97.

Goodlad, J. 1984. *A place called school: Prospects for the future.* New York: McGraw Hill.

Goodman, Y. M., and K. S. Goodman. 1990. Vygotsky in a whole-language perspective. In *Vygotsky and Education: Instructional implications and applications of sociohistorical psychology,* ed. L. C. Moll, 223–50. Cambridge, U.K.: Cambridge University Press.

Greenberg, P. 1992. Teaching about Native Americans? Or teaching about people including Native Americans? *Young Children* 79: 27–30.

Gregorc, A. F., and K. A. Butler. 1983. http://jaie.asu.edu/v32/V32S3AME.htm (accessed July 17, 2003).

Guba, E. G., and Y. S. Lincoln. 1981. *Effective evaluation.* San Francisco: Jossey Bass.

Gumperz, J. J., and E. Hernandez-Chavez. 1972. Bilingualism, bidialectalism, and classroom interaction. In *Functions of language in the classroom,* eds. C. Cazden, D. Hymes, and V. John, 84–110. New York: Teachers College Press.

Haladyna, T., and N. S. Haas. 1991. Raising standardized achievement test scores and the origins of test scores pollution. *Educational Researcher* 20 (5): 2–7.

Halliday, M. A. K. 1971. *Three aspects of children's language development: Learning language, learning through language, learning about language.* ERIC Document No. 214 184.

Halliday, M. A. K., and R. Hasan. 1976. *Cohesion in English.* London: Longman.

Hammerberg, D. D., and C. Grant. 2001. Monocultural literacy. In *Reconceptualizing literacy in the new age of multiculturalism and pluralism,* eds. P. R. Schmidt and P. B. Mosenthal, 65–88. Greenwich, Conn.: Information Age Publishing.

Hardaway, B. 1993. Setting a tone of acceptance: Impairment and the schools. In *Opening the American mind,* eds. G. M. Sill, M. T. Chapllin, J. Ritzke, and D. Wilson, 193–203. Newark, Del.: University of Delaware Press.

Harris, D. B. 1963. *Children's drawings as measures of intellectual maturity.* New York: Harcourt, Brace & World.

Hatano, G. 1993. Commentary: Time to merge Vygotskian and constructivist conceptions of knowledge acquisition. In *Contexts for learning: Sociocultural dynamics in children's development,* eds. E. A. Forman, N. Minick, and C. A. Stone, 153–66. New York: Oxford University Press.

Havighurst, R. J., M. K. Gunther, and I. E. Pratt. 1946. Environment and the Draw-a-Man test: The performance of Indian children. *Journal of Abnormal and Social Psychology* 41: 50–63.

Heath, S. B. 1981. Questioning at home and at school: A comparative study. In *Doing the ethnography of schooling: Educational Anthropology in action,* ed. G. Spindler, 102–31. New York: Holt, Rinehart & Winston.

———. 1983. *Ways with words.* New York: Cambridge University Press.

Hecht, S. A., and L. Close. 2002. Emergent literacy skills and training time uniquely predict variability in responses to phonemic awareness training in disadvantaged Kindergartners. *Journal of Experimental Child Psychology* 82: 93–115.

Hein, G. E. 2003. *Constructivist learning theory.* www.exploratorium.edu/IFI/resources/ constructivist learning.html (accessed June 21, 2003).

Herrnstein, R., and C. Murray. 1994. *The bell curve.* New York: Free Press.

Hess, R. D., and V. Shipman. 1965. Early experience and socialization of cognitive modes in children. *Child Development* 36: 869–86.

Hilberg, R. S., and R. G. Tharp. 2002. Theoretical perspectives, research findings and classroom implications of the learning styles of American Indian and Alaska Native students. Charleston, W. Va.: Rural Education and Small Schools ERIC Document No. 468 000.

Hirsch, E. D., Jr. 1988. *Cultural literacy: What every American needs to know.* New York: Random House.

Hirsch, E. D., Jr., J. F. Kett, and J. Trefil. 2002. *The new dictionary of cultural literacy.* Boston: Houghton Mifflin.

Hohensee, J. B., and L. Derman-Sparks. 1992. *Implementing the anti-bias curriculum in early childhood classrooms.* ERIC Document No. 351 146.

John, V. P. 1972. Styles of learning—styles of teaching: Reflections on the education of Navajo children. In *Functions of language in the classroom,* eds. C. Cazden, D. Hymes, and V. John, 132–54. New York: Teachers College Press.

Kamii, C., R. L. Long, M. Manning, and G. Manning. 1990. Spelling in kindergarten: A constructivist analysis comparing Spanish-speaking and English-speaking children. *Journal of Research in Childhood Education* 4: 91–97.

Kawakami, A. J., and K. H. Au. 1986. Encouraging reading and language development in cultural minority children. *Topics In Language Disorders* 6: 71–80.

Kewley, L. K. 1998. Peer collaboration versus teacher-directed instruction: How the two methods engage students in the learning process. *Journal of Research in Childhood Education* 13: 27–33.

Kohlberg, L., J. Yaeger, and E. Hjertholm. 1968. Private speech: Four studies and a review of theories. *Child Development* 39: 691–736.

Koki, S., D. van Broekhuizen, and D. L. Uehara. 2000. *Prevention and intervention for effective classroom organization and management in pacific classrooms.* www.prel .org/products/Products/prevenion-intervention.htm (accessed July 18, 2003).

Korzenik, D. 1977. Saying it with pictures. In *The arts and cognition,* eds. D. Perkins and B. Leondar, 192–207. Baltimore, Md.: The Johns Hopkins University Press.

Kozol, J. 1991. *Savage inequalities: Children in America's schools.* New York: Crown.

Labbo, L. D. 1996. Beyond storytime: A sociopsychological perspective on young children's opportunities for literacy development during story extension time. *Journal of Literacy Research* 28 (3): 405–28.

Labov, W. 1970. The logic of non-standard English. In *Language and Poverty,* ed. F. Williams, 153–87. Chicago: Markham Press.

Lakeshore. 2004. Early childhood education catalogue. Calif.: Lakeshore learning materials.

Lamme, L. L., and N. M. Childers. 1983. The composing process of three young children. *Research in the Teaching of English* 17 (1): 33–50.

Lampert, M. 1986. Knowing, doing, and teaching multiplication. *Cognition and Instruction* 3 (4): 305–42.

Laresse, S. 2002. Preserving the language. *New Mexico Magazine* (August): 32–36.

Lasky, L., and R. Mukerji. 1990. *Art: Basic for young children.* Washington, D.C.: NAEYC.

Laughlin, M. C., H. Martin, Jr., and C. E. Sleeter. 2001. Liberating literacy. In *Reconceptualizing literacy in the new age of multiculturalism and pluralism,* eds. P. R. Schmidt and P. B. Mosenthal, 89–109. Greenwich, Conn.: Information Age Publishing.

Lave, J. 2003. *Situated learning.* http://tip.psychology.org/lave.html (accessed July 16, 2003).

Lave, J., and E. Wenger. 1991. *Situated learning: Legitimate peripheral participation.* Cambridge, U.K.: Cambridge University Press.

Leacock, E. B. 1972. Abstract versus concrete speech: A false dichotomy. In *Functions of language in the classroom,* eds. C. Cazden, D. Hymes, and V. John, 111–34. New York: Teachers College Press.

Leap, W. L. 1992. American Indian English. In *Teaching American Indian students,* ed. J. Reyhner, 143–56. Norman: University of Oklahoma Press.

Lehiste, I. 2002. Phonetics. *Science and Technology* 13: 330–35. New York: McGraw Hill.

Levick, M. 1998. *See what I'm saying: What children tell us through art.* Dubuque, Iowa: Islewest Publishing.

Levin, H. M. 1991. *Building school capacity for effective teacher empowerment: Applications to Elementary Schools with at-risk students.* ERIC Document No. ED 337 856.

———. 2001. *Learning from school reform.* Prepared for the International Conference on Rejuvenating Schools through Partnership, May 22–24.

Leu, D. J., and C. K. Kinzer. 2000. The convergence of literacy instruction with networked technologies for information and communication. In *Envisioning the future of literacy,* eds. J. E. Redence and D. M. Barone, 88–105. Newark, Delaware: International Reading Association.

Lipka, J., and E. Yanez. 1998. Identifying and understanding cultural differences: Toward a culturally based pedagogy. In *Transforming the culture of schools: Yup'ik Eskimo examples,* edited by J. Lipka, J. and G. V. Mohatt, and the Ciulistet group, 11–137. New Jersey: Lawrence Erlbaum.

Litowitz, B. E. 1993. Deconstruction in the zone of proximal development. In *Contexts for learning: Sociocultural dynamics in children's development,* eds. E. A. Forman, N. Minick, and C. A. Stone, 184–96. New York: Oxford University Press.

Madden, N. A. et al. 1991. *Success for All: Multi-year effects of a schoolwide elementary restructuring program.* Paper presented at the annual meeting of the American Educational Research Association, Chicago.

Many, J. E. 2000. How will literacy be defined in the new millennium? In *Envisioning the future of literacy,* eds. J. E. Readence and D. M. Barone, 50–52. Newark, Del.: International Reading Association.

Marlowe, B. A., and M. L. Page. 1998. *Creating and sustaining the constructivist classroom.* Thousand Oakes, Calif.: Corwin Press.

Mays, B. 1985. *Indian villages of the southwest.* San Francisco, Calif.: Chronicle.

McCarty, T. L., and R. Schaffer. 1992. Language and literacy development. In *Teaching American Indian students,* ed. J. Reyhner, 115–31. Norman: University of Oklahoma Press.

McEachern, W. R. 1990. *Supporting emergent literacy among young American Indian students.* ERIC Document No. 319 581.

McLane, J. B. 1990. Writing as a social process. In *Vygotsky and Education: Instructional implications and applications of sociohistorical psychology,* ed. L. C. Moll, 304–18. Cambridge, U.K.: Cambridge University Press.

McQuillan, J. 1998. *The literacy crisis: False claims, real solutions.* Portsmouth, N.H.: Heinemann.

Mehan, H. 1993. On the use of videotape as an instrument in educational research. In *Qualitative voices in educational research,* ed. M. Schratz, 93–105. London: The Falmer Press.

Meier, D. 2000. Foreword to *Central Park East* by D. Bensman. New York: Teachers College Press.

Menchaca, M. 1997. Early racist discourse: Roots of deficit thinking. In *The evolution of deficit thinking: Educational thought and practice,* ed. R. Valencia, 13–40. London: The Falmer Press.

Merriam. 1973. *New Collegiate Dictionary.* Springfield, Mass.: G. and C. Merriam Co.

Miller, A. G., and R. Thomas. 1972. Cooperation and competition among Blackfoot Indian and urban Canadian children. *Child Development* 43: 1104–10.

Miller, A. G., and P. M. Gildea. 1987. How children learn words. *Scientific American* 257 (3): 94–99.

Miramontes, O. B., and N. L. Commins. 1991. Redefining literacy and literacy contexts: Discovering a community of learners. In *Literacy for a diverse society,* ed. E. H. Hiebert, 75–92. New York: Teachers College Press.

Mohatt, G., and F. Erickson. 1981. Cultural differences in teaching styles in an Odaawa school: A sociolinguistic approach. In *Culture and the bilingual classroom,* eds. H. Trueba, G. Guthrie, and K. Au, 105–19. Rowley, Mass.: Newbury House.

Moll, L. C. 1990. Introduction to *Vygotsky and Education: Instructional implications and applications of sociohistorical psychology,* ed. L. C. Moll, 1–30. Cambridge, U.K.: Cambridge University Press.

Moll, L. C., and K. F. Whitmore. 1993. Vygotsky in classroom practice. In *Contexts for learning: Sociocultural dynamics in children's development,* eds. E. A. Forman, N. Minick, C. A. Stone, 19–42. New York: Oxford University Press.

Montessori, M. 1995. *The absorbent mind.* New York: Henry Holt & Co.

Moustafa, M. 1997. *Beyond traditional phonics: Research discoveries and reading instruction.* Portsmouth, N.H: Heinemann.

———. 2000. Phonics instruction. In *Beginning reading and writing,* eds. D. S. Strickland and L. M. Morrow, 121–33. New York: Teachers College Press.

Neisser, U. 1986. New answers to an old question. In *The school achievement of minority children: New perspectives*, ed. U. Neisser, 1–15. Hillsdale, N.J.: Lawrence Erlbaum.

Nieto, S. 1992. *Affirming diversity: The sociopolitical context of multicultural education.* White Plains, N.Y.: Longman.

Oakes, J. 1986. Tracking, inequality, and the rhetoric of reform: Why schools don't change. *Journal of Education* 168 (1): 60–79.

O'Cadiz, M., and C. A. Torres. 1994. Literacy, social movements and class consciousness: Paths from Freire and the Sao Paulo experience. *Anthropology & Education Quarterly* 25: 208–25.

Office of Educational Research and Improvement. 1995. *Promising programs in Native education.* Native education initiative of the regional educational labs. ERIC Document No. 385 420.

Ogbu, J. 1995. Cultural problems in minority education: Their interpretations and consequences—part one: Theoretical background. *The Urban Review* 27: 189–205.

Oldfather, P., J. West, J. White, and J. Wilmarth. 1990. *Learning through children's eyes: Social constructivism and the desire to learn.* Washington, D.C.: American Psychological Association.

Ortiz, S. 1994. *The Pueblo.* New York: Chelsea Press.

Palinscar, A. S., A. L. Brown, and J. C. Campione. 1993. First-grade dialogues for knowledge acquisition and use. In *Contexts for Learning,* eds. E. A. Forman, N. Minick, and C. Addison Stone, 45–51. New York: Oxford University Press.

Paul, R. 1976. Invented spelling in kindergarten. *Young children* (March): 195–200.

Pavel, M. D. 1999. *Schools, principals and teachers serving American Indian and Alaska Native students.* ERIC Document 425 895.

Peacock, T., and E. Albert. 2000. *Our children's songs: American Indian students and the schools.* ERIC Document No. 459 045.

Pearl, A. 1997. Cultural and accumulated environmental deficit models. In *The evolution of deficit thinking: Educational thought and practice,* ed. R. Valencia, 132–59. London: The Falmer Press.

Perez, S. A. 1994. Responding differently to diversity. *Childhood Education* (Spring): 151–53.

Pewewardy, C. D. 1992. Culturally responsive pedagogy in action. In *Teaching diverse populations: Forming a knowledge base,* eds. E. R. Hollins, J. E. King, and W. C. Hayman, 77–92. New York: State University of New York Press.

Phillips, S. 1972. Participant structures and communicative competence: Warm Springs children in community and classroom. In *Functions of language in the classroom,* eds. C. Cazden, V. P. John, and D. Hymes, 370–94. New York: Teachers College Press.

Piaget, J. 1963. *The origins of intelligence in children.* New York: Norton.

Pogrow, S. 2000. Success for all does not produce success for students. *Phi Delta Kappan* 82: 67–80.

Polakow, V. 1997. Naming and blaming: Beyond a pedagogy of the poor. In *Children and families "at promise,"* eds. B. B. Swadner and S. Lubeck, 263–70. New York: State University of New York Press.

PWCS. 2003. http://www.pwcs.edu/curriculum/sol/reading.html (accessed July 16, 2003).

Quinn, A. 2003. *Social constructivism.* www.isye.gatech.edu/˜aquinn/paper/social.html (accessed June 17, 2003).

Read, C. 1971. Preschool children's knowledge of English phonology. *Harvard Educational Review* 41 (7): 1–34.

———. 1986. *Children's creative spelling.* London: Routledge & Kegan Paul.

Reder, S. 1994. Practice-Engagement theory: A sociocultural approach to literacy across languages and cultures. In *Literacy across languages and cultures,* eds. B. M. Ferdman, R. Weber, and A. G. Ramirez, 33–74. New York: State University of New York Press.

Reyes, R. 1998. A Native perspective on the school reform movement: A hot topics paper. ERIC Document No. 423 101.

Reyhner, J. 1992. Adapting curriculum to culture. In *Teaching American Indian students,* 96–103. Norman: University of Oklahoma Press.

———. 2001. *Teaching reading to American Indian/Alaska Native students.* ERIC Document No. 459 972.

Reyhner, J., and D. Davidson. 1992. Affective factors. *NABE NEWS* 16 (3): 1–2.

Reyhner, J., and W. Cockrum. 2001. Reading, language, culture and ethnic minority students. In *Reconceptualizing literacy in the new age of multiculturalism and plural-*

ism, eds. P. R. Schmidt and P. B. Mosenthal, 163–85. Greenwich, Conn.: Information Age Publishing.

Robinson, T. 1993. The intersections of gender, class, race, and culture: On seeing clients whole. *Journal of Multicultural Counseling and Development* 27 (1): 50–58.

Romero, M. E. 1994. Identifying giftedness among Keresan Pueblo Indians: The Keres study. *Journal of American Indian education* 31 (3): 35–58.

Rosenblatt, E., and E. Winner. 1989. The art of children's drawings. *Journal of Aesthetic Education* 22 (1): 3–15.

Rowe, D. W. 1993. *Preschoolers as authors: Literacy learning in the social world of the classroom.* London: Hampton Press.

Ruzic, R., and K. O'Connell. 2003. *Anchored Instruction.* www.cast.org/ncac/Anchored-Instruction1663.cfm (accessed July 16, 2003).

Ryan, W. 1971. *Blaming the Victim.* New York: Random House.

Saint-Laurent, L., and J. Giasson. 2001. The effects of a multicomponent literacy program and of supplemental phonological sessions on at-risk Kindergartners. *Educational Research and Evaluation,* vol. 7, no. 1, 2 (March): 1–33.

Samaha, N. V., and R. DeLisi. 2000. Peer collaboration on a nonverbal reasoning task by urban, minority students. *The Journal of Experimental Education* 69: 1–12.

Sando, J. 1992. *Pueblo nations: Eight centuries of Pueblo history.* Santa Fe, N.M.: Clear Light.

Schlessinger, A. M. 1994. Unity, multiculturalism and the American creed: An interview with Arthur Schlessinger, Jr., on National Public Radio. *Cultural Survival Quarterly* (Summer/Fall): 1–2.

Schmidt, P. R. 1995. Working and playing with others: Cultural conflict in a kindergarten literacy program. *The Reading Teacher* 48: 404–12.

———. 1999. Focus on Research: Know thyself and understand others. *Language Arts* 76: 332–40.

Scribner, S., and M. Cole. 1981. *The psychology of literacy.* Cambridge, Mass.: Harvard University Press.

Scully, V. J. 1975. *Pueblo: Mountain, village, dance.* New York: Viking.

Shannon, P. 2000. "What's my name?" A politics of literacy in the latter half of the 20th century. In *Envisioning the future of literacy,* eds. J. E. Redence and D. M. Barone, 72–87. Newark, Del.: International Reading Association.

Slavin, R. E., and R. Yampolsky. 1991. *Success for all: Effects on language minority students.* ERIC Document No. 331 294.

Slavin, R. E. et al. 1990. *Success for All: Effects of variations in duration and resources of a schoolwide elementary restructuring program.* Baltimore, Md.: Center for Research on Effective Schooling for Disadvantaged Students: The Johns Hopkins University.

Sleeter, C. E. 1996. *Multicultural education as social activism.* Albany, N.Y.: State University Press.

Soldier, L. L. 1992. Working with Native American children. *Young Children* (79): 5–21.

Soloman, D., M. Watson, V. Battistich, E. Schaps, and K. Delucchi. 1996. Creating classrooms that students experience as communities. *Journal of Community Psychology* 24 (6): 719–48.

Spring, J. 1994. *Deculturalization and the struggle for equality: A brief history of the education of dominated cultures in the United States.* New York: McGraw-Hill.

———. 1995. *The intersection of cultures: Multicultural education in the United States.* New York: McGraw-Hill.

Stake, R. E. 1995. *The art of case study research.* Thousand Oaks, Calif.: Sage.

Stevens, E. 1995. *The design, development, and evaluation of literacy education.* wwww.bjiao.com/tel7001/book/Reding%20WWriting%20Workshop.htm (accessed July 16, 2003).

Stipek, Deborah, R. Feiler, D. Daniels, and S. Milburn. 1995. Effects of different instructional approaches on young children's achievement and motivation. *Child Development* 66: 209–23.

Suina, J. 1985. And then I went to school. *New Mexico Journal of Reading* 2: 34–37.

———. 1992. Pueblo secrecy: Result of intrusions. *New Mexico Magazine* (January): 20–24.

Swadener, B. B. 1997. Children and families "at promise": Deconstructing the Discourse of risk. In *Children and families "at promise,"* eds. B. B. Swadner and S. Lubeck, 17–49. New York: State University of New York Press.

Swadener, B. B., and S. Lubeck. 1995. The social construction of children and families "at risk": An introduction. In *Children and families "at promise,"* eds. B. B. Swadner and S. Lubeck, 1–16. New York: State University of New York Press.

Sweet, J. D. 1985. *Dances of the Tewa Pueblo Indians.* Santa Fe, N.M.: School of American Research.

Swisher, K. 1991. *American Indian/Alaska Native learning styles: Research and practice.* ERIC Document No. 335 175.

Swisher, K. and D. Deyhle. 1992. Adapting instruction to culture. In *Teaching American Indian students,* ed. J. Reyhner, 81–95. Norman: University of Oklahoma Press.

Swisher, K. G., and J. W. Tippeconic II. 1999. *Research to support improved practice in Indian Education* ERIC Document No. 427 915.

Tangel, D. M., and B. A. Blachman. 1992. Effect of phoneme awareness instruction on kindergarten children's invented spelling. *Journal of Reading Behavior* 24: 233–61.

Taylor, D., and C. Dorsey-Gaines. 1988. *Growing up literate: Learning from inner-city families.* Portsmouth, N.H.: Heinemann.

Teale, W. H. 1986. Home background and literacy development. In *Emergent literacy: Writing and reading,* eds. W. Teale and E. Sulzby, 173–206. Norwood, N.J.: Ablex.

Thernstrom, A., and S. Thernstrom. 2003. *No Excuses: Closing the racial gap in learning.* New York: Simon & Schuster.

Tinzmann, M. B. et al. 1990. *What is the collaborative classroom?* www.ncrel.org/sdrs/areas/rpl_esys/collab.htm (accessed July 16, 2003).

Trueba, E. T., and L. I. Bartolome. 1997. *The education of Latino students: Is school reform enough?* ERIC Document No. 410 367.

Trueba, H. T. 1993. *From failure to success: Cultural conflict in the academic achievement of Chicano students.* ERIC Document No. 387 285.

Tudge, J. 1990. Vygotsky, the zone of proximal development, and peer collaboration: Implications for classroom practice. In *Vygotsky and Education: Instructional implications and applications of sociohistorical psychology,* ed. L. C. Moll, 155–74. Cambridge, U.K.: Cambridge University Press.

Tunley-Daymude, E., and Begay-Campbell. 2000. Early childhood education/language acquisition combined with teaching and learning styles. In *Deconstructing the myths: A research agenda for American Indian education,* ed. D. Chavers, 15–21. ERIC Document No. 447 985.

Turiel, E. 1989. The social construction of social construction. In *Child development today and tomorrow,* ed. W. Damon, 86–106. San Francisco, Calif.: Jossey-Bass.

Valencia, R. R. 1997. Conceptualizing the notion of deficit thinking. In *The evolution of deficit thinking: Educational thought and practice,* ed. R. R. Valencia, 1–12. London: The Falmer Press.

Valencia, R. R., and D. G. Solorzano. 1997. Contemporary deficit thinking. In *The evolution of deficit thinking: Educational thought and practice,* ed. R. R. Valencia, 160–210. London: The Falmer Press.

Vygotsky, L. S. 1962. *Thought and language.* Cambridge, Mass.: MIT Press.

———. 1978. *Mind in Society.* Cambridge, Mass.: Harvard University Press.

Watt, H. C. 2001. *Writing in kindergarten teaches phonological awareness.* Dissertation Abstracts International Section A: Humanities and Social Sciences 62 (4–A): University Microfilms International.

Wax, M. L., R. H. Wax, and R. V. Dumont, Jr. 1964. Formal education in an American Indian community. *Social Problems, An SSSP Monograph*: 1–145.

Wells, G. 1981a. Language as interaction. In *Learning through interaction: The study of language development,* ed. G. Wells, 24–72. Cambridge, U.K.: Cambridge University Press.

———. 1981b. Becoming a communicator. In *Learning through interaction: The study of language development,* ed. G. Wells, 72–115. Cambridge, U.K.: Cambridge University Press.

Wertsch, J., P. Tulviste, and F. Hagstrom. 1993. A sociocultural approach to agency. In *Contexts for learning: Sociocultural dynamics in childen's development,* eds. E. A. Forman, N. Minnick, and C. A. Stone, 336–56. New York: Oxford University Press.

Wiletto, A., and M. LeCompte. 1998. Vignette # 8 Mom, What if I forget how to talk Navajo?: Collisions of culture in the public schools: The Native American and Appalachian Experience. In *Ethnic diversity in communities and schools: Recognizing and Building on strengths,* by K. Borman, 141–49. Stamford, Conn.: Ablex.

Willis, A. I., and V. J. Harris. 2000. Political acts: Literacy learning and teaching. In *Envisioning the future of literacy,* eds. J. E. Readence and D. M. Barone, 57–71. Newark, Del.: International Reading Association.

Wilson, B. G. 1995. *Metaphors for instruction: Why we talk about learning environments.* http://carbon.cudenver.edu/~bwilson/construct.html (accessed July 17, 2003).

Winner, E. 1989. Development in the visual arts. In *Child development today and tomorrow,* ed. W. Damon, 199–221. San Francisco: Jossey Bass.

Wolf, D., and M. D. Perry. 1989. From endpoints to repertoires: Some new conclusions about children's drawings. In *Art, mind, and education: Research from project zero,* eds. H. Gardner and D. N. Perkins, 17–34. Urbana: University of Illinois Press.

Wray, D., and J. Medwell. 1990. *Language and literacy in the primary years.* London: Routledge.

Wright Group. 1992. *Sunshine: Level I teacher guide.* Bothell, Wash.: The Wright Group.

Yawkey, T. D., and T. J. Miller. 1984. The language of social play in young children. In *The development of oral and written language in social contexts,* eds. A. Pelligrini and T. Yawkey, 95–104. Norwood, N.J.: Ablex.

Index

abstract-random range learning, 148–49
Accelerated Schools, 175–76;
    empowerment and responsibil-
    ity, 175–76; purpose, unity of,
    175; strengths, use of, 176
accumulated environmental deficit
    theory, 4. *See also* cultural dep-
    rivation
administrative power, misuse of, 126–
    29
affective school of thought, 66, 73
affrication, 104
analytic/linear thinking, 148
anchored instruction, 167–68
Anti-Bias Curriculum, 177–79
artwork and drawing, 52–60, 65–83;
    affective school of thought, 66,
    73; artistic development, 73–83,
    149–50; bunnies, creation of,
    55–60, 78–79, 82; cognitive
    school of thought, 66–67, 73;

    Goodenough-Harris Draw-a-
    Person test, 67, 70, 71–72;
    multicultural materials, need
    for, 178; parts, create in, 5–6,
    80–83, 149–50; preschematic
    stage, 77; representation, 73–
    76; scribbles, 74–76; speech,
    81–83. *See also* symbol system
    of drawing
Au, K. H., 134
autonomous model of literacy, 28

balanced language, 169–70
Bartolome, Lilia, 6
basals, 117–19, 126. *See also* reading
    programs
basic skills education, 6, 21, 113–14,
    119–20, 122, 131, 149, 184;
    critical thinking versus, 111–13;
    "minimum competency" educa-
    tion, 142; as reductionist educa-

freedom: of choice, 159–60; of movement, 160–61
Freire, P., 138

games, 168–69
Gardner, Howard: artwork, view of, 73; multiple intelligences, 41
gesture, 5, 63; dramatic play and, 64–65; evolution of written language, element of, 85
Gliddon, George, 14, 16
globals, 71, 91. *See also* artwork and drawing, scribbles
Golomb, C., 74, 80
Goodenough-Harris Draw-a-Person test, 22, 67, 70, 71–72

Hawaiian Kamehamela Early Education Program (KEEP), 115–16, 157–58
hegemony, 133
holistic thinking, 6, 149, 154, 157, 170; analytic/linear thinking versus, 148; Indian learning, image of, 110, 148–51
home, cultural differences from school, 13, 15, 21, 25–28. *See also* cultural deprivation
Horowitz, David, 20

ideological model of literacy, 28
imaginary word cleaver, 94, 97, 99
invented spelling, 38, 95–96, 150; and phoneme awareness intervention, 86; Read's study, standard for, 99; Richgels test of, 95–96; sounds, focus on, 86; word lists, 95
intelligence test, 19–20; Stanford Revision and Extension of the Binet-Simon intelligence test, 19; Wechsler Intelligence Scale for Children-Revised (WISC-R), 148

joint story making, 47–48

Karen. *See* study of Pueblo Indian children
Kawakami, A. J., 134
Keres language, 2, 29, 32–33, 117, 183. *See also* Pueblo community
Klineberg, 23
knowledge-construction process, 126

Lampert, 164–65. *See also* situated learning
language development, 4, 16, 40, 143; learning, influences on, 159–60
learning styles, 3, 24–25, 27, 142–51; abstract-random range versus concrete-sequential range, 148–49. *See also* collaborative learning; holistic thinking; social constructivism; visual thinking
linguistic deficit, 17, 141–42; compensatory language, as antidote for, 17–18
Lipka, J., 134
literacy: autonomous model versus ideological model, 28; critical thinking, 113–14; cultural literacy, 179; differences from mainstream, 2–3, 11, 18–20, 110; "dipstick" method, 12; functional literacy, 122–23; Many's conception of, 119–20; process of becoming literate, 42, 150, 170; programs, choice of, 112; and sociocognitive view, 38–41; technology, convergence with, 119–20; word centers, 107, 108. *See also* emergent writing; invented spelling; writing time
lower-SES children: and basic skills education, 6, 113–14; middle-class children versus, 1–2, 11–12, 17, 152; Native Hawaiian and Polynesian children, 115–16; and reading programs, 112

Many, J. E., 119–20
Martin. *See* study of Pueblo Indian children

About the Author

*T*erese Fayden has worked as an elementary school teacher in the rural southwest for the past thirteen years. During much of that time, she taught Kindergarten children on a Pueblo Indian reservation. There, she developed her passion to institute and ensure a curriculum that fosters cognitive challenges for Native American and other minority students.

In addition to founding a Montessori program in her school district, she was conferred the honor of Teacher of the Year by the Concerned Parents of Native American Children in 1995. She is the recipient of many grants, including one from the prestigious McCune Foundation, and has taught literacy classes at the University of New Mexico. She is most interested in decolonization research and has published numerous articles related to the preservation of the integrity of underrepresented children's identity.